Ivory Apes and P

IVORY APES AND PEACOC

[Illustration: DOSTOIEVSKY, BY VALLOTON]

IVORY APES AND PEACOCKS

JOSEPH CONRAD, WALT WHITMAN,
JULES LAFORGUE, DOSTOIEVSKY AND TOLSTOY,
SCHOENBERG, WEDEKIND, MOUSSORGSKY,
CEZANNE, VERMEER, MATISSE, VAN GOGH, GAUGUIN,
ITALIAN FUTURISTS, VARIOUS LATTER-DAY POETS,
PAINTERS, COMPOSERS AND DRAMATISTS

BY
JAMES HUNEKER

NEW YORK
CHARLES SCRIBNER'S SONS
1917

COPYRIGHT, 1915, BY
CHARLES SCRIBNER'S SONS

PUBLISHED SEPTEMBER, 1915

To
JOHN QUINN

"Every three years once came the ships of Tarshish bringing gold and silver, ivory and apes, and peacocks."
  --_II Chronicles_ 9. 21.

CONTENTS

	PAGE
I. THE GENIUS OF JOSEPH CONRAD	1
II. A VISIT TO WALT WHITMAN	22
III. THE BUFFOON OF THE NEW ETERNITIES: JULES LAFORGUE	32
IV. DOSTOIEVSKY AND TOLSTOY, AND THE YOUNGER CHOIR OF RUSSIAN WRITERS	52
V. I. ARNOLD SCHOENBERG II. MUSIC OF TO-DAY AND TO-MORROW	89 104
VI. FRANK WEDEKIND	121
VII. THE MAGIC VERMEER	141
VIII. RICHARD STRAUSS AT STUTTGART	153

IX.	MAX LIEBERMANN AND SOME PHASES OF MODERN GERMAN ART	173
X.	A MUSICAL PRIMITIVE: MODESTE MOUSSORGSKY	190
XI.	NEW PLAYS BY HAUPTMANN, SUDERMANN, AND SCHNITZLER	203
XII.	KUBIN, MUNCH, AND GAUGUIN: MASTERS OF HALLUCINATION	222
XIII.	THE CULT OF THE NUANCE: LAFCADIO HEARN	240
XIV.	I. THE MELANCHOLY OF MASTERPIECES	249
	II. THE ITALIAN FUTURIST PAINTERS	262
XV.	IN THE WORKSHOP OF ZOLA	275
XVI.	A STUDY OF DE MAUPASSANT	288
XVII.	PUVIS DE CHAVANNES	301
XVIII.	THREE DISAGREEABLE GIRLS	311

IVORY APES AND PEACOCKS

I

THE GENIUS OF JOSEPH CONRAD

I

In these piping days when fiction plays the handmaid or prophet to various propaganda; when the majority of writers are trying to prove something, or acting as venders of some new-fangled social nostrums; when the insistent drums of the Great God Reclame are bruising human tympani, the figure of Joseph Conrad stands solitary among English novelists as the very ideal of a pure and disinterested artist. Amid the clamour of the market-place a book of his is a sea-shell which pressed to the ear echoes the far-away murmur of the sea; always the sea, either as rigid as a mirror under hard, blue skies or shuddering symphonically up some exotic beach. Conrad is a painter doubled by a psychologist; he is the psychologist of the sea--and that is his chief claim to originality, his Peak of Darien. He knows and records its every pulse-beat. His genius has the rich, salty tang of an Elizabethan adventurer and the spaciousness of those times. Imagine a Polish sailor who read Flaubert and the English Bible, who bared his head under equatorial few large stars and related his doings in rhythmic, sonorous, coloured prose; imagine a man from a landlocked country who "midway in his mortal life" began writing for the first time and in an alien tongue, and, added to an almost abnormal power of description, possessed the art of laying bare the human soul, not after the meticulous manner of the modern Paul Prys of psychology, but following the larger method of Flaubert, who believed that actions should translate character--imagine these paradoxes and you have partly imagined Joseph Conrad, who has so finely said that "imagination, and not invention, is the supreme master of art as of life."

He has taken the sea-romance of Smollett, Marryat, Melville, Dana, Clark Russell, Stevenson, Becke, Kipling, and for its well-worn situations has substituted not only many novel nuances, but invaded new territory, revealed obscure atavisms and the psychology lurking behind the mask of the savage, the transpositions of dark souls, and shown us a world of "kings, demagogues, priests, charlatans, dukes, giraffes, cabinet ministers, bricklayers, apostles, ants, scientists, Kaffirs, soldiers, sailors, elephants, lawyers, dandies, microbes, and constellations of a universe whose amazing spectacle is a moral end in itself." In his Reminiscences Mr. Conrad has told us, with the surface frankness of a Pole, the genesis of his literary debut of Almayer's Folly, his first novel, and in a quite casual fashion throws fresh light on that somewhat enigmatic character--reminding me in the juxtaposition of his newer psychologic procedure and the simple old tale, of Wagner's Venusberg ballet, scored after he had composed Tristan und Isolde. But, like certain other great Slavic writers, Conrad has only given us a tantalising peep into his mental workshop. We rise after finishing the Reminiscences realising that we have read once more romance, in whose half-lights and modest evasions we catch fleeting glimpses of reality. Reticence is a distinctive quality of this author; after all, isn't truth an idea that traverses a temperament?

That many of his stories were in the best sense "lived" there can be no doubt--he has at odd times confessed it, confessions painfully wrung from him, as he is no friend of the interviewer. The white-hot sharpness of the impressions which he has projected upon paper recalls Taine's dictum: "les sensations sont des hallucinations vraies." Veritable hallucinations are the seascapes and landscapes in the South Sea stories, veritable hallucinations are the quotidian gestures and speech of his anarchists and souls sailing on the winds of noble and sinister passions. For Conrad is on one side an implacable realist.... Unforgetable are his delineations of sudden little rivers never charted and their shallow, turbid waters, the sombre flux of immemorial forests under the crescent cone of night, and undergrowth overlapping the banks, the tragic chaos of rising storms, hordes of clouds sailing low on the horizon, the silhouettes of lazy, majestic mountains, the lugubrious magic of the tropical night, the mysterious drums of the natives, and the darkness that one can feel, taste, smell. What a gulf of incertitudes for white men is evoked for us in vivid, concrete terms. Unforgetable, too, the hallucinated actions of the student Razumov the night Victor Haldin, after launching the fatal bomb, seeks his room, his assistance, in that masterpiece, Under Western Eyes. But realist as Conrad is, he is also a poet who knows, as he says himself, that "the power of sound has always been greater than the power of sense." (Reason is a poor halter with which to lead mankind to drink at the well of truth.) He woos the ear with his singing prose as he ravishes the eye with his pictures. In his little-known study of Henry James he wrote: "All creative art is magic, is evocation of the unseen in forms persuasive, enlightening, familiar, and surprising," and finally, "Fiction is history, human history, or it is nothing." Often a writer tells us more of himself in criticising a fellow craftsman than in any formal aesthetic pronunciamiento. We soon find out the likes and dislikes of Mr. Conrad in this particular essay, and also what might be described as the keelson of his workaday philosophy: "All adventure, all love, every success, is resumed in the supreme energy of renunciation. It is the utmost limit of our power." No wonder his tutor, half in anger, half in sorrow, exclaimed: "You are an incorrigible, hopeless Don Quixote."

I suppose a long list might be made of foreigners who have mastered the English language and written it with ease and elegance, yet I cannot recall one who has so completely absorbed native idioms, who has made for himself an English mind (without losing his profound and supersubtle Slavic soul), as has Joseph Conrad. He is unique as stylist. He first read English literature in Polish translations, then in the original; he read not only the Bible and Shakespeare, but Dickens, Fenimore Cooper, and Thackeray; above all, Dickens. He followed no regular course, just as he belongs to no school in art, except the school of humanity; for him there are no types, only humans. (He detests formulae and movements.) His sensibility, all Slavic, was stimulated by Dickens, who was a powerful stimulant of the so-called "Russian pity," which fairly honeycombs the works of Dostoievsky. There is no mistaking the influence of the English Bible on Conrad's prose style. He is saturated with its puissant, elemental rhythms, and his prose has its surge and undertow. That is why his is never a "painted ship on a painted ocean"; by the miracle of his art his water is billowy and undulating, his air quivers in the torrid sunshine, and across his skies--skies broken into new, strange patterns--the cloud-masses either float or else drive like a typhoon. His rhythmic sense is akin to Flaubert's, of whom Arthur Symons wrote: "He invents the rhythm of every sentence, he changes his cadence with every mood, or for the convenience of every fact; ... he has no fixed prose tune." Nor, by the same token, has Conrad. He seldom indulges, as does Theophile Gautier, in the static paragraph. He is ever in modulation. There is ebb and flow in his sentences. A typical paragraph of his shows what might be called the sonata form: an allegro, andante, and presto. For example, the opening pages of Karain (one of his best stories, by the way) in Tales of Unrest:

"Sunshine gleams between the lines of those short paragraphs [he is writing of the newspaper accounts of various native risings in the Eastern Archipelago]--sunshine and the glitter of the sea. A strange name wakes up memories; the printed words scent the smoky atmosphere of to-day faintly, with the subtle and penetrating perfume as of land-breezes breathing through the starlight of bygone nights; a signal-fire gleams like a jewel on the high brow of a sombre cliff; great trees, the advanced sentries of immense forests, stand watchful and still over sleeping stretches of open water; a line of white surf thunders on an empty beach, the shallow water foams on the reefs; and green islets scattered through the calm of noonday lie upon the level of a polished sea like a handful of emeralds on a buckler of steel."

There is no mistaking the _coda_ of this paragraph--selected at random--beginning at "and"; it suggests the author of Salammbo, and it also contains within its fluid walls evocations of sound, odour, bulk, tactile values, the colour of life, the wet of the waves, and the whisper of the wind. Or, as a contrast, recall the rank ugliness of the night when Razumov visits the hideous tenement, expecting to find there the driver who would carry to freedom the political assassin, Haldin. Scattered throughout the books are descriptive passages with few parallels in our language. Indeed, Conrad often abuses his gift, forgetting that his readers do not possess his tremendously developed faculty of attention.

II

Invention he has to a plentiful degree, notwithstanding his giving it second place in comparison with imagination. His novels are the novels of ideas dear to Balzac, though tinged with romance--a Stendhal of the sea. Gustave Kahn called him un puissant reveur, and might have added, a wonderful spinner of yarns. Such yarns--for men and women and children! At times yarning seemingly for the sake of yarning--true art-for-art, though not in the "precious" sense. From the brilliant melochromatic glare of the East to the drab of London's mean streets, from the cool, darkened interiors of Malayan warehouses to the snow-covered allees of the Russian capital, or the green parks on the Lake of Geneva, he carries us on his magical carpet, and the key is always in true pitch. He never saves up for another book as Henry James once said of some author, and for him, as for Mr. James, every good story is "both a picture and an idea"; he seeks to interpret "the uncomposed, unrounded look of life with its accidents, its broken rhythms." He gets atmosphere in a phrase; a verbal nuance lifts the cover of some iniquitous or gentle soul. He contrives the illusion of time, and his characters are never at rest; even within the narrow compass of the short story they develop; they grow in evil or wisdom, are always transformed; they think in "character," and ideality unites his vision with that of his humans. Consider the decomposition of the moral life of Lord Jim and its slow recrudescence; there is a prolonged duel between the will and the intelligence. Here is the tesselation of mean and tragic happenings in the vast mosaic we call Life. And the force of fatuity in the case of Almayer--a book which has for me the bloom of youth. Sheer narrative could go no further than in The Nigger of the Narcissus (Children of the Sea), nor interior analysis in The Return.

What I once wrote of Henry James might be said of Joseph Conrad: "He is exquisitely aware of the presence of others." And this awareness is illustrated in Under Western Eyes and Nostromo--the latter that astonishing rehabilitation of the humming life on a South American seaboard. For Nostromo nothing is lost save honour; he goes to his death loving insensately; for Razumov his honour endures till the pressure put upon it by his love for Haldin's sister cracks it, and cracks, too, his reason. For once the novelist seems cruel to the pathological point--I mean in the punishment of Razumov by the hideous spy. I hope this does not betray parvitude of view-point. I am not thin-skinned, and Under Western Eyes is my favourite novel, but the closing section is lacerating music for the nerves. And what a chapter!--that thunder-storm driving down the valley of the Rhone, the haggard, haunted face of the Russian student forced, despite his convictions, to become an informer and a supposed anarchist (curious students will find the first hint of the leitmotiv of this monumental book in An Anarchist--A Set of Six; as Gaspar Ruiz may be looked on as a pendant to Nostromo). Under Western Eyes is a masterpiece of irony, observation, and pity. I once described it as being as powerful as Dostoievsky and as well written as Turgenieff. The truth is that it is Conrad at his best, although I know that I may seem to slight the Eastern tales. It has the colour and shape and gait of the marvellous stories of Dostoievsky and Turgenieff--with an absolutely original motive, and more modern. A magical canvas!

Its type of narrative is in the later style of the writer. The events are related by an English teacher of languages in Geneva, based on the diary of Razumov. It is a favourite device of Conrad's which might be described as, structurally progressing from the homogeneous to the heterogeneous. His novel, Chance, is a specific instance of his intricate and elliptical method. Several personages of the story relate in almost fugal manner, the heroine appearing to us in flashes as if reflected by some revolving mirror. It is a difficult and elusive method, but it presents us with many facets of character and is swift and secular. If Flaubert in Sentimental Education originated a novel structure in fiction, Conrad may claim the same honour; his edifice, in its contrapuntal presentation of character and chapter suspensions, is new, tantalisingly, bewilderingly, refreshingly, new. The colour is toned down, is more sober than the prose of the Eastern stories. Sometimes he employs the personal pronoun, and with what piquancy as well as poignancy may be noted in the volume Youth. This contains three tales, the first, which gives the title-key, has been called the finest short story in English, although it is difficult to discriminate. What could be more thrilling, with a well-nigh supernatural thrill (and the colouring of Baudelairian cruelty and blood-lust) than The Heart of Darkness, or what more pathetic--a pathos which recalls Balzac's Pere Goriot and Turgenieff's A Lear of the Steppe, withal still more pity-breeding--than The End of the Tether? This volume alone should place Conrad among the immortals.

That he must have had a "long foreground" we find after studying the man. Sailing a ship is no sinecure, and for Conrad a ship is something with human attributes. Like a woman, it must be lived with to be understood, and it has its ways and whims and has to be petted or humoured, as in The Brute--that monstrous personification of the treacherous sea's victim. Like all true artists, Conrad never preaches. His moral is in suffusion, and who runs may read. We recognise his emotional calibre, which is of a dramatic intensity, though never over-emphasising the morbid. Of his intellectual grasp there is no question. He possesses pathos, passion, sincerity, and humour. Wide knowledge of mankind and nature he has, and in the field of moral power we need but ask if he is a Yes-Sayer or a No-Sayer, as the Nietzschians have it. He says Yes! to the universe and of the eternal verities he is cognisant. For him there is no "other side of good and evil." No writers of fiction, save the very greatest, Flaubert, Tolstoy, Dostoievsky, or Turgenieff, have so exposed the soul of man under the stress of sorrow, passion, anger, or as swimming, a midget, in the immensities of sky, or burrowing, a fugitive, in suffocating virgin forests. The soul and the sea--they are the beloved provinces of this sailor and psychologue. But he also recognises the relativity of things. The ineluctable vastness and sadness of life oppress him. In Karain we read: "Nothing could happen to him unless what happens to all--failure and death." His heroes are failures, as are heroes in all great poetry and fiction, and their failure is recorded with muffled irony. The fundamental pessimism of the Slavic temperament must be reckoned with. But this pessimism is implied, and life has its large as well as its "little ironies." In Chance, which describes the hypertrophy of a dolorous soul, he writes:

"It was one of those dewy, starry nights, oppressing our spirit, crushing our pride, by the brilliant evidence of the awful loneliness, of the hopeless, obscure magnificence of our globe lost in the splendid revelation of a glittering, soulless universe.... Daylight is friendly to man toiling under a sun which warms his heart; and cloudy, soft nights are more kindly to our littleness."

To match that one must go to Thomas Hardy, to the eloquent passage describing the terrors of infinite space in Two on a Tower. However, Conrad is not often given to such Hamlet-like moods. The shock and recoil of circumstances, the fatalities of chance, and the vagaries of human conduct intrigue his intention more than the night side of the soul. Yet, how well he has observed the paralysis of will caused by fear. In An Outpost of Progress is the following: "Fear always remains. A man may destroy everything within himself, love and hate and belief, and even doubt; but as he clings to life he cannot destroy fear: the fear, subtle, indestructible, and terrible that pervades his being, that lurks in his heart; that watches on his lips the struggle of his last breath...."

III

It has been said that women do not read him, but according to my limited experience I believe the contrary. (Where, indeed, would any novelist be if it were not for women?) He has said of Woman: "She is the active partner in the great adventure of humanity on earth and feels an interest in all its episodes." He does not idealise the sex, like George Meredith, nor yet does he describe the baseness of the Eternal Simpleton, as do so many French novelists. He is not always complimentary: witness the portrait of Mrs. Fyne in Chance, and the mosaic of anti-feminist opinions to be found in that story. That he succeeded better with his men is a commonplace of all masculine writers, not that women always succeed with their sex, but to many masters of imaginative literature woman is usually a poet's evocation, not the creature of flesh and blood and bones, of sense and sentiment, that she is in real life. Conrad opens no new windows in her soul, but he has painted some full-length portraits and made many lifelike sketches, which are inevitable. From the shining presence of his mother, the assemblage of a few traits in his Reminiscences, to Flora de Barral in Chance, with her self-tortured temperament, you experience that "emotion of recognition" described by Mr. James. You know they live, that some of them go on marching in your memory after the book has been closed. Their actions always end by resembling their ideas. And their ideas are variegated.

In Under Western Eyes we encounter the lovely Natalie Haldin, a sister in spirit to Helena, to Lisa, to any one of the Turgenieff heroines.

Charm is hers, and a valiant spirit. Her creator has not, thus far, succeeded in bettering her. Only once does he sound a false note. I find her speech a trifle rhetorical after she learns the facts in the case of Razumov (p. 354). Two lines are superfluous at the close of this heart-breaking chapter, and in all the length of the book that is the only flaw I can offer to hungry criticism. The revolutionary group at Geneva--the mysterious and vile Madame de S----, the unhappy slave, Tekla, the much-tried Mrs. Haldin, and the very vital anarchist, surely a portrait sur le vif, Sophia Antonovna, are testimonies of the writer's skill and profound divination of the human heart. (He has confessed that for him woman is "a human being, very much like myself.") The dialogue between Razumov, the spiritual bankrupt, and Sophia in the park is one of those character-revealing episodes that are only real when handled by a supreme artist. Its involutions and undulations, its very recoil on itself as the pair face their memories, he haunted, she suspicious, touch the springs of desperate lives. As an etching of a vicious soul, the Eliza of Chance is arresting. We do not learn her last name, but we remember her brutal attack on little Flora, an attack that warped the poor child's nature. Whether the end of the book is justified is apart from my present purpose, which is chiefly exposition, though I feel that Captain Anthony is not tenderly treated. But "there is a Nemesis which overtakes generosity, too, like all the other imprudences of men who dare to be lawless and proud...." And this sailor, the son of the selfish poet, Carleon Anthony, himself sensitive, but unselfish, paid for his considerate treatment of his wife Flora. Only Hardy could have treated the sex question with the same tact as Conrad (he has done so in Jude the Obscure).

In his sea tales Conrad is a belated romanticist; and in Chance, while the sea is never far off, it is the soul of an unhappy girl that is shown us; not dissected with the impersonal cruelty of surgeon psychologists, but revealed by a sympathetic interpreter who knows the weakness and folly and tragedy of humanity.

The truth is, Conrad is always an analyst; that sets him apart from other writers of sea stories. Chance is different in theme, but not as different in treatment as in construction. His pattern of narration has always been of an evasive character; here the method is carried to the pitch of polyphonic intricacy. The richness of interest, the startling variety, and the philosophic largeness of view--the tale is simple enough otherwise for a child's enjoyment--are a few of its qualities. Coventry Patmore is said to be the poet alluded to as Carleon Anthony, and there are distinct judgments on feminism and the new woman, some wholesome truths uttered at a time when man has seemingly shrivelled up in the glorified feminine vision of mundane things. The moral is to be found on page 447. "Of all the forms offered to us by life it is the one demanding a couple to realise it fully which is the most imperative. Pairing off is the fate of mankind. And if two beings thrown together, mutually attracted, resist the necessity, fail in understanding, and stop voluntarily short ... they are committing a sin against life."

The Duel (published in America under the title of A Point of Honor) is a tour de force in story-telling that would have made envious Balzac. Then there is Winnie Verloc in the Secret Agent, and her cockney sentiment and rancours. She is remarkably "realised," and is a pitiful apparition at the close. The detective Verloc, her husband, wavers as a portrait between reality and melodrama. The minor female characters, her mother and the titled lady patron of the apostle Michaelis, are no mere supernumeraries.

The husband and wife in The Return are nameless but unforgettable. It is a profound parable, this tale. The man discovered in his judgment of his foolish wife that "morality is not a method of happiness." The image in the mirrors in this tale produces a ghastly effect. I enjoyed the amateur anarchist, the English girl playing with bombs in The Informer; she is an admirable foil for the brooding bitterness of the ruined Royalist's daughter in that stirring South American tale, Gaspar Ruiz. Conrad knows this continent of half-baked civilisations; life grows there like rank vegetations. Nostromo is the most elaborate and dramatic study of the sort, and a wildly adventurous romance into the bargain. The two women, fascinating Mrs. Gould and the proud, beautiful Antonia Avellanos, are finely contrasted. And what a mob of cutthroats, politicians, and visionaries! "In real revolutions the best characters do not come to the front," which statement holds as good in Paris as in Petrograd, in New York, or in Mexico. The Nigger of the Narcissus and Nostromo give us the "emotion of multitude."

A genuinely humorous woman is the German skipper's wife in Falk, and the niece, the heroine who turns the head of the former cannibal of Falk--this an echo, doubtless, from the anecdote of the dog-eating granduncle B---- of the Reminiscences--is heroic in her way. Funniest of all is the captain himself. Falk is almost a tragic figure. Amy Foster--in the same volume--is pathetic, and Bessie Carvil, of To-morrow, might have been signed by Hardy. In Youth the old sea-dog's motherly wife is the only woman. As for the impure witch in The Heart of Darkness, I can only say that she creates a new shudder. How she appeals to the imagination! The soft-spoken lady, bereft of her hero in this narrative, who lives in Brussels, is a specimen of Conrad's ability to make reverberate in our memory an enchanting personality, and with a few strokes of the brush. We cannot admire the daughter of poor old Captain Whalley in The End of Tether, but she is the propulsive force of his actions and final tragedy. For her we have "that form of contempt which is called pity." That particular story will rank with the best in the world's literature. Nina Almayer shows the atavistic "pull" of the soil and opposes finesse to force, while Alice Jacobus in 'Twixt Land and Sea (A Smile of Fortune) is half-way on the road back to barbarism. But Nina will be happy with her chief. In depicting the slow decadence of character in mixed races and the naive stammerings at the birth of their souls, Conrad is unapproachable.

In the selection of his titles he is always happy; how happy, may be noted in his new book, Victory. It is not a war book, though it depicts in his most dramatic manner the warring of human instincts. It was planned several years ago, but not finished until the writer's enforced stay in his unhappy native land, Poland. Like Goethe or Stendhal, Conrad can write in the midst of war's alarums about the hair's-breadth 'scapes of his characters. But, then, the Polish is the most remarkable race in Europe; from leading forlorn hopes to playing Chopin the Poles are unequalled. Mr. Conrad has returned to his old habitat in fiction. An ingenious map shows the reader precisely where his tragic tale is enacted. It may not be his most artistic, but it is an engrossing story. Compared with Chance, it seems a cast-back to primitive souls; but as no man after writing such an extraordinary book as Chance will ever escape its influence (after his Golden Bowl, Mr. James was quite another James), so Joseph Conrad's firmer grasp on the burin of psychology shows very plainly in Victory; that is, he deals with elemental causes, but the effects are given in a subtle series of reactions. He never drew a girl but once like Flora de Barral; and, till now, never a man like the Swede, Axel Heyst, who has been called, most appropriately, "a South Sea Hamlet." He has a Hamletic soul, this attractive young man, born with a metaphysical caul, which eventually strangles him. No one but Conrad would dare the mingling of such two dissociated genres as the romantic and the analytic, and if, here and there, the bleak rites of the one, and the lush sentiment of the other, fail to modulate, it is because the artistic undertaking is a well-nigh impossible one. Briefly, Victory relates the adventures of a gentleman and scholar in the Antipodes. He meets a girl, a fiddler in a "Ladies' Orchestra," falls in love, as do men of lofty ideals and no sense of the practical, goes off with her to a lonely island, there to fight for her possession and his own life. The stage-setting is magnificent; even a volcano lights the scene. But the clear, hard-blue sky is quite o'erspread by the black bat Melancholia, and the silence is indeed "dazzling." The villains are melodramatic enough in their behaviour, but, as portraits, they are artfully different from the conventional bad men of fiction. The thin chap, Mr. Jones, is truly sinister, and there is a horrid implication in his woman-hating, which vaguely peeps out in the bloody finale. The hairy servant might be a graduate from The Island of Doctor Moreau of Mr. Wells--one of the beast folk; while the murderous henchman, Ricardo, is unpleasantly put before us. I like the girl; it would have been so easy to spoil her with moralising; but the Baron is the magnet, and, as a counterfoil, the diabolical German hotel keeper. There is too much arbitrary handling at the close for my taste. Only in the opening chapters of Victory does Mr. Conrad pursue his oblique method of taletelling; the pomp and circumstance of a lordly narrative style roll to a triumphant conclusion. This Polish writer easily heads the present school of English fiction.

His most buoyant and attractive girl is Freya Nelson (or Nielsen) in the volume alluded to; she, however, is pure Caucasian, and perhaps more American than European. Her beauty caresses the eye. The story is a good one, though it ends unhappily--another cause for complaint on the part of the sentimentalists who prefer molasses to meat. But this is a tale which is also literature. Conrad will never be coerced into offering his readers sugar-coated tittle-tattle. And at a period when the distaff of fiction is too often in the hands of men the voice of the romantic realist and poetic ironist, Joseph Conrad, sounds a dynamic masculine bass amid the shriller choir. He is an aboriginal force. Let us close with the hearty affirmation of Walt Whitman: "Camerado! this is no book, who touches this, touches a man."

II

A VISIT TO WALT WHITMAN

My edition of Walt Whitman's Leaves of Grass is dated 1867, the third, if I am not mistaken, the first appearing in 1855. Inside is pasted a card upon which is written in large, clumsy letters: "Walt Whitman, Camden, New Jersey, July, 1877." I value this autograph, because Walt gave it to me; rather I paid him for it, the proceeds, two dollars (I think that was the amount), going to some asylum in Camden. In addition, the "good grey poet" was kind enough to add a woodcut of himself as he appeared in the 1855 volume, "hankering, gross, mystical, nude," and another of his old mother, with her shrewd, kindly face. Walt is in his shirt-sleeves, a hand on his hip, the other in his pocket, his neck bare, the pose that of a nonchalant workman--though in actual practice he was always opposed to work of any sort; on his head is a slouch-hat, and you recall his line: "I wear my hat as I please, indoors or out." The picture is characteristic, even to the sensual mouth and Bowery-boy pose. You almost hear him say: "I find no sweeter fat than sticks to my own bones." Altogether a different man from the later bard, the heroic apparition of Broadway, Pennsylvania Avenue, and Chestnut Street. I had convalesced from a severe attack of Edgar Allan Poe only to fall desperately ill with Whitmania. Youth is ever in revolt, age alone brings resignation. My favourite reading was Shelley, my composer among composers, Wagner. Chopin came later. This was in 1876, when the Bayreuth apotheosis made Wagner's name familiar to us, especially in Philadelphia, where his empty, sonorous Centennial March was first played by Theodore Thomas at the Exposition. The reading of a magazine article by Moncure D. Conway caused me to buy a copy, at an extravagant price for my purse, of The Leaves of Grass, and so uncritical was I that I wrote a parallel between Wagner and Whitman; between the most consciously artistic of men and the wildest among improvisators. But then it seemed to me that both had thrown off the "shackles of convention." (What prison-like similes we are given to in the heady, generous impulses of green adolescence.) I was a boy, and seeing Walt on Market Street, as he came from the Camden Ferry, I resolved to visit him. It was some time after the Fourth of July, 1877, and I soon found his little house on Mickle Street. A policeman at the ferry-house directed me. I confess I was scared after I had given the bell one of those pulls that we tremblingly essay at a dentist's door. To my amazement the old man soon stood before me, and cordially bade me enter.

"Walt," I said, for I had heard that he disliked a more ceremonious prefix, "I've come to tell you how much the Leaves have meant to me." "Ah!" he simply replied, and asked me to take a chair. To this hour I can see the humble room, but when I try to recall our conversation I fail. That it was on general literary subjects I know, but the main theme was myself. In five minutes Walt had pumped me dry. He did it in his quiet, sympathetic way, and, with the egoism of my age, I was not averse from relating to him the adventures of my soul. That Walt was a fluent talker one need but read his memoirs by Horace Traubel. Witness his tart allusion to Swinburne's criticism of himself: "Isn't he the damnedest simulacrum?" But he was a sphinx the first time I met him. I do recall that he said Poe wrote too much in a dark cellar, and that music was his chief recreation--of which art he knew nothing; it served him as a sounding background for his pencilled improvisations. I begged for an autograph. He told me of his interest in a certain asylum or hospital, whose name has gone clean out of my mind, and I paid my few dollars for the treasured signature. It is now one of my literary treasures.

If I forget the tenor of our discourse I have not forgotten the immense impression made upon me by the man. As vain as a peacock, Walt looked like a Greek rhapsodist. Tall, imposing in bulk, his regular features, mild, light-blue or grey eyes, clear ruddy skin, plentiful white hair and beard, evoked an image of the magnificently fierce old men he chants in his book. But he wasn't fierce, his voice was a tenor of agreeable timbre, and he was gentle, even to womanliness. Indeed, he was like a receptive, lovable old woman, the kind he celebrates so often. He never smoked, his only drink was water. I doubt if he ever drank spirits. His old friends say "No," although he is a terrible rake in print. Without suggesting effeminacy, he gave me the impression of a feminine soul in a masculine envelope. When President Lincoln first saw him he said: "Well, he _looks_ like a man!" Perhaps Lincoln knew, for his remark has other connotations than the speech of Napoleon when he met Goethe: "Voila un homme!" Hasn't Whitman asked in Calamus, the most revealing section of Leaves: "Do you suppose yourself advancing on real ground toward a real heroic man?" He also wrote of Calamus: "Here the frailest leaves of me.... Here I shade down and hide my thoughts. I do not express them. And yet they expose me more than all my other poems." Mr. Harlan, Secretary of the Interior, when he dismissed Walt from his department because of Leaves, did not know about the Calamus section--I believe they were not incorporated till later--but Washington was acquainted with Walt and his idiosyncrasies, and, despite W. D. Connor's spirited vindication, certain rumours would not be stifled. Walt was thirty-six when Leaves appeared; forty-one when Calamus was written.

I left the old man after a hearty hand-shake, a So long! just as in his book, and returned to Philadelphia. Full of the day, I told my policeman at the ferry that I had seen Walt. "That old gas-bag comes here every afternoon. He gets free rides across the Delaware," and I rejoiced to think that a soulless corporation had some appreciation of a great poet, though the irreverence of this "powerful uneducated person" shocked me. When I reached home I also told my mother of my visit. She was plainly disturbed. She said that the writings of the man were immoral, but she was pleased at my report of Walt's sanity, sweetness, mellow optimism, and his magnetism, like some natural force. I forgot, in my enthusiasm, that it was Walt who listened, I who gabbled. My father, who had never read Leaves, had sterner criticism to offer: "If I ever hear of you going to see that fellow you'll be sorry!" This coming from the most amiable of parents, surprised me. Later I discovered the root of his objection, for, to be quite frank, Walt did not bear a good reputation in Philadelphia, and I have heard him spoken of so contemptuously that it would bring a blush to the shining brow of a whitmaniac. Yet dogs followed him and children loved him. I saw Walt accidentally at intervals, though never again in Camden. I met him on the streets, and several times took him from the Carl Gaertner String Quartet Concerts in the foyer of the Broad Street Academy of Music to the Market Street cars. He lumbered majestically, his hairy breast exposed, but was a feeble old man, older than his years; paralysis had maimed him. He is said to have incurred it from his unselfish labours as nurse in the camp hospitals at Washington during the Civil War; however, it was in his family on the paternal side, and at thirty he was quite grey. The truth is, Walt was not the healthy hero he celebrates in his book. That he never dissipated we know; but his husky masculinity, his posing as the Great God Priapus in the garb of a Bowery boy is discounted by the facts. Parsiphallic, he was, but not of Pan's breed. In the Children of Adam, the part most unfavourably criticised of Leaves, he is the Great Bridegroom, and in no literature, ancient or modern, have been the "mysteries" of the temple of love so brutally exposed. With all his genius in naming certain unmentionable matters, I don't believe in the virility of these pieces, scintillating with sexual images. They leave one cold despite their erotic vehemence; the abuse of the vocative is not persuasive, their raptures are largely rhetorical. This exaltation, this ecstasy, seen at its best in William Blake, is sexual ecstasy, but only when the mood is married to the mot lumiere is there authentic conflagration. Then his "barbaric yawp is heard across the roofs of the world"; but in the underhumming harmonics of Calamus, where Walt really loafs and invites his soul, we get the real man, not the inflated hum-buggery of These States, Camerados, or My Message, which fills Leaves with their patriotic frounces. His philosophy is fudge. It was an artistic misfortune for Walt that he had a "mission," it is a worse one that his disciples endeavour to ape him. He was an unintellectual man who wrote conventionally when he was plain Walter Whitman, living in Brooklyn. But he imitated Ossian and Blake, and their singing robes ill-befitted his burly frame. If, in Poe, there is much "rant and rococo," Whitman is mostly yawping and yodling. He is destitute of humour, like the majority of "prophets" and uplifters, else he might have realised that a Democracy based on the "manly love of comrades" is an absurdity. Not alone in Calamus, but scattered throughout Leaves, there are passages that fully warrant unprejudiced psychiatrists in styling this book the bible of the third sex.

But there is rude red music in the versicles of Leaves. They stimulate, and, for some young hearts, they are as a call to battle. The book is a capital hunting-ground for quotations. Such massive head-lines--that soon sink into platitudinous prose; such robust swinging rhythms, Emerson told Walt that he must have had a "long foreground." It is true. Notwithstanding his catalogues of foreign countries, he was hardly a cosmopolitan. Whitman's so-called "mysticism" is a muddled echo of New England Transcendentalism; itself a pale dilution of an outworn German idealism--what Coleridge called "the holy jungle of Transcendental metaphysics." His concrete imagination automatically rejected metaphysics. His chief asset is an extraordinary sensitiveness to the sense of touch; it is his distinguishing passion, and tactile images flood his work; this, and an eye that records appearances, the surface of things, and registers in phrases of splendour the picturesque, yet seldom fuses matter and manner into a poetical synthesis. The community of interest between his ideas and images is rather affiliated than cognate. He has a tremendous, though ill-assorted vocabulary. His prose is jolting, rambling, tumid, invertebrate. An "arrant artist," as Mr. Brownell calls him, he lacks formal sense and the diffuseness and vagueness of his supreme effort--the Lincoln burial hymn--serves as a nebulous buffer between sheer over-praise and serious criticism. He contrives atmosphere with facility, and can achieve magical pictures of the sea and the "mad naked summer night." His early poem, Walt Whitman, is for me his most spontaneous offering. He has at times the primal gift of the poet--ecstasy; but to attain it he often wades through shallow, ill-smelling sewers, scales arid hills, traverses dull drab levels where the slag covers rich ore, or plunges into subterrene pools of nocturnal abominations--veritable regions of the "mother of dead dogs." Probably the sexlessness of Emerson's, Poe's, and Hawthorne's writings sent Whitman to an orgiastic extreme, and the morbid, nasty-nice puritanism that then tainted English and American letters received its first challenge to come out into the open and face natural facts. Despite his fearlessness, one must subscribe to Edmund Clarence Stedman's epigram: "There are other lights in which a dear one may be regarded than the future mother of men." Walt let in a lot of fresh air on the stuffy sex question of his day, but, in demanding equal sexual rights for women, he meant it in the reverse sense as propounded by our old grannies' purity leagues. Continence is not the sole virtue or charm in womanhood; nor, by the same token, is unchastity a brevet of feminine originality. But women, as a rule, have not rallied to his doctrines, instinctively feeling that he is indifferent to them, notwithstanding the heated homage he pays to their physical attractions. Good old Walt sang of his camerados, capons, Americanos, deck-hands, stagecoach-drivers, machinists, brakemen, firemen, sailors, butchers, bakers, and candlestick makers, and he associated with them; but they never read him or understood him. They prefer Longfellow. It is the cultured class he so despises that discovered, lauded him, believing that he makes vocal the underground world; above all, believing that he truly represents America and the dwellers thereof--which he decidedly does not. We are, if you will, a commonplace people, but normal, and not enamoured of "athletic love of comrades." I remember a dinner given by the Whitman Society about twenty years ago, at the St. Denis Hotel, which was both grotesque and pitiable. The guest of honour was "Pete" Doyle, the former car-conductor and "young rebel friend of Walt's," then a middle-aged person. John Swinton, who presided, described Whitman as a troglodyte, but a cave-dweller he never was; rather the avatar of the hobo. As John Jay Chapman wittily wrote: "He patiently lived on cold pie, and tramped the earth in triumph." Instead of essaying the varied, expressive, harmonious music of blank verse, he chose the easier, more clamorous, and disorderly way; but if he had not so chosen we should have missed the salty tang of the true Walt Whitman. Toward the last there was too much Camden in his Cosmos. Quite appropriately his dying word was le mot de Cambronne. It was the last victory of an organ over an organism. And he was a gay old pagan who never called a sin a sin when it was a pleasure.

III

THE BUFFOON OF THE NEW ETERNITIES: JULES LAFORGUE

I

"Jules Laforgue: Quelle joie!"
--J.-K.-HUYSMANS.

All victories are alike; defeat alone displays an individual profile. And the case of Jules Laforgue wears this special aspect. Dying on the threshold of his twenty-seventh year, coming too old into a world too young, his precocity as poet and master of fantastic prose has yet not the complexion of a Chatterton or a Keats. In his literary remains, slender enough as to quantity, there is little to suggest a fuller development if he had lived. Like his protagonist Arthur Rimbaud--surely the most extraordinary poetic apparition of the nineteenth century--Jules Laforgue accomplished his destiny during the period when most poets are moulding their wings preparatory to flight. He flew in youth, flew moonward, for his patron goddess was Selene, he her faithful worshipper, a true lunalogue. His transcendental indifferentism saved him from the rotten-ripe maturity of them that are born "with a ray of moonlight in their brains," as Villiers de l'Isle Adam hath it. And Villiers has also written: "When the forehead alone contains the existence of a man, that man is enlightened only from above his head; then his jealous shadow, prostrate under him, draws him by the feet, that it may drag him down into the invisible." Like Watteau, Laforgue was "condemned" from the beginning to "a green thought in a green shade." The spirit in him, the "shadow," devoured his soul, pulverised his will, made of him a Hamlet without a propelling cause, a doubter in a world of cheap certitudes and insolent fatuities, but barred him proffering his pearls to pigs. He came before Nietzsche, yet could he have said with Zarathustra: "I love the great despisers because they are the great adorers, they are arrows of longing for the other shore." Now Laforgue was a great despiser.

But he made merry over the ivory, apes, and peacocks of existence. He seems less French than he is in his self-mockery, yet he is a true son of his time and of his country. This young Hamlet, who doubted the constancy of his mother the moon, was a very buffoon; I am the new buffoon of dusty eternities, might have been his declaration; a buffoon making subtle somersaults in the metaphysical blue. He was a metaphysician complicated by a poet. Von Hartmann it was who extorted his homage. "All is relative," was his war-cry on schools and codes and generalisations. His urbanity never deserted him, though it was an exasperated urbanity. His was an art of the nerves. Arthur Symons has spoken of his "icy ecstasy" and Maurice Maeterlinck described his laughter as "laughter of the soul." Like Chopin or Watteau, he danced on roses and thorns. All three were consumptives and the aura of decay floats about their work; all three suffered from the nostalgia of the impossible. The morbid decadent aquafortist that is revealed in the corroding etchings of Laforgue is germane to men in whom irony and pity are perpetually disputing. We think of Heine and his bitter-sweetness. Again with Zarathustra, Laforgue could say: "I do not give alms. I am not poor enough for that." He possesses the sixth sense of infinity. A cosmical jester, his badinage is well-nigh dolorous. His verse and prose form a series of personal variations. The lyric in him is through some temperamental twist reversed. Fantastic dreams overflow his reality, and he always dreams with wide-open eyes. Watteau's l'Indifferent! A philosophical vaudevillist, he juggles with such themes as a metaphysical Armida, the moon and her minion, Pierrot; with celestial spasms and the odour of mortality, or the universal sigh, the autumnal refrains of Chopin, and the monotony of love. "Life is quotidian!" he has sung, and women are the very symbol of sameness, that is their tragedy--or comedy. "Stability thy name is Woman!" exclaims the Hamlet of this most spiritual among parodists.

One never gets him with his back to the wall. He vanishes in the shining cloud of a witty abstraction when cornered. His prose is full of winged neologisms, his poetry heavy with the metaphysics of ennui. Remy de Gourmont speaks of his magnificent work as the prelude to an oratorio achieved in silence. Laforgue, himself, called it an intermezzo, and in truth it is little more. His intellectual sensibility and his elemental soul make for mystifications. As if he knew the frailness of his tenure on life, he sought azure and elliptical routes. He would have welcomed Maeterlinck's test question: "Are you of those who name or those who only repeat names?" Laforgue was essentially a namer--with Gallic glee he would have enjoyed renaming the animals as they left the Noachian ark; yes, and nicknaming the humans, for he is a terrible disrespecter of persons and rank and of the seats of the mighty.

Some one has said that a criticism is negative if it searches for what a writer lacks instead of what he possesses. We should soon reach a zero if we only registered the absence of "necessary" traits in our poet. He is so unlike his contemporaries--with a solitary exception--that his curious genius seems composed of a bundle of negatives. But behind the mind of every great writer there marches a shadowy mob of phrases, which mimics his written words, and makes them untrue indices of his thoughts. These shadows are the unexpressed ideas of which the visible sentences are only eidolons; a cave filled with Platonic phantoms. The phrase of Laforgue has a timbre capable of infinite prolongations in the memory. It is not alone what he says, nor the manner, but his power of arousing overtones from his keyboard. His aesthetic mysticism is allied with a semi-brutal frankness. Feathers fallen from the wings of peri adorn the heads of equivocal persons. Cosmogonies jostle evil farceurs, and the silvery voices of children chant blasphemies. Laforgue could repeat with Arthur Rimbaud: "I accustomed myself to simple hallucinations: I saw, quite frankly, a mosque in place of a factory, a school of drums kept by the angels; post-chaises on the road to heaven, a drawing-room at the bottom of a lake; the title of a vaudeville raised up horrors before me. Then I explained my magical sophisms by the hallucination of words! I ended by finding something sacred in the disorder of my mind" [translation by Arthur Symons]. But while Laforgue with all his "spiritual dislocation" would not deny the "sacred" disorder, he saw life in too glacial a manner to admit that his were merely hallucinations. Rather, correspondences, he would say, for he was as much a disciple of Baudelaire and Gautier in his search for the hidden affinity of things as he was a lover of the antique splendours in Flaubert's Asiatic visions. He, too, dreamed of quintessentials, of the sheer power of golden vocables and the secret alchemy of art. He, too, promenaded his incertitudes, to use a self-revealing phrase of Chopin's. An aristocrat, he knew that in the country of the idiot the imbecile always will be king, and, "like many a one who turned away from life, he only turned away from the rabble, and cared not to share with them well and fire and fruit." His Kingdom of Green was consumed and became grey by the regard of his coldly measuring eye. For him modern man is an animal who bores himself. Laforgue is an essayist who is also a causeur. His abundance is never exuberance. Without sentiment or romance, nevertheless, he does not suggest ossification of the spirit. To dart a lance at mythomania is his delight, while preserving the impassibility of a Parnassian. His travesties of Hamlet, Lohengrin, Salome, Pan, Perseus enchant, their plastic yet metallic prose denotes the unique artist; above all they are modern, they graze the hem of the contemporaneous. From the sublime to the arabesque is but a semitone in his antic mien. Undulating in his desire to escape the automatic, doubting even his own scepticism, Jules Laforgue is a Hamlet a rebours. Old Fletcher sings:

"Then stretch our bones in a still, gloomy valley,
Nothing's so dainty sweet as lovely melancholy."

II

He seems to have been of an umbrageous character. His life was sad and simple. He was born August 20, 1860, at Montevideo--"Ville en amphitheatre, toits en terrasses, rues en daumiers, rade enorme"--of Breton parentage. He died at Paris, 1887. Gustave Kahn, the symbolist poet, describes Laforgue in his Symbolistes and Decadents as a serious young man, with sober English manners and an extreme rectitude in the matter of clothes. Not the metaphysical Narcissus that was once Maurice Barres--whose early books show the influence of Laforgue. He adored the philosophy of the Unconscious as set forth by Von Hartmann, was erudite, collected delicate art, thought much, read widely, and was an ardent advocate of the Impressionistic painters. I have a pamphlet by Mederic Dufour, entitled Etude sur l'AEthetique de Jules Laforgue: une Philosophie de l'Impressionisme, which is interesting, though far from conclusive, being an attack on the determinism of Taine, and a defence of Monet, Pissarro, and Sisley. But then we only formulate our preferences into laws. The best thing in it is the phrase: "There are no types, there is only humanity," to the wisdom of which we must heartily subscribe. From 1880 to 1886 Laforgue was

reader to the Empress Augusta at Berlin and was admired by the
cultivated court circle, as his letters to his sister and M.
Ephrussi, his friend, testify. He was much at home in Germany and
there is no denying the influence of Teutonic thought and spirit on
his susceptible nature. Naturally prone to pessimism (he has called
himself a "mystic pessimist") as was Amiel, the study of Hegel,
Schopenhauer, and Hartmann solidified the sentiment. He met an English
girl, Leah Lee, by name, and after giving her lessons in French, fell
in love, and in 1887 married her. It is interesting to observe the
sinister dandy in private life, as a tender lover, a loving brother.
This spiritual dichotomy is not absent in his poetry. He holds back
nothing in his self-revelations, except the sad side, though there is
always an exquisite tremulous sensibility in his baffling art. A few
months after his marriage he was attacked by the fatal malady, as was
his unfortunate wife, and he was buried on his twenty-seventh
birthday. Gustave Kahn notes that few followed him to the grave. He
was unknown except to some choice spirits, the dozen superior persons
of Huysmans, scattered throughout the universe. His wife survived him
only a short time. Little has been written of him, the most complete
estimate being that of Camille Mauclair, with an introduction by
Maeterlinck--who calls his Hamlet more Hamlet than Shakespeare's. In
addition to these, and Dufour, Kahn, De Gourmont and Felix Feneon, we
have in English essays by George Moore, Arthur Symons, Philip Hale,
the critic of music, and Aline Gorren. Mr. Moore introduced Laforgue
in company with Rimbaud to the English reading world and Mr. Symons
devoted to him one of his sensitive studies in The Symbolist Movement
in Literature. Mr. Hale did the same years ago for American readers in
a sympathetic article, The Fantastical Jules Laforgue. He also
translated with astonishing fidelity to the letter and spirit of the
author, his incomparable Lohengrin, Fils de Parsifal. I regret having
it no longer in my possession so that I might quote from its delicious
prose. As to the verse, I know of few attempts to translate the
untranslatable. Perhaps Mr. Symons has tried his accomplished hand at
the task. How render the sumptuous assonance and solemn rhythms of
Marche Funebre: O convoi solennel des soleils magnifiques?

III

"Je ne suis qu'un viveur lunaire
Qui faits des ronds dans les bassins
Et cela, sans autre dessin
Que devenir un legendaire...."

Sings our poet in the silver-fire verse of L'Imitation de Notre-Dame
la Lune, wherein he asks--Mais ou sont les Lunes d'Antan. This Pierrot
lunaire, this buffoon of new and dusty eternities, wrote a sort of
vers libres, which, often breaking off with a smothered sob,
modulates into prose and sings the sorrows and complaints of a world
peopled by fantastic souls, clowns, somnambulists, satyrs, poets,
harlots, dainty girls, Cheret posters, pierrots, kings of pyschopathic
tastes, blithe birds, and sad-coloured cemeteries. The poet is a
mocking demon who rides on clouds dropping epigrams earthward, the
earth that grunts and sweats beneath the sun or cowers and weeps under
the stellar prairies. He mockingly calls himself "The Grand Chancellor
of Analysis." Like Nietzsche he dances when his heart is heavy, and
trills his roundelays and his gamut of rancorous flowers with an
enigmatic smile on his lips. It is a strange and disquieting music, a
pageantry of essences, this verse with its resonance of emerald.
Appearing in fugitive fashion, it was gathered into a single volume
through the efforts of friends and with the Moralites legendaires
comprises his life-work, for we can hardly include the Melanges
posthumes, which consist of scraps and fragments (published in 1903)
together with some letters, not a very weighty addition to the dead
poet's fame. His translations of Walt Whitman I've not seen. Perhaps
his verse is doomed; it was born in the hectic flush of early
dissolution, but it is safe to predict that as long as lovers of rare
literature exist the volume of prose will survive. It has for the

gourmet of style an unending charm, the charm en sourdine of its creator, to whom a falling leaf or an empire in dissolution was of equal value. "His work," wrote Mr. Symons, "has the fatal evasiveness of those who shrink from remembering the one thing which they are unable to forget. Coming as he does after Rimbaud, turning the divination of the other into theories, into achieved results, he is the eternally grown-up nature to the point of self-negation, as the other is the eternal enfant terrible." Tout etait pour le vieux dans le meilleur des mondes, Laforgue would have cried in the epigram of Paul Bourget.

The prose of Jules Laforgue recalls to me his description of the orchestra in Salome, the fourth of the Moralites legendaires. Sur un mode allegre et fataliste, un orchestre aux instruments d'ivoire improvisait une petite overture unanime. That his syllables are of ivory I feel, and improvised, but his themes are pluralistic, the immedicable and colossal ennui of life the chiefest. Woman--the "Eternal Madame," as Baudelaire calls her--is a being both magical and mediocre; she is also an escape from the universal world-pain. La fin de l'homme est proche ... Antigone va passer du menage de la famille au menage de la planete (prophetic words). But when lovely woman begins to talk of the propagation of the ideal she only means the human species. With Lessing he believes: "There is, at most, but one disagreeable woman in the world; a pity then that every man gets her for himself."

It is rather singular to observe in the writings of Marinetti, the self-elected leader of the so-called Futurists, the hopeless deliquescence of the form invented by Louis Bertrand in his Gaspard de la Nuit, and developed with almost miraculous results in Baudelaire and terminating with Huysmans, Maeterlinck, and Francis Poictevin ("Paysages"). Rimbaud had intervened. In his Illuminations we read that "so soon as the Idea of the Deluge had sunk back into its place, a rabbit halted amid the sainfoin and the small swinging bells, and said its prayers to the rainbow through the spider's web. Oh! The precious stones in hiding, the flowers already looking out ... Madame X established a piano in the Alps.... The caravans started. And the Splendid Hotel was erected upon the chaos of ice and night of the Pole" (from the translation by Aline Gorren). This, apparently mad sequence of words and dissociation of ideas, has been deciphered by M. Kahn, and need not daunt any one who has patience and ingenuity. I confess I prefer Laforgue, who at his most cryptic is never so wildly tantalising as Rimbaud.

Moralites legendaires contains six sections. I don't know which to admire the most, the Hamlet or the Lohengrin, the Salome or the Persee et Andromede. Le Miracle des Roses is of an exceeding charm, though dealing with the obvious, while Pan et la Syrinx has a quality which I can recall nowhere else in literature; perhaps in the cadences charged with the magic and irony of Chopin, or in the half-dreams of Watteau, colour and golden sadness intermingled, may evoke the spiritual parodies of Laforgue, but in literature there is no analogue, though Pan is of classic flavour despite his very modern Weltanschauung. Syrinx is a woodland creature nebulous and exquisite. Pursued by Pan--the Eternal Male in rut--she does not succumb to his pipes, and after she has vanished in the lingering wind, he blows sweeter music through his seven reeds. The symbol is not difficult to decipher. And who would not succumb to the languorous melancholy of Andromede, not chained to a rock but living on the best of terms with her monster, who calls her Bebe! The sea bores her profoundly. She looks for Perseus, who doesn't come; the sea, always the sea without a moment's weakness; in brief, not the stuff of which friends are made! When the knight appears and kills her monster, he loses his halo for Andromede, who cherishes her monstrous guardian. Perseus, a prig disgusted by the fickleness of the Young Person, flees, and the death of the monster brings to life a lovely youth--put under the spell of malignant powers--who promptly weds his ward. In Lohengrin, Son of Parsifal, the whole machinery of the Wagner opera is transposed to the key of lunar parody. What ambrosia from the Walhalla of topsyturvy is this Elsa with her "eyes hymeneally illumined" as she awaits her saviour. He appears and they are married. Alas! The pillow of the nuptial couch becomes a swan that carries off Lohengrin weary of the tart queries made by his little bride concerning love and sex and other unimportant questions of daily life. This Elsa is a sensual goose. She is also a stubborn believer in the biblical injunction: "Crescite et multiplicamini," and she would willingly allow the glittering stranger Knight to brise le sceau de ses petites solitudes, as the Vicar of Diane-Artemis phrases it. The landscapes of these tales are fantastically beautiful, and scattered through the narrative are fragments of verse, vagrant and witty, that light up the stories with a glowworm phosphorescence.

Salome and her celebrated eyebrows is a spiritual sister of Flaubert's damsel, as Elsa is nearly related to his Salammbo. She dwells in the far-off Iles Blanches Esoteriques, and she, too, is annoyed by the stupidity of the sea, always new, always respectable! She is the first of the Salomes since Flaubert who has caught some of her prototype's fragrance. (Oscar Wilde's attempt proved mediocre. He introduced a discordant pathological note, but the music of Richard Strauss may save his pasticcio. It interprets the exotic prose of the Irishman with tongues of fire; it laps up the text, encircles it, underlines, amplifies, comments, and in nodules of luminosity, makes clear that which is dark, ennobles much that is vain, withal it never insists on leading; the composer appears to follow the poet.) Laforgue's Salome tries to sport with the head of John the Baptist, stumbles, loses her footing, and falls from the machicolated wall on jagged rocks below, as the head floats out to sea, miraculously alight. There are wit and philosophy and the hint of high thoughts in Salome, though her heart like glass is cold, empty, and crystalline.

The subtitle of Hamlet, which heads the volume, is--Or, the Results of Filial Devotion--and the story, as Mr. Hale asserts, is Laforgue's masterpiece. Here is a Hamlet for you, a prince whose antics are enough to disturb the dust of Shakespeare and make the angels on high weep with hysterical laughter. Not remotely hinting at burlesque, the character is delicately etched. By the subtle withdrawal of certain traits, this Hamlet behaves as a man would who has been trepanned and his moral nature removed by an analytical surgeon. He is irony personified and is the most delightful company for one weary of the Great Good Game around and about us, the game of deceit, treachery, politics, love, social intercourse, religion, and commerce. Laforgue's Hamlet sees through the hole in the mundane millstone and his every phrase is like the flash of a scimitar.

It is the irony of his position, the irony of his knowledge that he is Shakespeare's creation and must live up to his artistic paternity; the irony that he is au fond a cabotin, a footlight strutter, a mouther of phrases metaphysical and a despiser of Ophelia (chere petite glu he names her) that are all so appealing. Intellectual braggart, this Hamlet resides after his father Horwendill's "irregular decease" in a tower hard by the Sound, from which Helsingborg may be seen. An old, stagnant canal is beneath his windows. In his chamber are waxen figures of his mother, Gerutha, and his uncle-father, Fengo. He daily pierces their hearts with needles after a bad old-fashioned mediaeval formula of witchcraft. But it avails naught. With a fine touch he seeks for his revenge by having enacted before their Majesties of Denmark his own play. They incontinently collapse in mortal nausea, for they are excellent critics.

Such a play scene, withal Shakespearian! "Stability thy name is woman!" he exclaims bitterly, for he fears love with the compromising domesticity of marriage. It is his rigorous transvaluation of all moral values and conventionalities that proclaims this Hamlet a man of the future. No half-way treaties with the obvious in life, no crooking the pregnant hinges of his opinions to the powers that be. An anarch, pure and complex, he despises all methods. What soliloquies, replete with the biting, cynical wisdom of a disillusionised soul!

"Ah," he sighs, "there are no longer young girls, they are all nurses. Ophelia loves me because, as Hobbes claims: 'Nothing is more agreeable in our ownership of goods than the thought that they are superior to the goods of others.' Now I am socially and morally superior to the 'goods' of her little friends. She wishes to make me, Hamlet, comfortable. Ah, if I could only have met Helen of Narbonne!" A Hamlet who quotes the author of The Leviathan is a Hamlet with a vengeance.

To him enter the players William and Kate. He reads them his play. Kate's stage name is Ophelia. "Comment!" cries Hamlet, "encore une Ophelia dans ma potion!" William doesn't like the play because his part is not "sympathetic." After they retire Hamlet indulges in a passionate outburst reproaching the times with its hypocrisy and des hypocrites et routinieres jeunes filles. If women but knew they would prostrate themselves before him as did the weeping ones upon the body of the dead Adonis! The key of this discourse is high-pitched and cutting. Laforgue, a philosopher, a pessimist, makes his art the canvas for his ironic temperament. The Prince's interview with Ophelia is full of soundless mirth. And how he lavishes upon his own deranged head offensive abuse: "Piteous provincial! Cabotin! Pedicure!" This last is his topmost term of contempt.

His parleying with the grave-diggers is another stroke of wit. One of them tells him that Polonius is carried off by apoplexy--a bust has been erected to his memory bearing the inscription, "Words! Words! Words!" He also learns that Yorick was his half-brother, the son of a gipsy woman. Ophelia dies--he hears this with mixed feelings--and he is informed that the young Prince Hamlet is quite mad. The grave-digger is a philosopher, he thinks that Fortinbras is at hand, that the best investment for his money will be in Norwegian bonds. The funeral cortege approaches. Hamlet hides.

His soliloquy upon the skull of Yorick has been partly done into English by Mr. Symons.

"Alas, poor Yorick! As one seems to hear in this little shell, the multitudinous roar of the ocean, so I hear the whole quenchless symphony of the universal soul, of whose echoes this box was its cross-roads. There's a solid idea!... Perhaps I have twenty or thirty years to live, and I shall pass away like the others. Like the others? O Totality, the misery of being there no longer! Ah! I would like to set out to-morrow and search all through the world for the most adamantine processes of embalming. They, too, were the little people of History, learning to read, trimming their nails, lighting the dirty lamp every evening, in love, gluttonous, vain, fond of compliments, handshakes, and kisses, living on bell-town gossip, saying, 'What sort of weather shall we have to-morrow? Winter has really come.... We have had no plums this year.' Ah! Everything is good, if it would not come to an end. And thou, Silence, pardon the earth; the little madcap hardly knows what he is doing; on the day of the great summing-up before the Ideal, she will be labelled with a piteous _idem_ in the column of the miniature evolutions of the Unique Evolution, in the column of negligible quantities.... To die! Evidently, one does without knowing it, as, every night, one enters upon sleep. One has no consciousness of the passing of the last lucid thought into sleep, into swooning, into death. Evidently. But to be no more, to be here no more, to be ours no more! Not even to be able, any more, to press against one's human heart, some idle afternoon, the ancient sadness contained in one little chord on the piano!"

And this "secular sadness" pursues the heartless Hamlet to the cemetery; he returns after dark in company with the buxom actress Kate. They have eloped.

But the fatal irresolution again overtakes him. He would see Ophelia's tomb for the last time, and as he attempts to decipher its inscription, Laertes--idiot d'humanite, the average sensible man--approaches and the pair hold converse. It is a revelation of the face of foolishness. Laertes reproaches Hamlet. He has by his trifling with Ophelia caused her death. Laertes calls him a poor demented one, exclaims over his lack of moral sense, and winds up by bidding the crazy Prince leave the cemetery. Quand on finit par folie, c'est qu'on a commence par le cabotinage. (Which is a consoling axiom for an actor.) Hamlet with his naïve irony calmly inquires:

"And thy sister!" This is too much for the distracted brother, who poignards the Prince. Hamlet expires with Nero's cry on his lips:

"Ah! Ah! _Qualis ... artifex ... pereo!_" And, as the author remarks: "He rendered to immutable nature his Hamletic soul." William enters and, discovering his Kate, gives her a sound beating; not the first or the last, as she apprises us. The poem ends with this motto: Un Hamlet de moins; la race n'en est pas perdue, qu'on se le dise! Which is chilly truth.

The artistic beauty of the prose, its haunting assonance, its supple rhythms make this Hamlet impossible save in French. Nor can the fine edge of its wit, its multiple though masked ironies, its astounding transposition of Shakespearian humour and philosophy be aught else than loosely paraphrased. Laforgue's Hamlet is of to-morrow, for every epoch orchestrates anew its own vision of Hamlet. The eighteenth century had one; the nineteenth had another; and our generation a fresher. But we know of none so vital as this fantastic thinker of Laforgue's. He must have had his ear close to the Time Spirit, so aptly has he caught the vibrations of his whirring loom, so closely to these vibrations has he attuned the key-note of his twentieth-century Hamlet.

IV

DOSTOIEVSKY AND TOLSTOY
AND THE YOUNGER CHOIR OF RUSSIAN WRITERS

I

"It is terrible to watch a man who has the Incomprehensible in his grasp, does not know what to do with it, and sits playing with a toy called God."
--_Letter to his brother Michael._

In his Criticism and Fiction, Mr. Howells wrote: "It used to be one of the disadvantages of the practice of romance in America, which Hawthorne more or less whimsically lamented, that there were few shadows and inequalities in our broad level of prosperity; and it is one of the reflections suggested by Dostoievsky's novel, The Crime and the Punishment, that whoever struck a note so profoundly tragic in American fiction would do a false and mistaken thing--as false and as mistaken in its way as dealing in American fiction with certain nudities which the Latin peoples seem to find edifying."

Who cares nowadays for the hard-and-fast classifications of idealist, realist, romanticist, psychologist, symbolist, and the rest of the phrases, which are only so much superfluous baggage for literary camp-followers. All great romancers are realists, and the converse may be true. You note it in Dumas and his gorgeous, clattering tales--improbable, but told in terms of the real. For my part, I often find them too real, with their lusty wenches and heroes smelling of the slaughter-house. Turn now to Flaubert, master of all the moderns; you may trace the romancer dear to the heart of Hugo, or the psychologist in Madame Bovary, the archaeological novel in Salammbo, or cold, grey realism as in L'Education Sentimentale, while his very style, with its sumptuous verbal echoes, its resonant, rhythmic periods--is not all this the beginning of that symbolism carried to such lengths by Verlaine and his followers? Shakespeare himself ranged from gross naturalism to the quiring of cherubim.

Walter Scott was a master realist if you forget his old-fashioned operatic scenery and costumes. It is to Jane Austen we must go for the realism admired of Mr. Howells, and justly. Her work is all of a piece. The Russians are realists, but with a difference; and that deviation forms the school. Taking Gogol as the norm of modern Russian fiction--Leo Wiener's admirable anthology surprises with its specimens of earlier men--we see the novel strained through the rich, mystic imagination of Dostoievsky; viewed through the more equable, artistic, and pessimistic temperament of Turgenieff, until it is seized by Leo Tolstoy and passionately transformed to serve his own didactic purposes. Realism? Yes, such as the world has never before seen, and yet at times as idealistic as Shelley. It is not surprising that Mr. John M. Robertson wrote, as far back as 1891: "In that strange country where brute power seems to be throttling all the highest life of the people ... there yet seems to be no cessation in the production of truthful literary art ... for justice of perception, soundness and purity of taste, and skill of workmanship, we in England, with all our freedom, can offer no parallel."

Perhaps "freedom" is the reason.

And what would this critic have said of the De Profundis of Maxim Gorky? Are there still darker depths to be explored? Little wonder Mr. Robertson calls Kipling's "the art of a great talent with a cheap culture and a flashy environment." Therefore, to talk of such distinctions as realism and romance is sheer waste of time. It is but a recrudescence of the old classic _vs._ romantic conflict. Stendhal has written that a classicist is a dead romanticist. It still holds good. But here in America, "the colourless shadow land of fiction," is there no tragedy in Gilead for souls not supine? Some years ago Mr. James Lane Allen, who cannot be accused of any hankerings after the flesh-pots of Zola, made an energetic protest against what he denominated the "feminine principle" in our fiction. He did not mean the books written by women--in sooth, they are for the most part boiling over with the joy of life--but he meant the feminism of so much of our novel writing put forth by men.

The censor in Russia by his very stringency caused a great fictional literature to blossom, despite his forbidding blue pencil. In America the sentiment of the etiolated, the brainless, the prudish, the hypocrite is the censor. (Though something might be said now about the pendulum swinging too far in the opposite direction.) Not that Mr. Howells is strait-laced, prudish, narrow in his views--but he puts his foot down on the expression of the tragic, the unusual, the emotional. With him, charming artist, it is a matter of temperament. He admires with a latitude quite foreign to English-speaking critics such diverse genius as Flaubert, Tolstoy, Turgenieff, Galdos, Jane Austen, Emilia Pardo Bazan, Mathilde Serao--greater than any modern woman writer of fiction--Henry James, and George Moore. But he admires each on his or her native heath. That their particular methods might be given universal application he does not admit. And when he wrote the above about Dostoievsky New York was not so full of Russians and Poles and people from southeastern Europe as it is now. Dostoievsky, if he were alive, would find plenty of material, tragedy and comedy alike, on our East Side.

The new translation of Dostoievsky in English by Constance Garnett is significant. A few years ago Crime and Punishment was the only one of his works well known. The Possessed, that extraordinary study of souls obsessed by madness and crime, The Brothers Karamazov, The House of the Dead, and The Idiot are to-day in the hands of American readers who indorse what Nietzsche said of the Russian master: "This profound man ... has perceived that Siberian convicts, with whom he lived for a long time (capital criminals for whom there was no return to society), were persons carved out of the best, the hardest and the most valuable material to be found in the Russian dominions.... Dostoievsky, the only psychologist from whom I had anything to learn." George Moore once had dubbed the novelist, "Gaboriau with psychological sauce." Since then, Mr. Moore has contributed a charming introduction to Poor Folk, yet there is no denying the force and wit of his hasty epigram. Dostoievsky is often melodramatic and violent; his "psychology" vague and tortuous.

And in the letters exchanged between Nietzsche and Georg Brandes, the latter writes of Dostoievsky after his visit to Russia: "He is a great poet but a detestable fellow, altogether Christian in his emotions, and quite _sadique_ at the same time. All his morality is what you have christened 'Slave's' morality.... Look at Dostoievsky's face: half the face of a Russian peasant, half the physiognomy of a criminal, flat nose, little penetrating eyes, under lids trembling with nervousness, the forehead large and well-shaped, the expressive mouth telling of tortures without count, of unfathomable melancholy, of morbid desires, endless compassion, passionate envy. An epileptic genius whose very exterior speaks of the stream of mildness that fills his heart, of the wave of almost insane perspicuity that gets into his head, finally the ambition, the greatness of endeavour, and the envy that small-mindedness begets.... His heroes are not only poor and crave sympathy, but are half imbeciles, sensitive creatures, noble drabs, often victims of hallucinations, talented epileptics, enthusiastic seekers after martyrdom, the very types that we are compelled to suppose probable among the apostles and disciples of the early Christian era. Certainly no mind stands further removed from the Renaissance."

Of all Dostoievsky's portraits after Sonia, the saintly prostitute, that of Nastasia Philipovna in The Idiot is the most lifelike and astounding. The career of this half-mad girl is sinister and tragic; she is half-sister in her temperamental traits to Paulina in the same master's admirable story The Gambler. Grushenka in The Brothers Karamazov is another woman of the demoniac type to which Nastasia belongs. Then there are high-spirited, hysterical girls such as Katarina in Karamazov, Aglaia Epanchin in The Idiot, or Liza in The Possessed (Besi). The border-land of puberty is a favourite theme with the Russian writer. And consider the splendidly fierce old women, mothers, aunts, grandmothers (Granny in The Gambler is a full-length portrait worthy of Hogarth) and befuddled old men--retired from service in state and army; Dostoievsky is a masterly painter of drunkards, drabs, and neuropaths. Prince Mushkin (or Myshkin) the semi-idiot in The Idiot is depicted with surpassing charm. He is half cracked and an epileptic, but is one of the most lovable young men in fiction. Thinking of him, you recall what Nietzsche wrote of Christ: "One regrets that a Dostoievsky did not live in the neighbourhood of this most interesting decadent, I mean some one who knew just how to perceive the thrilling charm of such a mixture of the sublime, the sickly, and the childish." Here is a "moral landscape of the dark Russian soul," and an exemplification in the Prince Myshkin of The Idiot, who is evidently an attempt to portray a latter-day Christ.

Raskolnikov in Crime and Punishment, like Rogozhin in The Idiot, Stavrogin in The Possessed were supermen before Nietzsche, but all half mad. A famous alienist has declared that three-fourths of Dostoievsky's characters are quite mad. This is an exaggeration, though there are many about whom the aura of madness and melancholy hovers. Dostoievsky himself was epileptic; poverty and epilepsy were his companions through a life crowded with unhappiness. (Born 1822, died 1881.) He was four years in Siberia, condemned though innocent as a member of the Petrachevsky group. He tells us that the experience calmed his nerves. His recollections of his Dead House are harrowing, and make the literature of prison life, whether written by Hugo, Zola,

Tolstoy, or others, like the literary exercise of an amateur. It is this sense of reality, of life growing like grass over one's head, that renders the novels of Dostoievsky "human documents." Calling himself a "proletarian of letters" this tender-hearted man denied being a psychologist--which pre-eminently he was: "They call me a psychologist; it is not true. I am only a realist in the highest sense of the word, _i. e._, I depict all the soul's depths."

If he has shown us the soul of the madman, drunkard, libertine, the street-walker, he has also exposed the psychology of the gambler.

He knew. He was a desperate gambler and in Baden actually starved in company with his devoted wife. These experiences may be found depicted in The Gambler.

He has been called the "Bossuet of the detraques," but I prefer that other and more appropriate title, the Dante of the North. His novels are infernos. How well Nietzsche studied him; they were fellow spirits in suffering. All Dostoievsky is in his phrase: "There are no ugly women"--put in the mouth of the senile, debauched Karamazov, a companion portrait to Balzac's Baron Hulot. His love for women has a pathological cast. His young girls discuss unpleasant matters. Even Frank Wedekind is anticipated in his Spring's Awakening by the Russian in The Brothers Karamazov: "How can Katarina have a baby if she isn't married?" cries one of the youngsters, a question which is the very nub of the Wedekind play. "Two parallel lines may meet in eternity," which sounds like Ibsen's query: "Two and two may make five on the planet Jupiter." He was deeply pious, nevertheless a questioner. His books are full of theological wranglings. Consider the "prose-poem" of the Grand Inquisitor and the second coming of Christ. Or such an idea as the "craving for community of worship is the chief misery of man, of all humanity from the beginning of time." We recognise Nietzsche in Dostoievsky's "the old morality of the old slave man," and a genuine poet in "the secret of the earth mingles with the mystery of the stars." His naive conception of eternity as "a chamber something like a bathhouse, long neglected, and with spider's webs in its corners" reminds us of Nietzsche when he describes his doctrine of the Eternal Recurrence. The Russian has told us in memorable phrases of the blinding, intense happiness, a cerebral spasm, which lasts the fraction of a second at the beginning of an epileptic attack. For it he declares, for that brief moment during which paradise is disclosed, he would sacrifice a lifetime. Little wonder in the interim of a cold, grey, miserable existence he suffered from what he calls "mystic fear," the fear of fear, such as Maeterlinck shows us in The Intruder. As for the socialists he says their motto is: "Don't dare to believe in God, don't dare to have property, fraternity or death, two millions of heads!"

The foundational theme of his work is an overwhelming love for mankind, a plea for solidarity which too often degenerates into sickly sentimentalism. He imitated Dickens, George Sand, and Victor Hugo--the Hugo of Les Miserables. He hated Turgenieff and caricatured him in The Possessed. It is true that in dialogue he has had few superiors; his men and women talk as they would talk in life and only in special instances are mouthpieces for the author's ideas--in this quite different from so many of Tolstoy's characters. Merejkowski has said without fear of contradiction that Dostoievsky is like the great dramatists of antiquity in his "art of gradual tension, accumulation, increase, and alarming concentration of dramatic action." His books are veritably tragic. In Russian music alone may be found a parallel to his poignant pathos and gloomy imaginings and shuddering climaxes. What is more wonderful than Chapter I of The Idiot with its adumbration of the entire plot and characterisation of the book, or Chapter XV and its dramatic surprises.

His cardinal doctrine of non-resistance is illustrated in the following anecdote. One evening while walking in St. Petersburg, evidently in meditation a beggar asked for alms. Dostoievsky did not answer. Enraged by his apparent indifference, the man gave him such a violent blow that he was knocked off his legs. On arising he picked up his hat, dusted his clothes, and walked away; but a policeman who saw the attack came running toward the beggar and took him to the lock-up. Despite his protest Dostoievsky accompanied them. He refused to make a charge, for he argued that he was not sure the prisoner was the culpable one; it was dark and he had not seen his face. Besides, he might have been sick in his mind; only a sick person would attack in such a manner. Sick, cried the examining magistrate, that drunken good-for-nothing sick! A little rest in jail would do him good. You are wrong, contradicted the accused, I am not drunk but hungry. When a man has eaten, he doesn't believe that another is starving. True, answered Dostoievsky, this poor chap was crazy with hunger. I shan't make a complaint. Nevertheless the ruffian was sentenced to a month's imprisonment. Dostoievsky gave him three roubles before he left. Now this kind man was, strange as it may seem, an anti-Semite. His diary revealed the fact after his death. In life he kept this prejudice to himself. I always think of Dostoievsky as a man in shabby clothes mounting at twilight an obscure staircase in some St. Petersburg hovel, the moon shining dimly through the dirty window-panes, and cobwebs and gloom abounding. "I love to hear singing to a street organ; I like it on cold, dark, damp autumn evenings, when all the passers-by have pale, green, sickly faces, or when wet snow is falling straight down; the night is windless ... and the street lamps shine through it," said Raskolnikov. Here is the essential Dostoievsky.

And his tenacious love of life is exemplified in Raskolnikov's musing: "Where is it I've read that some one condemned to death says or thinks an hour before his death, that if he had to live on some high rock, on such a narrow ledge that he would only have room to stand, and the ocean, everlasting darkness, everlasting solitude, everlasting tempest around him, if he had to remain standing on a square yard of space all his life, a thousand years, eternity, it were better to live than to die at once." We feel the repercussion of his anguish when death was imminent for alleged participation in a nihilistic conspiracy. Or, again, that horrid picture of a "boxed eternity": "We always imagine eternity as something beyond our conception, something vast, vast! But why must it be vast? Instead of all that, what if it's one little room, like a bath-house in the country, black and grimy and spiders in every corner, and that's all eternity is? I sometimes fancy it is that." The grotesque and the sinister often nudge elbows in these morbid, monstrous pages.

His belief in the unchanging nature of mankind is pure fatalism. "Afterwards I understand ... that men won't change and that nobody can alter it and that it's not worth wasting efforts over it.... Whoever is strong in mind and spirit will have power over them. He who despises most things will be a lawgiver among them, and he who dares most of all will be most in right. Any one who is greatly daring is right in their eyes. So it has been till now, and so it always will be." Thus Rodion, the student to the devoted Sonia. It sounds like Nietzsche avant la lettre. Or the cynicism of: "Every one thinks of himself, and he lives most gaily who knows best how to deceive himself." He speaks of his impending exile to Siberia: "But I wonder shall I in those fifteen or twenty years grow so meek that I shall humble myself before people and whimper at every word that I am a criminal. Yes, that's it, that's it, that's what they are sending me there for, that's what they want. Look at them running to and fro about the streets, every one of them a scoundrel and a criminal at heart, and worse still, an idiot. But try to get me off and they'd be wild with righteous indignation. Oh, how I hate them all!" (The above excerpts are from the admirable translation by Constance Garnett.)

As for his own mental condition, Dostoievsky gives us a picture of it in Injury and Insult: "As soon as it grew dusk I gradually fell into that state of mind which so often overmasters me at night since I've been ill, and which I shall call mystic fear. It is a crushing anxiety about something which I can neither define nor even conceive, which does not actually exist, but which perhaps is about to be realised, at this very moment, to appear and rise up before me like an inexorable, horrible misshapen fact." This "frenzied anguish" is a familiar stigma of epilepsy. Its presence denotes the approach of an attack.

But the "sacred malady" had, in the case of Dostoievsky, its compensations. Through this fissure in the walls of his neurotic soul he peered and saw its strange perturbations, divined their origins in the very roots of his being, and recorded--as did Poe, Baudelaire, and Nietzsche--the fluctuations of his sick will. With this Russian, his Hamlet-like introspection becomes vertigo, and life itself fades into a dream compounded of febrile melancholy or blood lust. It was not without warrant that he allows Rogoszin, in The Idiot, to murder Nastasia Philipovna, because of her physical charms. The aura of the man foredoomed to morbid crime is unmistakable.

The letters of Fyodor Michailovitch Dostoievsky came as a revelation to his admirers. We think of him as overflowing with sentiment for his fellow man, a socialist, one who "went to the people" long before Tolstoy dreamed of the adventure, a man four years in prison in Siberia, and six more in that bleak country under official inspection; truly, a martyr to his country, an epileptic and a genius. You may be disappointed to learn from these telltale documents--translated by Ethel Colburn Mayne--that the Russian writer while in exile avoided his fellow convicts, was very unpopular with them, and that throughout his correspondence there are numerous contemptuous references to socialism and "going to the people." He preferred solitude, he asserts more than once, to the company of common folk or mediocre persons. He gives Tolstoy at his true rating, but is cruel to Turgenieff--who never wished him harm. The Dostoievsky caricature portrait of Turgenieff--infinitely the superior artist of the two--in The Possessed is absurd. Turgenieff forgave, but Dostoievsky never forgave Turgenieff for this forgiveness. Another merit of these letters is the light they shed on the true character of Tolstoy, who is shown in his proper environment, neither a prophet nor a heaven-storming reformer. Dostoievsky invented the phrase: "land-proprietor literature," to describe the fiction of both Tolstoy and Turgenieff. He was abjectly poor, gambled when he got the chance (which was seldom), hated Western Europe, France and Germany in particular, but admired the novels of George Sand, Victor Hugo, and Charles Dickens. He tells us much of his painful methods of writing ("what do I want with fame when I'm writing for daily bread?" he bitterly asks his brother), and the overshadowing necessity that compelled him to turn in "copy" when he lacked food, fire, friends. No wonder this private correspondence shows us anything but a lover of mankind, no matter how suffused in humanitarianism are his books, with their drabs, tramps, criminals, and drunkards. Turgenieff divined in him Sadistic predispositions; he was certainly a morbid man; while Tolstoy wrote of him: "It never entered my head to compare myself with him.... I am weeping now over the news of his death ... and I never saw the man." Dostoievsky was a profound influence on the art and life of Tolstoy.

It may interest musical persons to learn that it was through the efforts of Adolphe Henselt, piano virtuoso and composer, that Dostoievsky was finally allowed to leave Siberia and publish his writings. Henselt, who was at the time court pianist and teacher of the Czarina, appealed to her, and thus the ball was set rolling that ended in the clemency of the Czar. To Henselt, then, Russian literature is indebted for the "greater Dostoievsky." Why he was ever sent to Siberia is still a mystery. He had avowed his disbelief in the teachings of the Petrachevsky group, and only frequented their meetings because "advanced" European literature was read aloud. Dostoievsky was never a nihilist, and in his open letter to some St. Petersburg students he gives them sound advice as to the results of revolution. Poor man! He knew from harsh experience.

Thanks to the Count Melchoir de Voguee, who introduced Tolstoy to the French in Le Roman Russe (containing studies of Pushkin, Gogol, Turgenieff, Dostoievsky) literary Paris was for a time saturated in Russian mysticism, and what the clear-headed Alphonse Daudet called "Russian pity." It was Count de Voguee, member of the Academy and Neo-Catholic (as the group headed by Ernest Lavisse elected to style itself), who compressed all Tolstoy in an epigram as having ("the mind of an English chemist in the soul of a Hindoo Buddhist") On dirait l'esprit d'un chimiste anglais dans l'ame d'un buddhiste hindou.

The modulation of a soul, at first stagnant, then plunged into the gulf of hopelessness, and at last catching a glimpse of light, is most clearly expressed by Leo Nikolaievitch in his Resurrection. That by throwing yourself again into the mire you may atone for early transgressions--the muddy sins of your youth--is one of those deadly ideas born in the crazed brain of an East Indian jungle-haunting fanatic. It possibly grew out of the barbarous custom of blood sacrifices. Waiving the tales told of his insincerity by Frau Anna Seuron, we know that Tolstoy wrestled with the five thousand devils of doubt and despair, and found light, his light, in a most peculiar fashion. But he is often the victim of his own illusions. That, Voguee, a great admirer, pointed out some years ago. Turgenieff understood Tolstoy; so did Dostoievsky, and so does latterly the novelist Dmitri Merejkowski.

Turgenieff's appeal to Tolstoy is become historic, and all the more pathetic because written on the eve of his death.

> Dear and beloved Leo Nikolaievitch: I have not written to you for a long time, for I lie on my deathbed. I cannot get well; that is not to be thought of. But I write in order to tell you how glad I am to have been your contemporary, and to make my last earnest request. My friend, return to literary work. This talent of yours has come from where all else comes. Oh, how happy I should be could I believe that my entreaty would prevail with you. My friend, our great national writer, grant my request.

This may be found, if we remember aright, in the Halperine-Kaminsky memoir.

Turgenieff, who was the greater artist of the pair, knew that Tolstoy was on the wrong path with his crack-brained religious and social notions; knew that in his becoming the writer of illogical tracts and pamphlets, Russia was losing a great artist. What would he have said if he had lived to read the sad recantation and artistic suicide of Tolstoy: "I consign my own artistic productions to the category of bad art, except the story, God Sees the Truth, which seeks a place in the first class, and The Prisoner of the Caucasus, which belongs to the second." Also sprach Tolstoy in that madman's book called What is Art? a work wherein he tried to outvie Nordau's abuse of beautiful art.

The Ninth Symphony of Beethoven, Hamlet, Macbeth, Dante, and Goethe, are all consigned to the limbo of bad art; bad because not "understanded of the people." The peasant, the moujik, is to be the criterion of art, an art which, in that case, ought to be a cross between fireworks and the sign-writing of the Aztecs. Voguee declared that Tolstoy had, like an intrepid explorer, leaped into an abysm of philosophical contradictions. Even the moderate French critic Faguet becomes enraged at the puerilities of the Russian. He wrote: "Tolstoy, comme createur, comme romancier, comme poete epique, pour mieux dire, est un des quatre ou cinq plus grands genies de notre siecle. Comme penseur, il est un des plus faibles esprits de l'Europe."

Not all that, replies Remy de Gourmont; Tolstoy may be wildly mistaken, but he is never weak-minded. We think it is his strength, his intensity that sends him caracoling on a dozen different roads in search of salvation.

How a man lacking the critical faculty may be misled is to be seen in What is Art? To master his subject the deluded novelist read all the essays, disquisitions, and works he could find on the theme of aesthetics. This as a preparation for clear thinking. It reminds one of that comical artist Pellerin, in Flaubert's L'Education Sentimentale, who devoured all the aesthetic treatises, ancient and modern, in search of a true theory of the beautiful before he painted a picture; and he had so thoroughly absorbed the methods of various painters that he could not sit down at his easel in the presence of his model without asking himself: Shall I "do" her a la Gainsborough, or, better still, in the romantic and mysterious manner of M. Delacroix, with fierce sunsets, melting moons, guitars, bloodshed, balconies, and the cries of them that are assassinated for the love of love?

Tolstoy reaches, after many hundred pages of his essay, the astoundingly original theory that art "is to establish brotherly union among men," which was better said by Aristotle, and probably first heard by him as a Socratic pearl of wisdom. It remained for Merejkowski to set right the Western world in its estimate of Tolstoy as man and artist. In his frank study, the facts in the case are laid bare by a skilled, impartial hand. What he writes is well known among Russians; it may shock English-speaking worshippers, who do not accept Tolstoy as a great artist, but as the prophet of a new dispensation--and it may be said, without beating about the bush, he rather liked the niche in which he was placed by these uncritical zealots.

The fate of the engineer hoist by his own petard is Tolstoy's. The peasants of his country understand him as little as they understand Beethoven, that Beethoven he so bitterly, so unjustly assailed in The Kreutzer Sonata. (Poor Beethoven. Why did not Tolstoy select Tristan and Isolde if he wished some fleshly music, some sensualistic caterwauling, as Huxley phrased it? But a melodious violin and piano sonata!) Tolstoy may go barefoot, dig for potatoes, wear his blouse hanging outside, but the peasantry will never accept him as one of their own. He has written volumes about "going to the people," and the people do not want him, do not comprehend him. And that is Tolstoy's tragedy, as it was the tragedy of Walt Whitman.

Curious students can find all they wish of Tolstoy's psychology in Merejkowski's book. One thing we cannot forbear dwelling upon--Dostoievsky's significance in any discussion of Tolstoy. Dostoievsky was a profounder nature, greater than Tolstoy, though he was not the finished literary artist. All that Tolstoy tried to be, Dostoievsky was. He did not "go to the people" (that pose of dilettantish anarchy)--he was born of them; he did not write about Siberian prisons from hearsay, he lived in them; he did not attempt to dive into the deep, social waters of the "submerged tenth," because he himself seldom emerged to the surface. In a word, Dostoievsky is a profounder psychologist than Tolstoy; his faith was firmer; his attacks of epilepsy gave him glimpses of the underworld of the soul, terrifying visions of his subconscious self, of his subliminal personality. And he had the courage of his chimera.

Tolstoy feared art as being too artificial, and, as Merejkowski shows: "From the dread mask of Caliban peeps out the familiar and by no means awe-inspiring physiognomy of the obstinate Russian democrat squire, the gentleman Positivist of the sixties." He never took writing as seriously as Dostoievsky; in Tolstoy there is a strong leaven of the aristocrat, the man who rather despises a mere pen worker. Contrast Dostoievsky's attitude before his work, recall the painful parturition of books, his sweating, remorseful days and nights when he could not produce. And now Tolstoy tells us that Uncle Tom's Cabin is greater than Shakespeare. Is it any wonder Turgenieff remonstrated with him? Is it any wonder if, after reading one of his latter-day tracts, we are reminded of The Washerwoman of Finchley Common, that classic in the polemics of sniffling piety? The truth is that Tolstoy, a wonderful artist in plastic portraiture, consciously or unconsciously fashioned the Tolstoy legend, as did Richard Wagner the Wagner legend, Victor Hugo the Hugo legend. Men of genius and imagination are nearly all play-actors in matters autobiographical.

It is to Dostoievsky, once the despised outcast, that we must go for the human documents of misery, the naked soul, the heart of man buffeted by fate. If you think Resurrection strong, then read Dostoievsky's The House of the Dead. If Anna Karenina has wooed you--as it must--take up The Idiot; and if you are impressed by the epic magnitude of War and Peace, study that other epic of souls, The Brothers Karamazov, which illuminates, as if with ghastly flashes of lightning, the stormy hearts of mankind. Tolstoy wrote of life; Dostoievsky lived it, drank its sour dregs--for he was a man accursed by luck and, like the apocalyptic dreamer of Patmos, a seer of visions denied to the robust, ever fleshly Tolstoy. His influence on Tolstoy was more than Stendhal's--Stendhal whom Tolstoy called his master.

Tolstoy denies life, even hates it after having enjoyed it to the full. His religion in the last analysis is nihilism, and if carried to its logical conclusion would turn the civilised world into a desert. Our great man, after his family was in bed, sometimes ate forbidden slices of beef, and he had been seen enjoying a sly cigarette, all of which should endear him to us, for it proves his unquenchable humanity. Yet that roast-beef sandwich shook the faith of thousands. No--it will not do to take Tolstoy seriously in his attempts at evolving a parody of early Christianity. He is doubtlessly sincere, but sincerity is often the cloak for a multitude of errors.

His Katusha--Maslova, as she is more familiarly known in Resurrection--is a far less appealing figure than the street-walker Sonia in Dostoievsky's Crime and Punishment. The latter lives, while poor Maslova, a crude silhouette in comparison, as soon as she begins the march to Siberia is transformed into a clothes-horse upon which Tolstoy drapes his moral platitudes. She is at first much more vital than her betrayer, who is an unreal bundle of theories; but in company with the rest of the characters she soon goes up in metaphysical smoke. Walizewski asserts that all Tolstoy's later life was a regrettable pose. "But this is the usual price of every kind of human greatness, and in the case of this very great man, it is an atavistic feature of the national ... education, which in his case was originally of the most hasty and superficial description."

In As the Hague Ordains, the anonymous author attacks "our great reformer and humbug," Count Leo Tolstoy. She claims that there was hardly a village in China so abounding in filth and ignorance as the Tula village of Yasnaya Polyana, beside Tolstoy's country home.

"I wonder," she writes, "why the procession of foreign visitors who go to Yasnaya Polyana, who lavish adulation and hysterical praises upon that crass socialist and mischief-maker of his day, never think to look around them and use their reasoning powers. Would it not be the logical thing for Yasnaya Polyana to be the model village of Russia? Something cleaner than Edam or Marken? A little of his magnificent humanitarianism and benevolence poured upon that unsanitary village on his own estate would be more practical, it seems to me, than the thin treacle of it spread over the whole universe. Talk is cheap in Yasnaya Polyana, and the Grand Poseur plays his part magnificently. Every visitor goes away completely hypnotised, especially the Americans, with their frothing about equality and the universal brotherhood of man. Universal grandmother! All men are just as equal as all noses or all mouths are equal. The world gets older, but learns nothing, and it cherishes delusions, and the same ones, just as it did in the time of the Greek philosophers. Leo Tolstoy might well have lived in a tub or carried a lantern by day, like the most sensational and theatrical of the ancients. He is only a past master of reclame, of the art of advertising. The Moujik blouse and those delightful tableaux of a real nobleman shoemaking and haymaking make his books sell. That is all. And, under the unsuspecting blouse of the humanitarian is the fine and perfumed linen of the dandy. Leo Tolstoy, the Beau Brummel of his corps in my father's day--the dandy in domino to-day."

III

Tolstoy the artist! When his vagaries are forgotten, when all his books are rags, when his very name shall be a vague memory, there will live the portrait of Anna Karenina. How dwarfed are his other achievements compared with the creation of this woman, and to create a living character is to be as the gods. Tolstoy has painted one of the three women in the fiction of the nineteenth century. If the roll-call of the century is ever sounded, these three women shall have endured "the drums and tramplings" of many conquests, and the contiguous dust of those fictional creatures not built for immortality. Balzac's Valreie Marneffe, the Emma Bovary of Flaubert, and the Russian's Anna Karenina are these daughters of earth--flesh and blood, tears and lust, and the pride of life that killeth.

Despite Tolstoy's religious mania, I have never doubted his sincerity for a moment. It is a mysterious yet potent factor in the psychology of such an artist as he that whatever he did he did with tremendous sincerity. That is the reason his fiction is nearer reality than all other fictions, and the reason, too, that his realities, _i. e._, his declarations of faith, are nearer other men's fictions. When he writes of his conversion, like John Bunyan, he lets you see across the very sill of his soul. And he does it artistically. He is not conscious that art enters into the mechanism of this spiritual evisceration; but it does. St. Augustine, John Bunyan, John Henry Newman wrote of their adventures of the spirit in letters of fire, and in all three there is a touch of the sublime naivete of childhood's outpourings.

I agree with the estimate of Tolstoy by Merejkowski. The main points of this study have been known to students who followed Tolstoy's extraordinary career for the past quarter of a century. Ibsen's individualism appeals. Better his torpedo exploding a thousand times under the social ark than the Oriental passivity of the Russian. There is hope in the message of Brand; none in Tolstoy's nihilism. One glorifies the will, the other denies, rejects it. No comparison can be made between the two wonderful men as playwrights. Yet Tolstoy's Powers of Darkness is brutal melodrama when compared to Ibsen's complex dramatic organisms. But what a nerve-shattering revelation is The Death of Ivan Ilyitch. This is the real Tolstoy.

How amateurish is the attitude of the Tolstoy disciple who cavils at his masterpieces. What is mere art compared to the message! And I say: what are all his vapourings and fatidical croonings on the tripod of pseudo-prophecy as compared to Anna Karenina? There is implicit drama, implicit morality in its noble pages, and a segment of the life of a nation in War and Peace. With preachers and saviours with quack nostrums the world is already well stocked. Great artists are rare. Every day a new religion is born somewhere--and it always finds followers. But art endures, it outlives dynasties, religions, divinities. It is with Tolstoy the artist we are enamoured. He may deliver his message of warning to a careless world--which only pricks up its ears when that message takes on questionable colour, as in the unpalatable Kreutzer Sonata. (Yes; that was eagerly devoured for its morbid eroticism.) We prefer the austerer Ibsen, who presents his men and women within the frame of the drama, absolutely without personal comment or _parti pris_--as before his decadence did Tolstoy in his novels. Ibsen is the type of the philosophical anarch, the believer in man's individuality, in the state for the individual, not the individual for the state. It is at least more dignified than the other's flood of confessions, of hysterical self-accusations, of penitential vows, and abundant lack of restraint. Yet no one doubts Tolstoy's repentance. Like Verlaine's it carried with it its own proofs.

But why publish to the world these intimate soul processes, fascinating as they are to laymen and psychologists alike? Why not keep watch with his God in silence and alone? The reason was (only complicated with a thousand other things, for Tolstoy was a complex being and a Slav), the plain reason was, we repeat, because Leo Nikolaievitch was an artist. He obeyed that demon known to Socrates and Goethe, and minutely recorded his mental and emotional fluctuations. And with Richard Wagner and Dostoievsky, Tolstoy is one of the three most emotional temperaments of the nineteenth century. Unlike Ibsen or Nietzsche, he does not belong to the twentieth century; his religion, his social doctrines are atavistic, are of the past. Tolstoy is what the French call _un cerebral_, which, as Arthur Symons points out, is by no means a man of intellect. "_Un cerebral_ is a man who feels through his brain, in whom emotion transforms itself into idea, rather than in whom idea is transformed by emotion." How well that phrase fits Tolstoy--the fever of the soul! He has had the fever of the soul, has subdued it, and his recital of his struggles makes breathless reading. They are depicted by an artist, an emotional artist, and, despite his protestations, by one who will die an artist and be remembered, not as the pontiff of a new dispensation, but as a great world artist.

An admirer has said of him that "confession has become his second nature"; rather it was a psychological necessity. The voice that cried from the comfortable wilderness of Yasnaya Polyana furnished unique "copy" for newspapers. Alas! the pity of it all. The moral dyspepsia that overtook Carlyle in middle life was the result of a lean, spoiled, half-starved youth; the moral dyspepsia that seized the soul of the wonderful Tolstoy was the outcome of a riotous youth, a youth overflowing with the "joy of life." Ibsen, like Carlyle, battled in his early days with poverty; but his message--if you will have a definite message (Oh, these literal, unimaginative folk of the Gradgrind sort, who would wring from the dumb mysterious beauty of nature definite meanings--as if sheer existence itself is not its own glorious vindication!)--may be a hopeful one. The individual is all in all; he is the evangel of the future; his belief is buoyant and Northern; whereas Tolstoy's sour outlook, his constant girding at the vanities of life (after he had, Solomon-like, tasted of them to the full) is Eastern; his is the Oriental fatalism, the hopeless doctrine of determinism. He discovers a new sin every day. Better one hour of Nietzsche's dancing madness than a cycle of Tolstoy's pessimistic renunciations. And all his ethical propaganda does not shake in the least our conviction of the truth and grandeur of Tolstoy's art.

Of the disciples the son of Tolstoy, Count Ilya, tells us in no uncertain accents:

My father had good reason for saying that the "Tolstoyites" were to him the most incomprehensible sect and the furthest removed from his way of thinking that he had ever come across. "I shall soon be dead," he sadly predicted, "and people will say that Tolstoy taught men to plough and reap and make boots; while the chief thing that I have been trying so hard to say all my life, the thing I believe in the most important of all, they will forget."

IV

THE YOUNGER CHOIR

Let us believe that Gogol, Pushkin, Lermontov, Nekrasov, Dostoievsky, Turgenieff, and Tolstoy are classics. As long as Russian, sonorous and beautiful tongue, is spoken, they will never die. And their successors? What is the actual condition of Russian literature at the present time? It is the bare truth to say that a period of stagnation set in during the decade after Turgenieff's death. Emigration carried with it the best brains of the land. We need not dwell upon the publicists, nor yet stir the muddy stream of agitation. It has been the misfortune of Russian literary men to be involved in dangerous political schisms and revolutionary movements; their misfortune, and perhaps their good luck. For dramatic material they have never been at a loss, though their art has suffered, and depth of feeling has been gained at a sad waste of other qualities. That grand old humourist Gogol has had no successors. Humour in Russia is a suspected thing. Even if there were a second Gogol he would never be allowed to put on the boards a second Revizor. We do not mean to assert that humour has died out altogether in literature, but it is not the special gift of those who write nowadays. Since Gogol or coeval with him, only men of secondary importance have been humourists: Uspenski, Ostrovski, Saltykov (Chtchedrine), or the author of the novel Oblomov, Gontcharov by name.

Maikov, Nadsohn, Polonski, Garchin, Korolenko, Tchekov were all men of talent; the last in particular, preceptor and friend to Gorky in his days of want, was a novelist of high artistic if morbid powers. He is dead. It is when we turn to the living that we realise what a flatland is Russian literature now. A writer and critic, Madame Z. Hippius, attempted in the Paris _Mercure de France_ to give an idea of the situation. She admitted the inadequacy of her sketch. The troubled political map of Russia has not been conducive to ripe artistic production. As she says, even the writers who refused to meddle with politics are marked men; politics in the shape of the secret police comes to them. Madame Hippius makes the assertion that literature in Russian has never existed in the sense of a literary _milieu_, as an organic art possessing traditions and continuity; for her, Tolstoy, Dostoievsky, and Turgenieff are but isolated men of genius. A glance back at the times and writings of such critics as Bielinski, Dobroliubov, and Nekrasov--a remarkable poet--disproves this statement. Without a Gogol the later novelists would be rather in the air. He first fashioned the bricks and mortar of native fiction. Read Kropotkin, Osip-Luri, E. Semenov, Walizewski, Melchior de Voguee, and Leo Wiener if you doubt the wealth and variety of this literature.

Among living prose writers two names are encountered: Maxim Gorky and Leonide Andreiev. Of the neurotic Gorky there is naught to be said that is encouraging. He was physically ill when in America and as an artist in plain decadence. He had shot his bolt in his tales about his beloved vagabonds. He had not the long-breathed patience or artistic skill for a novel. His novels, disfigured by tirades and dry attempts at philosophical excursions, are all failures. When his tramps begin to spout Nietzsche on their steppes the artificial note is too apparent. His plays are loose episodes without dramatic action or climax, sometimes moving, as in the case of Nachtasyl, and discordant in The Children of the Sun. Gorky had a natural talent; in his stories a submerged generation became eloquent. And he became a doctrinaire. Nietzsche finished the ruin that Marx had begun; his art, chiefly derived from Dostoievsky and Tchekov, succumbed to a sentimental socialism.

Andreiev is still strong, though enveloped in "mystic anarchism." He is as naturally gifted as Gorky and a thinker of more precision. His play, Les Tenebres, reveals the influences of Dostoievsky and Tolstoy. It is a shocking arraignment of self-satisfied materialism. A young revolutionary is the protagonist. The woman in the case belongs to the same profession as Dostoievsky's Sonia. Not encouraging, this. Yet high hopes are centred upon Andreiev. For the rest there is Vladimir Soloviev, who is a poet-metaphysician with a following. He has mystic proclivities. Scratch a Russian writer and you come upon a mystic. He is against clericalism and believes in an "anti-clerical church"! There is a little circle at Moscow, where a Muscovite review, _La Balance_ (founded 1903), is the centre of the young men. V. Brusoff, a poet, is the editor. Balmont and Sologub write for its pages, as do Rosanow and Merejkowski. In 1898 there was a review started called _Mir Iskousstva_. Its director was Serge Diaghilev, and it endured until 1904. Sologub is one of the most promising poets. Block, Remisov, Ivanov are also poets of much ability. There are romancers such as Zensky, Kuzmin, Ivanov, Ropshin, Chapygin, Serafimovitch, Zaitzeff, Volnoff; some of these wrote on risky themes. But when the works of these new writers are closely scrutinised their lack of originality and poverty of invention are noticeable.

The "poisonous honey" of French decadents and symbolists has attracted one party; and the others are being swallowed up in the pessimistic nebula of "mystic anarchy" and fatalism. "Russian pity" suffuses their work. There is without doubt a national sentiment and a revolt against western European culture, particularly the French. Russia for the Russians is the slogan of this group. But thus far nothing in particular has come of their patriotic efforts; no overwhelming personality has emerged from the rebellious froth of new theories. If ever the "man on horseback" does appear in Russia, it is very doubtful if he will bestride a Pegasus.

Of bigger and sterner calibre than any of the productions of the others is Sanine, a novel by Michael Artzibaschev, that is being widely read not only in Russia but in all the world. It was written as long ago as 1903 the author tells us. He is of Tartar origin, born 1878, of parents in whose veins flowed Russian, French, Georgian, and Polish blood. He is of humble origin, as is Gorky, and being of a consumptive tendency, he lives in the Crimea. He began as a journalist. His photograph reveals him as a young man of a fine, sensitive type, truly an apostle of pity and pain. He passionately espouses the cause of the poor and downtrodden, as his extraordinary revolutionary short stories--The Millionaire among the rest--show. Since Turgenieff's Fathers and Sons, no tale like Metal Worker Schevyrjow has appeared in European literature. In it the bedrock of Slavic fatalism, an anarchistic pessimism is reached. It has been done into French by Jacques Povolozky. The Russian author reveals plentiful traces of Tolstoy, Turgenieff, Dostoievsky, and Gorky in his pages; Tchekov, too, is not absent. But the new note is the influence of Max Stirner. Michael Artzibaschev calmly grafts the disparate ideas of Dostoievsky and Max Stirner in his Sanine, and the result is a hero who is at once a superman and a scoundrel--or are the two fairly synonymous? This clear-eyed, broad-shouldered Sanine passes through the little town where he was born, leaving behind him a trail of mishaps and misfortunes. He is depicted with a marvellous art, though it is impossible to sympathise with him. He upsets a love-affair of his sister's, he quarrels with and insults her lover, who commits suicide; he also drives to self-destruction a wretched little Hebrew who has become a freethinker and can't stand the strain of his apostasy; he is the remote cause of another suicide, that of a weakling, a student full of "modern" ideas, but whose will is quite sapped. Turgenieff's Fathers and Sons is recalled more than once, especially the character of Bazarov, the nihilist. Furthermore, when this student fails to reap the benefit of a good girl's love, Sanine steps in and ruins her. Even incest is hinted at. All this sounds incredible in our bare recital, but in the flow and glow of the richly coloured narrative everything is plausible, nay, of the stuff of life. As realists the Russians easily lead all other nations in fiction. There are descriptions of woodlands that recall a little scene from Turgenieff's Sportsman's Sketches; there are episodes, such as the bacchanal in the monastery, a moonlit ride in the canoe with a realistic seduction episode, and the several quarrels that would have pleased both Tolstoy and Dostoievsky; there is an old mujik who seems to have stepped out of Dostoievsky, yet is evidently a portrait taken from life. The weak mother, the passionate sister, the sweet womanly quality of the deceived girl, these are portraits worthy of a master. Sanine is not the Rogoszin, and his sister is not the Nastasia Philipovna, of Dostoievsky's The Idiot; for all that they are distinct and worthy additions to the vast picture-gallery of Russian fiction.

Sanine himself hardly appeals to our novel readers, for whom a golf-stick and a motor-car are symbols of the true hero. In a word, he is real flesh and blood. He goes as mysteriously as he came. The novel that followed, Breaking Point, is a lugubrious orgy of death and erotic madness, a symphony of suicide and love and the disgust of life. Artzibaschev is now in English garb. Thus far Sanine is his masterpiece.

V

ARNOLD SCHOENBERG

I

Two decades ago, more or less, John M. Robertson published several volumes chiefly concerned with the gentle art of criticism. Mr. Robertson introduced to the English-reading world the critical theories of Emile Hennequin, whose essays on Poe, Dostoievsky, and Turgenieff may be remembered. It is a cardinal doctrine of Hennequin and Robertson that, as the personal element plays the chief role in everything the critic writes, he himself should be the first to submit to a grilling; in a word, to be put through his paces and tell us in advance of his likes and dislikes, his prejudices and passions. Naturally, it doesn't take long to discover the particular bias of a critic's mind. He writes himself down whenever he puts pen to paper.

For instance, there is the historic duel between Anatole France, a free-lance among critics, and Ferdinand Brunetiere, intrenched behind the bastions of tradition, not to mention the _Revue des Deux Mondes_. That discussion, while amusing, was so much threshing of academic straw. M. France disclaimed all authority--he, most erudite among critics; M. Brunetiere praised impersonality in criticism--he, the most personal among writers--not a pleasing or expansive personality, be it understood; but, narrow as he was, his personality shone out from every page.

Now, says Mr. Robertson, why not ask every critic about to bring forth an opinion for a sort of chart on which will be shown his various qualities of mind, character; yes, and even his physical temperament; whether sanguine or melancholic, bilious or eupeptic, young or old, peaceful or truculent; also his tastes in literature, art, music, politics, and religion. This reminds one of an old-fashioned game. And all this long-winded preamble is to tell you that the case of Arnold Schoenberg, musical anarchist, and an Austrian composer who has at once aroused the ire and admiration of musical Germany, demands just such a confession from a critic about to hold in the balance the music or unmusic (the Germans have such a handy word) of Schoenberg. Therefore, before I attempt a critical or uncritical valuation of the art of Arnold Schoenberg let me make a clean breast of my prejudices in the manner suggested by Hennequin and Robertson. Besides, it is a holy and unwholesome idea to purge the mind every now and then.

First: I place pure music above impure, _i. e._, instrumental above mixed. I dislike grand opera as a miserable mishmash of styles, compromises, and arrant ugliness. The moment the human voice intrudes in an orchestral work, my dream-world of music vanishes. Mother Church is right in banishing, from within the walls of her temples the female voice. The world, the flesh, and the devil lurk in the larynx of the soprano or alto, and her place is before the footlights, not as a vocal staircase to paradise. I say this, knowing in my heart that nothing is so thrilling as Tristan and Isolde, and my memory-cells hold marvellous pictures of Lilli Lehmann, Milka Ternina, and Olive Fremstad. So, I'm neither logical nor sincere; nevertheless, I maintain the opinion that absolute music, not programme, not music-drama, is the apogee of the art. A Beethoven string quartet holds more genuine music for me than the entire works of Wagner.

There's a prejudiced statement for you!

Second: I fear and dislike the music of Arnold Schoenberg, who may be called the Max Stirner of music. Now, the field being cleared, let us see what the music of the new man is like. Certainly, he is the hardest musical nut to crack of his generation, and the shell is very bitter in the mouth.

Early in December, 1912, the fourth performance of a curious composition by Schoenberg was given at the Choralionsaal in the Bellevuestrasse, Berlin. The work is entitled Lieder des Pierrot Lunaire, the text of which is a fairly good translation of a poem cycle by Albert Guiraud. This translation was made by the late Otto Erich Hartleben, himself a poet and dramatist. I have not read the original French verse, but the idea seems to be faithfully represented in the German version. This moon-stricken Pierrot chants--rather declaims--his woes and occasional joys to the music of the Viennese composer, whose score requires a reciter (female), a piano, flute (also piccolo), clarinet (also bass clarinet), violin (also viola), and violoncello. The piece is described as a melodrama. I listened to it on a Sunday morning, and I confess that Sunday at noon is not a time propitious to the mood musical. It was also the first time I had heard a note of Schoenberg's. In vain I had tried to get some of his scores; not even the six little piano pieces could I secure. Instead, my inquiries were met with dubious or pitying smiles--your music clerk is a terrible critic betimes, and his mind oft takes upon it the colour of his customer's orders. So there I was, to be pitched overboard into a new sea, to sink or float, and all the while wishing myself miles away.

A lady of pleasing appearance, attired in a mollified Pierrot costume, stood before some Japanese screens and began to intone--to cantillate, would be a better expression. She told of a monstrous moon-drunken world, then she described Columbine, a dandy, a pale washer-woman--"Eine blasse Waescherin waescht zur Nachtzeit bleiche Tuecher"--and always with a refrain, for Guiraud employs the device to excess. A valse of Chopin followed, in verse, of course (poor suffering Frederic!), and part one--there are seven poems, each in three sections--ended with one entitled Madonna, and another, the Sick Moon. The musicians were concealed behind the screens (dear old Mark Twain would have said, to escape the outraged audience), but we heard them only too clearly!

It is the decomposition of the art, I thought, as I held myself in my seat. Of course, I meant decomposition of tones, as the slang of the ateliers goes.

What did I hear? At first, the sound of delicate china shivering into a thousand luminous fragments. In the welter of tonalities that bruised each other as they passed and repassed, in the preliminary grip of enharmonics that almost made the ears bleed, the eyes water, the scalp to freeze, I could not get a central grip on myself. It was new music (or new exquisitely horrible sounds) with a vengeance. The very ecstasy of the hideous! I say "exquisitely horrible," for pain can be at once exquisite and horrible; consider toothache and its first cousin, neuralgia. And the border-land between pain and pleasure is a territory hitherto unexplored by musical composers. Wagner suggests poetic anguish; Schoenberg not only arouses the image of anguish, but he brings it home to his auditory in the most subjective way. You suffer the anguish with the fictitious character in the poem. Your nerves--and remember the porches of the ears are the gateways to the brain and ganglionic centres--are literally pinched and scraped.

I wondered that morning if I were not in a nervous condition. I looked about me in the sparsely filled hall. People didn't wriggle; perhaps their souls wriggled. They neither smiled nor wept. Yet on the wharf of hell the lost souls disembarked and wept and lamented. What was the matter with my own ego? My conscience reported a clean bill of health, I had gone to bed early the previous night wishing to prepare for the ordeal. Evidently I was out of condition (critics are like prize-fighters, they must keep in constant training else they go "stale"). Or was the music to blame? Schoenberg is, I said to myself, the crudest of all composers, for he mingles with his music sharp daggers at white heat, with which he pares away tiny slices of his victim's flesh. Anon he twists the knife in the fresh wound and you receive another horrible thrill, all the time wondering over the fate of the Lunar Pierrot and--hold on! Here's the first clew. If this new music is so distractingly atrocious what right has a listener to bother about Pierrot? What's Pierrot to him or he to Pierrot? Perhaps Schoenberg had caught his fish in the musical net he used, and what more did he want, or what more could his listeners expect?--for to be hooked or netted by the stronger volition of an artist is the object of all the seven arts.

How does Schoenberg do it? How does he pull off the trick? It is not a question to be lightly answered. In the first place the personality of the listener is bound to obtrude itself; dissociation from one's ego--if such a thing were possible--would be intellectual death; only by the clear, persistent image of ourselves do we exist--banal psychology as old as the hills. And the ear, like the eye, soon "accommodates" itself to new perspectives and unrelated harmonies.

I had felt, without clearly knowing the reason, that when Albertine Zehme so eloquently declaimed the lines of Madonna, the sixth stanza of part one, beginning "Steig, o Mutter aller Schmerzen, auf den Altar meiner Toene!" that the background of poignant noise supplied by the composer was more than apposite, and in the mood-key of the poem. The flute, bass clarinet, and violoncello were so cleverly handled that the colour of the doleful verse was enhanced, the mood expanded; perhaps the Hebraic strain in the composer's blood has endowed him with the gift of expressing sorrow and desolation and the abomination of living. How far are we here from the current notion that music is a consoler, is joy-breeding, or should, according to the Aristotelian formula, purge the soul through pity and terror. I felt the terror, but pity was absent. Blood-red clouds swept over vague horizons. It was a new land through which I wandered. And so it went on to the end, and I noted as we progressed that Schoenberg, despite his ugly sounds, was master of more than one mood; witness the shocking cynicism of the gallows song Die duerre Dirne mit langen Halse. Such music is shameful--"and that's the precise effect I was after"--could the composer triumphantly answer, and he would be right. What kind of music is this, without melody, in the ordinary sense; without themes, yet every acorn of a phrase contrapuntally developed by an adept; without a harmony that does not smite the ears, lacerate, figuratively speaking, the ear-drums; keys forced into hateful marriage that are miles asunder, or else too closely related for aural matrimony; no form, that is, in the scholastic formal sense, and rhythms that are so persistently varied as to become monotonous--what kind of music, I repeat, is this that can paint a "crystal sigh," the blackness of prehistoric night, the abysm of a morbid soul, the man in the moon, the faint sweet odours of an impossible fairy-land, and the strut of the dandy from Bergamo? (See the Guiraud poem.) There is no melodic or harmonic line, only a series of points, dots, dashes, or phrases that sob and scream, despair, explode, exalt, blaspheme.

I give the conundrum the go-by; I only know that when I finally surrendered myself to the composer he worked his will on my fancy and on my raw nerves, and I followed the poems, loathing the music all the while, with intense interest. Indeed, I couldn't let go the skein of the story for fear that I might fall off somewhere into a gloomy chasm and be devoured by chromatic wolves. I recalled one extraordinary moment at the close of the composition when a simple major chord was sounded and how to my ears it had a supernal beauty; after the perilous tossing and pitching on a treacherous sea of no-harmonies it was like a field of firm ice under the feet.

Ivory Apes and Peacocks.txt

I told myself that it served me right, that I was too old to go gallivanting around with this younger generation, that if I would eat prickly musical pears I must not be surprised if I suffered from aural colic. Nevertheless, when certain of the Schoenberg compositions reached me from Vienna I eagerly fell to studying them. I saw then that he had adopted as his motto: Evil, be thou my good! And that a man who could portray in tone sheer ugliness with such crystal clearness is to be reckoned with in these topsyturvy times.

I have called Arnold Schoenberg a musical anarchist, using the word in its best estate--anarchos, without a head. Perhaps he is a superman also, and the world doesn't know it. His admirers and pupils think so, however, and several of them have recorded their opinion in a little book, published at Munich, 1912, by R. Piper & Co.

The life of Arnold Schoenberg, its outer side, has thus far been uneventful, though doubtless rich in the psychical sense. He is still young, born in Vienna, September 13, 1874. He lived there till 1901, then in the December of that year he went to Berlin, where he was for a short time conductor in Wolzogen's Bunten Theatre, and also teacher of composition at Stern's Conservatory. In 1903 he returned to Vienna, where he taught--he is pre-eminently a pedagogue, even pedantic as I hope to presently prove--in the K. K. Akademie fuer Musik. In 1911 Berlin again beckoned to him, and as hope ever burns in the bosom of composers, young and old, he no doubt believes that his day will come. Certainly, his disciples, few as they may be, make up by their enthusiasm for the public and critical flouting. I can't help recalling the Italian Futurists when I think of Schoenberg. The same wrath may be noted in the galleries where the young Italian painters exhibit. So it was at the end of the concert. One man, a sane person, was positively purple with rage (evidently he had paid for his seat), and swore that the composer was verrueckt.

His compositions are not numerous. Schoenberg appears to be a reflective rather than a spontaneous creator. Here is an abridged list: Opus 1, 2, and 3 (composed, 1898-1900); Opus 4, string sextet, which bears the title, Verklaerte Nacht (1899); Gurrelieder, after J. P. Jacobsen, for solos; chorus and orchestra (1900), published in the Universal Edition, Vienna; Opus 5, Pelleas et Melisande, symphonic poem for orchestra (1902), Universal Edition aforesaid; Opus 6, eight lieder (about 1905); Opus 7, E string quartet, D minor (1905); Opus 8, six orchestral lieder (1904); Opus 9, Kammersymphonie (1906); two ballads for voice and piano (1907); Peace on Earth, mixed chorus a capella (1908), manuscript; Opus 10, II, string quartet, F-sharp minor (1907-8); fifteen lieder, after Stefan George, a talented Viennese poet, one of the Jung-Wien group (1908), manuscript; Opus 11, three piano pieces (1908); five pieces for orchestra (1909) in the Peters Edition; monodrama, Erwartung (1909); Glueckliche Hand, drama with music, text by composer, not yet finished (1910); and six piano pieces (1911). His book on harmony appeared in 1910 and was universally treated as the production of a madman, and, finally, as far as this chronicle goes, in 1911-12 he finished Pierrot Lunaire, which was first produced in Berlin.

   * * * * *

One thing is certain, and this hardly need assure my musical readers, the old tonal order has changed for ever; there are plenty of signs in the musical firmament to prove this. Moussorgsky preceded Debussy in his use of whole-tone harmonies, and a contemporary of Debussy, and an equally gifted musician, Martin Loeffler, was experimenting before Debussy himself in a dark but delectable harmonic region. The tyranny of the diatonic and chromatic scales, the tiresome revolutions of the major and minor modes, the critical Canutes who sit at the seaside and say to the modern waves: Thus far and no farther; and then hastily abandon their chairs and rush to safety else be overwhelmed, all these things are of the past, whether in music, art, literature, and--let

Nietzsche speak--in ethics. Even philosophy has become a plaything, and logic "a dodge," as Professor Jowett puts it. Every stronghold is being assailed, from the "divine" rights of property to the common chord of C major. With Schoenberg, freedom in modulation is not only permissible, but is an iron rule; he is obsessed by the theory of overtones, and his music is not only horizontally and vertically planned, but, so I pretend to hear, also in a circular fashion. There is no such thing as consonance or dissonance, only imperfect training of the ear (I am quoting from his Harmony, certainly a bible for musical supermen). He says: "Harmonie fremde Toene gibt es also nicht"--and a sly dig at the old-timers--"sondern nur dem Harmoniesystem fremde." After carefully listening I noted that he too has his mannerisms, that in his chaos there is a certain order, that his madness is very methodical. For one thing he abuses the interval of the fourth, and he enjoys juggling with the chord of the ninth. Vagabond harmonies, in which the remotest keys lovingly hold hands, do not prevent the sensation of a central tonality somewhere--in the cellar, on the roof, in the gutter, up in the sky. The inner ear tells you that the D-minor quartet is really thought, though not altogether played, in that key. As for form, you must not expect it from a man who declares: "I decide my form during composition only through feeling." Every chord is the outcome of an emotion, the emotion aroused by the poem or idea which gives birth to the composition. Such antique things as the cyclic form or community of themes are not to be expected in Schoenberg's bright lexicon of anarchy. He boils down the classic form to one movement and, so it seemed to my hearing, he begins developing his idea as soon as it is announced.

Such polyphony, such interweaving of voices--eleven and twelve and fifteen are a matter of course--as would make envious the old tonal weavers of the Netherlands! There is, literally, no waste ornament or filling in his scores; every theme, every subsidiary figure, is set spinning so that you dream of fireworks spouting in every direction, only the fire is vitriolic and burns the tympani of the ears. Seriously, like all complex effects, the Schoenberg scores soon become legible if scrutinised without prejudice. The string sextet, if compared to the later music, is sunny and Mozartian in its melodic and harmonic simplicity. They tell me that Schoenberg once wrote freely in the normal manner, but finding that he could not attract attention he deliberately set himself to make abnormal music. I don't know how true this may be; the same sort of thing was said of Mallarme and Paul Cezanne and Richard Strauss, and was absolutely without foundation.

Schoenberg is an autodidact, the lessons in composition from Alexander von Zemlinsky not affecting his future path-breaking propensities. His mission is to free harmony from all rules. A man doesn't hit on such combinations, especially in his acrid instrumentation, without heroic labour. His knowledge must be enormous, for his scores are as logical as a highly wrought mosaic; that is, logical, if you grant him his premises. He is perverse and he wills his music, but he is a master in delineating certain moods, though the means he employs revolt our ears. To call him "crazy," is merely amusing. No man is less crazy, few men are so conscious of what they are doing, and few modern composers boast such a faculty of attention. Concentration is the key-note of his work; concentration--or condensation formal, concentration of thematic material--to the vanishing-point; and conciseness in treatment, although every license is allowed in modulation.

Every composer has his aura; the aura of Arnold Schoenberg is, for me, the aura of subtle ugliness, of hatred and contempt, of cruelty, and of the mystic grandiose. He is never petty. He sins in the grand manner of Nietzsche's Superman, and he has the courage of his chromatics. If such music-making is ever to become accepted, then I long for Death the Releaser. More shocking still would be the suspicion that in time I might be persuaded to like this music, to embrace, after abhorring it.

As for Schoenberg, the painter--he paints, too!--I won't take even the guarded praise of such an accomplished artist as Kandinsky as sufficient evidence. I've not seen any of the composer's "purple cows," and hope I never shall see them. His black-and-white reproductions look pretty bad, and not nearly as original as his music. The portrait of a lady (who seems to be listening to Schoenbergian harmonies) hasn't much colour, a critic tells us, only a sickly rose in her dress. He also paints grey-green landscapes and visions, the latter dug up from the abysmal depths of his subconsciousness. Schoenberg is, at least, the object of considerable curiosity. What he will do next no man may say; but at least it won't be like the work of any one else. The only distinct reminiscence of an older composer that I could discover in his Pierrot was Richard Wagner (toujours Wagner, whether Franck or Humperdinck or Strauss or Debussy), and of him, the first page of the Introduction to the last act of Tristan und Isolde, more the mood than the actual themes. Schoenberg is always atmospheric. So is a tornado. He is the poet whose flowers are evil; he is the spirit that denies; never a realist, like Strauss, ingeniously imitating natural sounds, he may be truthfully described as a musical symbolist.

II

MUSIC OF TO-DAY AND TO-MORROW

Despite the fact that he played the flute and ranked Rossini above Wagner, Arthur Schopenhauer said some notable things about music. "Art is ever on the quest," is a wise observation of his, "a quest, and a divine adventure"; though this restless search for the new often ends in plain reaction, progress may be crab-wise and still be progress. I fear that "progress" as usually understood is a glittering "general idea" that blinds us to the truth. Reform in art is not like reform in politics; you can't reform the St. Matthew Passion or the Fifth Symphony. Is Parsifal a reformation of Gluck? This talk of reform is only confusing the historic with the aesthetic. Art is a tricksy quantity and like quicksilver is ever mobile. As in all genuine revolutions the personal equation counts the heaviest, so in dealing with the conditions of music at the present time one must study the temperament of our music-makers and let prophecy sulk in its tent as it may.

If Ruskin had written music-criticism, he might have amplified the meaning of his once-famous phrase, the "pathetic fallacy," for I consider it a pathetic fallacy--though not in the Ruskinian sense--in criticism to be over-shadowed by the fear that, because some of our critical predecessors misjudged Wagner or Manet or Ibsen, we should be too merciful in criticising our contemporaries. Here is the "pathos of distance" run to sentimental seed. The music of to-day may be the music of to-morrow, but if it is not, what then? It may satisfy the emotional needs of the moment, yet to-morrow be a stale formula. But what does that prove? Though Bach and Beethoven built their work on the bases of eternity (employing this tremendous term in a limited sense), one may nevertheless enjoy the men whose music is of slighter texture and "modern." Nor is this a plea for mediocrity. Mediocrity we shall always have with us: mediocrity is mankind in the normal, and normal man demands of art what he can read without running, hear without thinking. Every century produces artists who are forgotten in a generation, though they fill the eye and the ear for a time with their clever production. This has led to another general idea, that of transition, of intermediate types. After critical perspective has been attained, it may be seen that the majority of composers fall into this category not a consoling notion, but an unavoidable. Richard Wagner has his epigones; the same is the case with Haydn, Mozart, Beethoven. Mendelssohn was a delightful feminine variation on Bach, and after Schumann came Brahms.

The Wagner-Liszt tradition of music-drama, so-called, and the symphonic poem have been continued with personal modifications by Richard Strauss; Max Reger has pinned his faith to Brahms and absolute music, though not without a marked individual variation. In considering his Sinfonietta, the Serenade, the Hiller Variations, the Prologue to a Tragedy, the Lustspiel Overture, the two concertos respectively for pianoforte and violin, we are struck not as much by the easy handling of old forms, as by the stark emotional content of these compositions. Reger began as a Brahmsianer, but he has not thus far succeeded in fusing form and theme as wonderfully as did his master. There is a Dionysian strain in his music that too often is in jarring discord with the intellectual structure of his work. But there is no denying that Max Reger is the one man in Germany to-day who is looked upon as the inevitable rival of Richard Strauss. Their disparate tendencies bring to the lips the old query, Under which king? Some think that Arnold Schoenberg may be a possible antagonist in the future, but for the present it is Reger and Strauss, and no third in opposition.

The Strauss problem is a serious one. In America much criticism of his performances has contrived to evade the real issue. He has been called hard names because he is money-loving, or because he has not followed in the steps of Beethoven, because of a thousand and one things of no actual critical value. That he is easily the greatest technical master of his art now living there can be no question. And he has wound up a peg or two the emotional intensity of music. Whether this striving after nerve-shattering combinations is a dangerous tendency is quite beside the mark. Let us register the fact. Beginning in the path made by Brahms, he soon came under the influence of Liszt, and we were given a chaplet of tone-poems, sheer programme-music, but cast in a bigger and more flexible mould than the thrice-familiar Liszt pattern. Whatever fate is reserved for Death and Transfiguration, Till Eulenspiegel, Also Sprach Zarathustra, Hero's Life, and Don Quixote, there is no denying their significance during the last decade of the nineteenth century. For me it seemed a decided step backward when Strauss entered the operatic field. One so conspicuously rich in the gift of music-making (for the titles of his symphonies never prevented us from enjoying their colouring and eloquence) might have avoided the more facile triumphs of the stage. However, Elektra needs no apology, and the joyous Rosenkavalier is a distinct addition to the repertory of high-class musical comedy. Strauss is an experimenter and no doubt a man for whom the visible box-office exists, to parody a saying of Gautier's. But we must judge him by his own highest standard, the standard of Elektra, Don Quixote, and Till Eulenspiegel, not to mention the beautiful songs. Ariadne on Naxos was a not particularly successful experiment, and what the Alp Symphony will prove to be we may only surmise. Probably this versatile tone-poet has said his best. He is not a second Richard Wagner, not yet has he the charm of the Lizst personality, but he bulks too large in contemporary history to be called a decadent, although in the precise meaning of the word, without its stupid misinterpretation, he is a decadent inasmuch as he dwells with emphasis on the technique of his composition, sacrificing the whole for the page, putting the phrase above the page, and the single note in equal competition with the phrase. In a word, Richard Strauss is a romantic, and flies the red flag of his faith. He has not followed the advice of Paul Verlaine in taking eloquence by the neck and wringing it. He is nothing if not eloquent and expressive, magnifying his Bavarian song-birds to the size of Alpine eagles. The newer choir has avoided the very things in which Strauss has excelled, for that way lie repetition and satiety. [Since writing the above, Strauss has given the world his ballet The Legend of Joseph, in which he has said nothing novel, but has with his customary skill mixed anew the old compound of glittering colours and sultry, exotic harmonies.]

* * * * *

However, Strauss is not the only member of the post-Wagnerian group, but he is the chief one who has kept his individual head above water in the welter and chaos of the school. Where are Cyrill Kistner, Hans

Sommer, August Bungert, and the others? Humperdinck is a mediocrity, even more so than Puccini. And what of the banalities of Bruckner? His Wagnerian cloak is a world too large for his trifling themes. Siegfried Wagner does not count, and for anything novel we are forced to turn our eyes and ears toward the direction of France. After Berlioz, a small fry, indeed, yet not without interest. The visit made by Claude Debussy to Russia in 1879 and during his formative period had consequences. He absorbed Moussorgsky, and built upon him, and he had Wagner at his finger-ends; like Charpentier he cannot keep Wagner out of his scores; the Bayreuth composer is the King Charles's head in his manuscript. Tristan und Isolde in particular must have haunted the composers of Louise, and Pelleas et Melisande. The Julien of Charpentier is on a lower literary and musical level than Louise, which, all said and done, has in certain episodes a picturesque charm; the new work is replete with bad symbolism and worse music-spinning. Debussy has at least a novel, though somewhat monotonous, manner. He is "precious," and in ideas as constipated as Mallarme, whose Afternoon of a Faun he so adequately set. Nevertheless, there is, at times, magic in his music. It is the magic of suggestiveness, of the hinted mystery which only Huysmans's superior persons scattered throughout the universe may guess. After Debussy comes Dukas, Ravel, Florent Schmitt, Rogier-Ducasse, men who seem to have caught anew the spirit of the eighteenth-century music and given it to us not through the poetic haze of Debussy, but in gleaming, brilliant phrases. There is promise in Schmitt. As to Vincent d'Indy, you differ with his scheme, yet he is a master, as was Cesar Franck a master, as are masters the two followers of D'Indy, Albert Roussel and Theodat de Severac. Personally I admire Paul Dukas, though without any warrant whatever for placing him on the same plane with Claude Debussy, who, after all, has added a novel nuance to art. But they are all makers of anxious mosaics; never do they carve the block; exquisite miniaturists, yet lack the big brush work and epical sweep of the preceding generation. Above all, the entire school is minus virility; its music is of the distaff, and has not the masculine ring of crossed swords.

It is hardly necessary to consider here the fantastic fashionings of Erik Satie, the "newest" French composer. He seems to have out-Schoenberged Schoenberg in his little piano pieces bearing the alluring titles of Embryons desseches, preludes and pastorales. Apart from the extravagant titles, the music itself is ludicrous qua music, but not without subtle irony. That trio of Chopin's Funeral March played in C and declared as a citation from the celebrated mazurka of Schubert does touch the rib risible. There are neither time signature nor bars. All is gentle chaos and is devoted to the celebration, in tone, of certain sea-plants and creatures. This sounds like Futurism or the passionate patterns of the Cubists, but I assure you I've seen and tried to play the piano music of Satie. That he is an arch-humbug I shall neither maintain nor deny. After Schoenberg anything is possible in this vale of agonising dissonance. I recall with positive satisfaction a tiny composition for piano by Rebikoff, which he calls a setting of The Devil's Daughters, a mural design by Franz von Stuck of Munich. To be sure, the bass is in C and the treble in D flat, nevertheless the effect is almost piquant. The humour of the new composers is melancholy in its originality, but Gauguin has said that in art one must be either a plagiarist or a revolutionist. Satie is hardly a plagiarist, though the value of his revolution is doubtful.

The influence of Verdi has been supreme among the Verdists of young Italy, though not one has proved knee-high to a grasshopper when compared with the composer of that incomparable Falstaffo. Ponchielli played his part, and under his guidance such dissimilar talents as Puccini, Mascagni, and Leoncavallo were fostered. Puccini stopped with La Boheme, all the rest is repetition and not altogether admirable repetition. That he has been the hero of many phonographs has nothing to do with his intrinsic merits. Cleverness is his predominating vice, and a marked predilection for time-serving; that is, he, like the excellent musical journalist that he is, feels the public pulse, spreads his sails to the breeze of popular favour, and while he is never as banal as Humperdinck or Leoncavallo, he exhibits this quality in suffusion. Above all, he is not original. If Mascagni had only followed the example of Single-Speech Hamilton, he would have spared himself many mortifications and his admirers much boredom. The new men, such as Wolf-Ferrari, Montemezzi, Giordano, and numerous others are eclectics; they belong to any country, and their musical cosmopolitanism, while affording agreeable specimens, may be dismissed with the comment that their art lacks pronounced personal profile. This does not mean that L'Amore dei Tre Re is less delightful. The same may be said of Ludwig Thuille and also of the Neo-Belgian group. Sibelius, the Finn, is a composer with a marked temperament. Among the English Delius shows strongest. He is more personal and more original than Elgar. Not one of these can tie the shoe-strings of Peter Cornelius, the composer of short masterpieces, The Barber of Bagdad--the original, not the bedevilled version of Mottl.

In Germany there is an active group of young men: Ernest Boehe, Walter Braunfels, Max Schillings, Hans Pfitzner, F. Klose, Karl Ehrenberg, Dohnany--born Hungarian--H. G. Noren. The list is long. Fresh, agreeable, and indicative of a high order of talent is a new opera by Franz Schreker, Das Spielwerk und die Prinzessin (1913). Schreker's earlier opera, Der ferne Klang, I missed, but I enjoyed the later composition, charged as it is with fantasy, atmosphere, bold climaxes, and framing a legendary libretto. The influence of Debussy is marked.

Curiously enough, the Russian Moussorgsky, whose work was neglected during his lifetime, has proved to be a precursor to latter-day music. He was not affected in his development by Franz Liszt, whose influence on Tschaikovsky, Borodin, Rimsky-Korsakof, Glazounof--he less than the others--was considerable. Like Dostoievsky, Moussorgsky is _ur_-Russian, not a polished production of western culture, as are Turgenieff, Tschaikovsky, Tolstoy, or Rubinstein. He is not a romantic, this Russian bear; the entire modern school is at one in their rejection of romantic moods and attitudes. Now, music is pre-eminently a romantic art. I once called it a species of emotional mathematics, yet so vast is its kingdom that it may contain the sentimentalities of Mendelssohn, the Old world romance of Schumann, the sublimated poetry of Chopin, and the thunderous epical accents of Beethoven.

Moussorgsky I have styled a "primitive," and I fancy it is as good an ascription as another. He is certainly as primitive as Paul Gauguin, who accomplished the difficult feat of shedding his Parisian skin as an artist and reappearing as a modified Tahitian savage. But I suspect there was a profounder sincerity in the case of the Muscovite. Little need now to sing the praises of Boris Godunoff, though not having seen and heard Ohaliapine, New York is yet to receive the fullest and sharpest impression of the role notwithstanding the sympathetic reading of Arturo Toscanini. Khovanchtchina is even more rugged, more Russian. Hearing it after Tschaikovsky's charming, but weak, setting of Eugen Onegin, the forthright and characteristic qualities of Moussorgsky are set in higher relief. All the old rhetoric goes by the board, and sentiment, in our sense of the word, is not drawn upon too heavily. Stravinsky is a new man not to be slighted, nor are Kodaly and Bartok. I mention only the names of those composers with whose music I am fairly familiar. Probably Stravinsky and his musical fireworks will be called a Futurist, whatever that portentous title may mean. However, the music of Tschaikovsky, Rimsky-Korsakof, Rachmaninof, and the others is no longer revolutionary, but may be considered as evolutionary. Again the theory of transitional periods and types comes into play, but I notice this theory has been applied only to minor masters, never to creators. We don't call Bach or Handel or Mozart or Beethoven intermediate types. Perhaps some day Wagner will seem as original to posterity as Beethoven does to our generation. Wasn't it George Saintsbury who once remarked that all discussion of contemporaries is conversation, not criticism? If this be the case, then it is suicidal for a critic to pass judgment upon the music-making of his day, a fact obviously at variance with daily practice. Yet it is a dictum not to be altogether contravened. For instance, my first impressions of Schoenberg were neither flattering to his composition nor to my indifferent critical acumen. If I had begun by listening to the comparatively mellifluous D-minor string quartet, played by the Flonzaley Quartet, as did my New York colleagues, instead of undergoing the terrifying aural tortures of Lieder des Pierrot Lunaire, I might have been as amiable as the critics. The string sextet has been received here with critical cordiality. Its beauties were exposed by the Kneisel Quartet. But circumstances were otherwise, and it was later that I heard the two string quartets--the latter in F-sharp minor (by courtesy, this tonality), with voices at the close--the astounding Gurrelieder and the piano pieces. The orchestral poem of Pelleas et Melisande I have yet to enjoy or execrate; there seems to be no middle term for Schoenberg's amazing art. If I say I hate or like it that is only a personal expression, not a criticism standing foursquare. I fear I subscribe to the truth of Mr. Saintsbury's epigram.

It may be considered singular that the most original "new" music hails from Austria, not Germany. No doubt that Strauss is the protagonist of the romantics, dating from Liszt and Wagner; and that Max Reger is the protagonist of the modern classicists, counting Brahms as their fount (did you ever read what Wagner, almost a septuagenarian, wrote of Brahms: "Der juedische Czardas-Aufspieler"?). But they are no longer proclaimed by those ultramoderns who dare to call Strauss an intermediate type. So rapidly doth music speed down the grooves of time. From Vienna comes Schoenberg; in Vienna lives and composes the youthful Erich Korngold, whose earlier music seems to well as if from some mountain spring, although with all its spontaneity it has no affinity with Mozart. It is distinctively "modern," employing the resources of the "new" harmonic displacements and the multicoloured modern orchestral apparatus. Korngold is so receptive that he reveals just now the joint influences of Strauss and Schoenberg. Yet I think the path lies straight before this young genius, a straight and shining path.

The little Erich Korngold--in reality a plump, good-looking boy--presents few problems for the critic. I know his piano music, replete with youthful charm, and I heard his overture produced by the Berlin Philharmonic Orchestra (the fifth concert of the season) under the leadership of Arthur Nikisch. Whether or not the youth is helped by his teacher, as some say, there can be no doubt as to his precocious talent. His facility in composition is Mozartian. Nothing laboured, all as spontaneous as Schoenberg is calculating. He scores conventionally, that is, latter-day commonplaces are the rule in his disposition and treatment of the instrumental army. Like Mozart, he is melodious, easy to follow, and, like Mozart, he begins by building on his immediate predecessor, in his case Strauss. Debussy is not absent, nor is Fritz Delius.

I heard not a little of Der Rosenkavalier. But who would suspect a lad of such a formal sense--even if it is only imitative--of such clear development, such climaxes, and such a capital coda! The chief test of the music--would you listen to it if you did not know who composed it?--is met. The overture is entertaining, if not very original. Truly a wonder child.

Hugo Wolf was a song writer who perilously grazed genius, but he rotted before he was ripe. Need we consider the respective positions of Bruckner or Mahler, one all prodigality and diffuseness, the other largely cerebral? And Mahler without Bruckner would hardly have been possible. Those huge tonal edifices, skyscrapers in bulk, soon prove barren to the spirit. A mountain in parturition with a mouse! Nor need we dwell upon the ecstatic Scriabine who mimicked Chopin so deftly in his piano pieces, "going" Liszt and Strauss one better--or ten, if you will--and spilt his soul in swooning, roseate vibrations. Withal, a man of ability and vast ambitions. (He died in 1915.)

More than two years ago I heard in Vienna Schoenberg's Gurrelieder, a setting to a dramatic legend by Jens Peter Jacobsen. This choral and orchestral work was composed in 1902, but it sounds newer than the quartets or the sextet. In magnitude it beats Berlioz. It demands five solo singers, a dramatic reader, three choral bodies, and an orchestra of one hundred and forty, in which figure eight flutes, seven clarinets, six horns, four Wagner tubas. Little wonder the impression was a stupendous one. There were episodes of great beauty, dramatic moments, and appalling climaxes. As Schoenberg has decided both in his teaching and practice that there are no unrelated harmonies, cacophony was not absent. Another thing: this composer has temperament. He is cerebral, as few before him, yet in this work the bigness of the design did not detract from the emotional quality. I confess I did not understand at one hearing the curious dislocated harmonies and splintered themes--melodies they are not--in the Pierrot Lunaire. I have been informed that the ear should play a secondary role in this "new" music; no longer through the porches of the ear must filter plangent tones, wooing the tympanum with ravishing accords. It is now the "inner ear," which is symbolic of a higher type of musical art. A complete disassociation of ideas, harmonies, rhythmic life, architectonic is demanded. To quote an admirer of the Vienna revolutionist: "The entire man in you must be made over before you can divine Schoenberg's art." Perhaps his aesthetik embraces what the metaphysicians call the Langley-James hypothesis; fear, anxiety, pain are the "content," and his hearers actually suffer as are supposed to suffer his characters or moods or ideas. The old order has changed, changed very much, yet I dimly feel that if this art is to endure it contains, perhaps in precipitation, the elements without which no music is permanent. But his elliptical patterns are interesting, above all bold. There is no such thing as absolute originality. Even the individual Schoenberg, the fabricator of nervous noises, leans heavily on Wagner. Wagner is the fountainhead of the new school, let them mock his romanticism as they may.

Is all this to be the music of to-morrow? Frankly, I don't know, and I'm sure Schoenberg doesn't know. He is said to be guided by his daimon, as was Socrates; let us hope that familiar may prompt him to more comprehensible utterances. But he must be counted with nowadays. He is significant of the reaction against formal or romantic beauty. I said the same more than a decade ago of Debussy. Again the critical watchmen in the high towers are signalling Schoenberg's movements, not without dismay. Cheer up, brethren! Preserve an open mind. It is too soon to beat reactionary bosoms, crying aloud, Nunc dimittis! Remember the monstrous fuss made over the methods of Richard Strauss and Claude Debussy. I shouldn't be surprised if ten years hence Arnold Schoenberg proves quite as conventional a member of musical society as those other two "anarchs of art."

VI

FRANK WEDEKIND

A very deceptive mask is literature. Here is your Nietzsche with his warrior pen slashing away at the conventional lies of civilisation, a terrific figure of outraged manhood, though in private life he was the gentlest of men, self-sacrificing, lovable, modest, and moral to a painful degree. But see what his imitators have made of him. And in all the tons of rubbish that have been written about Tolstoy, the story told by Anna Seuron is the most significant. But a human being is better than a half-god.

Bearing this in mind I refused to be scared in advance by the notorious reputation of Frank Wedekind, whose chief claim to recognition in New York is his Spring's Awakening, produced at the Irving Place Theatre seasons ago. I had seen this moving drama of youth more than once in the Kammerspielhaus of the Deutsches Theatre, Berlin, and earlier the same poet's drama Erdgeist (in the summer, 1903), and again refused to shudder at its melodramatic atrocities. Wedekind wore at that time the mask Mephistophelian, and his admirers, for he had many from the beginning, delighted in what they called his spiritual depravity--forgetting that the two qualities cannot be blended. Now, while I have termed Frank Wedekind the naughty boy of the modern German drama, I by no means place him among those spirits like Goethe's Mephisto, who perpetually deny. On the contrary, he is one of the most affirmative voices in the new German literature.

He is always asserting. If he bowls away at some rickety ninepin of a social lie, he does it with a gusto that is exhilarating. To be sure, whatever the government is, he is against it; which only means he is a rebel born, hating constraint and believing with Stendhal that one's first enemies are one's own parents. No doubt, after bitter experience, Wedekind discovered that his bitterest foe was himself. That he is a tricky, Puck-like nature is evident. He loves to shock, a trait common to all romanticists from Gautier down. He sometimes says things he doesn't mean. He contradicts himself as do most men of genius, and, despite his poetic temperament, there is in him much of the lay preacher. I have noticed this quality in men such as Ibsen and Strindberg, who cry aloud in the wilderness of Philistia for freedom, for the "free, unhampered life" and then devise a new system that is thrice as irksome as the old, that puts one's soul into a spiritual bondage. Wedekind is of this order; a moralist is concealed behind his shining ambuscade of verbal immoralism. In Germany every one sports his Weltanschauung, his personal interpretation of life and its meanings. In a word, a working philosophy--and a fearsome thing it is to see young students with fresh sabre cuts on their honest countenances demolishing Kant, Schopenhauer, or Nietzsche only to set up some other system.

Always a system, always this compartmentising of the facts of existence. Scratch the sentimentalism and aestheticism of a German, and you come upon a pedant. Wedekind has not altogether escaped this national peculiarity. But he writes for to-morrow, not yesterday; for youth, and not to destroy the cherished prejudices of the old. His admirers speak of him as a unicum, a man so original as to be without forerunners, without followers. A monster? For no one can escape the common law of descent, whether physical or spiritual. Wedekind has had plenty of teachers, not excepting the most valuable of all, personal experience. The sinister shadow cast by Ibsen fell across the shoulders of the young poet, and he has read Max Stirner and Nietzsche not wisely, but too well. He is as frank as Walt Whitman (and as shameless) concerning the mysteries of life, and as healthy (and as coarse) as Rabelais. Furthermore, Strindberg played a marked role in his artistic development. Without the hopeless misogyny of the Swede, without his pessimism, Wedekind is quite as drastic. And the realism of the Antoine Theatre should not be omitted.

He exhibits in his menagerie of types--many of them new in the theatre--a striking collection of wild animals. In the prologue to one of his plays he tells his audience that to Wedekind must they come if they wish to see genuine wild and beautiful beasts. This sounds like Stirner. He lays much stress on the fact that literature, whether poetic or otherwise, has become too "literary"--hardly a novel idea; and boasts that none of his characters has read a book. The curse of modern life is the multiplication of books. Very true, and yet I find that Wedekind is "literary," that he could exclaim with Stephan Mallarme: "La chair est triste, helas! et j'ai lu tous les livres."

Regarding the modern stage he is also positive. He believes that for the last twenty years dramatic literature is filled with half-humans, men who are not fit for fatherhood, women who would escape the burden of bearing children because of their superior culture. This is called "a problem play," the hero or heroine of which commits suicide at the end of the fifth act to the great delight of neurotic, dissatisfied ladies and hysterical men. Weak wills--in either sex--have been the trump card of the latter-day dramatist; not a sound man or woman who isn't at the same time stupid, can be found in the plays of Ibsen or Hauptmann or the rest. Wedekind mentions no names, but he tweaks several noses prominent in dramatic literature.

He is the younger generation kicking in the panels of the doors in the old houses. There is a hellish racket for a while, and then when the dust clears away you discern the revolutionist calmly ensconced in the seats of the bygone mighty and passionately preaching from the open window his version of New Life; he is become reformer himself and would save a perishing race--spiritually speaking--from damnation by the gospel of beauty, by shattering the shackles of love--especially the latter; love to be love must be free, preaches Wedekind; love is still in the swaddling clothes of Oriental prejudice. George Meredith once said the same in Diana of the Crossways, although he said it more epigrammatically. For Wedekind religion is a symbol of our love of ourselves; nevertheless, outside of his two engrossing themes, love and death, he is chiefly concerned with religion, not alone as material for artistic treatment, but as a serious problem of our existence. A Lucifer in pride, he tells us that he has never made of good evil, or vice versa; he, unlike Baudelaire, has never deliberately said: Evil, be thou my good! That he has emptied upon the boards from his Pandora-box imagination the greatest gang of scoundrels, shady ladies, master swindlers, social degenerates, circus people, servants, convicts, professional strong men, half-crazy idealists, irritable rainbow-eaters--the demi-monde of a subterranean world--that ever an astonished world saw perform their antics in front of the footlights is not to be denied, but it must be confessed that his criminal supermen and superwomen usually get their deserts. Like Octave Mirbeau, he faces the music of facts, and there are none too abhorrent that he doesn't transform into something significant.

On the technical side Strindberg has taught him much; he prefers the one-act form, or a series of loosely joined episodes. Formally he is not a master, nor despite his versatility is he objective. With Strindberg he has been called "Shakespearian"--fatal word--but he is not; that in the vast domain of Shakespeare there is room for them both I do not doubt; room in the vicinity of the morbid swamps and dark forests, or hard by the house of them that are melancholy mad.

The oftener I see or read Wedekind the more I admire his fund of humour. But I feel the tug of his theories. The dramatist in him is hampered by the theorist who would "reform" all life--he is neither a socialist nor an upholder of female suffrage--and when some of his admiring critics talk of his "ideals of beauty and power," then I know the game is up--the prophet, the dogmatist, the pedant, not the poet, artist, and witty observer of life, are thrust in the foreground.

There is Hermann Sudermann, for example, the precise antipodes of Wedekind--Sudermann, the inexhaustible bottle of the German theatre, the conjurer who imperturbably pours out any flavour, colour, or liquid you desire from his bottle; presto, here is Ibsen, or Dumas, or Hauptmann, or Sardou; comedy, satire, tragedy, farce, or the marionettes of the fashionable world! Frank Wedekind is less of the stage prestidigitator and more sincere. We must, perforce, listen to his creatures as they parade their agony before us, and we admire his clever rogues--the never-to-be-forgotten Marquis of Keith heads the list--and smile at their rough humour and wisdom. For me, the real Frank Wedekind is not the prophet, but the dramatist. As there is much of his stark personality in his plays, it would not be amiss to glance at his career.

He has "a long foreground," as Emerson said of Walt Whitman. He was born at Hanover, July 24, 1864, and consequently was only twenty-seven years old when, in 1891, he wrote his most original, if not most finished, drama, Spring's Awakening. He studied law four terms at Munich, two at Zurich: but for this lawless soul jurisprudence was not to be; it was to fulfil a wish of his father's that he consented to the drudgery. A little poem which has been reproduced in leaflet form, Felix and Galathea, is practically his earliest offering to the muse. Like most beginnings of fanatics and realists, it fairly swims and shimmers with idealism. His father dead, a roving existence and a precarious one began for the youthful Frank. He lived by his wits in Paris and London, learned two languages, met that underworld which later was to figure in his vital dramatic pictures, wrote advertisements for a canned soup--in Hauptmann's early play, Friedensfest, Wedekind is said to figure as Robert, who is a reclame agent--was attached to circuses, variety theatres, and fairs, was an actor in tingletangles, cabarets, and saw life on its seamiest side, whether in Germany, Austria, France, or England. Such experiences produced their inevitable reaction--disillusionment. Finally in 1905 Director Reinhardt engaged him as an actor and he married the actress Tilly Niemann-Newes, with whom he has since lived happily, the father of a son, his troubled spirit in safe harbour at last, but not in the least changed, to judge from his play, Franziska, a Modern Mystery.

Personally, Wedekind was never an extravagant, exaggerated man. A sorrowful face in repose is his, and when he appeared on Hans von Wolzogen's Ueberbrettl, or sang at the Munich cabaret called the Eleven Hangmen, his songs--he composes at times--Ilse, Goldstueck, Brigitte B, Mein Liebchen, to the accompaniment of his guitar, there was a distinct individuality in his speech and gesture very attractive to the public.

But as an actor Wedekind is not distinguished, though versatile. I've only seen him in two roles, as Karl Hetman in his play of Hidalla (now renamed after the leading role), and as Ernest Scholtz in The Marquis of Keith. As Jack the Ripper in The Box of Pandora I am glad to say that I have not viewed him, though he is said to be a gruesome figure during the few minutes that he is in the scene. His mimetic methods recalled to me the simplicity of Antoine--who is not a great actor, yet, somehow or other, an impressive one. Naturally, Wedekind is the poet speaking his own lines, acting his own creations, and there is, for that reason, an intimate note in his interpretations, an indescribable sympathy, and an underscoring of his meanings that even a much superior actor might miss. He is so absolutely unconventional in his bearing and speech as to seem amateurish, yet he secures with his naturalism some poignant effects. I shan't soon forget his Karl Hetman, the visionary reformer.

Wedekind, like Heine, has the faculty of a cynical, a consuming self-irony. He is said to be admirable in Der Kammersaenger. It must not be forgotten that he has, because of a witty lampoon in the publication Simplicissimus, done his "little bit" as they say in penitentiary social circles. These few months in prison furnished him with scenic opportunities; there is more than one of his plays with a prison set. And how he does lay out the "system." He, like Baudelaire, Flaubert, and De Maupassant, was summoned before the bar of justice for outraging public morals by the publication of his play, The Box of Pandora, the sequel to Erdgeist. He had to withdraw the book and expunge certain offensive passages, but he escaped fine and imprisonment, as did his publisher, Bruno Cassirer. He rewrote the play, the second act of which had been originally printed in French, the third in English, and its republication was permitted by the sensitive authorities of Berlin.

If a critic can't become famous because of his wisdom he may nevertheless attain a sort of immortality, or what we call that elusive thing, by writing himself down an ass. The history of critical literature would reveal many such. Think of such an accomplished practitioner as the late M. Brunetiere, writing as he did of Flaubert and Baudelaire. And that monument to critical ineptitude, Degeneration, by Max Nordau. A more modern instance is the judgment of

Julius Hart in the publication, _Tag_ (1901), concerning our dramatist. He wrote: "In German literature to-day there is nothing as vile as the art of Frank Wedekind." Fearing this sparkling gem of criticism might escape the notice of posterity, Wedekind printed it as a sort of motto to his beautiful poetic play (1902), Such Is Life. However, the truth is that our poet is often disconcerting. His swift transition from mood to mood disturbs the spectator, especially when one mood is lofty, the next shocking. He has also been called "the clown of the German stage," and not without reason, for his mental acrobatics, his grand and lofty tumblings from sheer transcendentalism to the raw realism, his elliptical style, are incomprehensible even to the best trained of audiences. As Alfred Kerr rightfully puts it, you must learn to see anew in the theatre of Wedekind. All of which is correct, yet we respectfully submit that the theatre, like a picture, has its optics: its foreground, middle distance, background, and foreshortening. Destroy the perspective and the stage is transformed into something that resembles staring post-Impressionist posters. The gentle arts of development, of characterisation, of the conduct of a play may not be flouted with impunity. The author more than the auditor is the loser. Wedekind works too often in bold, bright primary colours; only in some of his pieces is the modulation artistic, the character-drawing summary without being harsh. His climaxes usually go off like pistol-shots. Fruehlings Erwachen (1891), the touching tale of Spring's Awakening in the heart of an innocent girl of fourteen, a child, Gretchen, doomed to tragic ending, set all Germany by the ears when it was first put on in the Kammerspielhaus, Berlin, by Director Reinhardt at the end of 1906. During fifteen years two editions had been sold, and the work was virtually unknown till its stage presentation. Mr. Shaw is right in saying that if you wish to make swift propaganda seek the theatre, not the pulpit, nor the book. With the majority Wedekind's name was anathema. A certain minority called him the new Messiah, that was to lead youth into the promised land of freedom. For a dramatist all is grist that makes revolve the sails of his advertising mill, and as there is nothing as lucrative as notoriety, Wedekind must have been happy.

He is a hard hitter and dearly loves a fight--a Hibernian trait--and his pen was soon transformed into a club, with which he rained blows on the ribs of his adversaries. That he was a fanatical moralist was something not even the broadest-minded among them suspected; they only knew that he meddled with a subject that was hitherto considered tacenda, and with dire results. Nowadays the thesis of Spring's Awakening is not so novel. In England Mr. H. G. Wells was considerably exercised over the problem when he wrote in The New Machiavelli such a startling sentence as "Multitudes of us are trying to run this complex, modern community on a basis of 'hush,' without explaining to our children or discussing with them anything about love or marriage."

I find in Spring's Awakening a certain delicate poetic texture that the poet never succeeded in recapturing. His maiden is a dewy creature; she is also the saddest little wretch that was ever wept over in modern fiction. Her cry when she confesses the worst to her dazed mother is of a poignancy. As for the boys, they are interesting. Evidently, the piece is an authentic document, but early as it was composed it displayed the principal characteristics of its author: Freakishness, an abnormal sense of the grotesque--witness that unearthly last scene, which must be taken as an hallucination--and its swift movement; also a vivid sense of caricature--consider the trial scene in the school; but created by a young poet of potential gifts. The seduction scene is well managed at the Kammerspielhaus. We are not shown the room, but a curtain slightly divided allows the voices of the youthful lovers to be overheard. A truly moving effect is thereby produced. Since the performance of this play, the world all over has seen a great light. Aside from the prefaces of Mr. Shaw on the subject of children and their education, plays, pamphlets, even legislation have dealt with the theme. A reaction was bound to follow, and we do not hear so much now about "sex initiation" and coeducation. Suffice it to say that Frank Wedekind was the first man to put the question plumply before us in dramatic shape.

A favourite one-act piece is Der Kammersaenger (1899), which might be translated as The Wagner Singer, for therein is laid bare the soul of the Wagnerian tenor, Gerardo, whose one week visit to a certain city results in both comedy and tragedy. He has concluded a brilliantly successful Gastspiel, singing several of the Wagnerian roles, and when the curtain rises we see him getting his trunks in order, his room at the hotel filled with flowers and letters. He must sing Tristan the next night in Brussels, and has but an hour to spare before his train departs. If he misses it his contract will be void, and in Europe that means business, tenor or no tenor. He sends the servant to pack his costumes, snatches up the score of Tristan, and as he hums it, he is aware that some one is lurking behind one of the window-curtains. It is a young miss, presumably English--she says: "Oh, yes"--and she confesses her infatuation. Vain as is our handsome singer he has no time for idle flirtations. He preaches a tonic sermon, the girl weeps, promises to be good, promises to study the music of Wagner instead of his tenors, and leaves with a paternal kiss on her brow. The comedy is excellent, though you dimly recall a little play entitled: Frederic Lemaitre. It is a partial variation on that theme. But what follows is of darker hue. An old opera composer has sneaked by the guard at the door and begs with tears in his eyes that the singer will listen to his music. He is met with an angry refusal. Gradually, after he has explained his struggles of a half-century, he, the friend of Wagner, to secure a hearing of his work, the tenor, who is both brutal and generous, consents, though he is pressed for time. Then the tragedy of ill luck is unfolded. The poor musician doesn't know where to begin, fumbles in his score, while the tenor, who has just caught another woman behind a screen, a piano teacher--here we begin to graze the edge of burlesque--grows impatient, finally interrupts the composer, and in scathing terms tells him what "art" really means to the world at large and how useless has been his sacrifice to that idol "art" with a capital "A." I don't know when I ever enjoyed the exposition of the musical temperament. The Concert, by Bahr, is mere trifling in comparison, all sawdust and simian gestures. We are a luxury for the bourgeois, the tenor tells his listener, who do not care for the music or words we sing. If they realised the meanings of Walkuere they would fly the opera-house. We singers, he continues, are slaves, not to our "art," but to the public; we have no private life.

He dismisses the old man.

Then a knock at the door, a fresh interruption. This time it is surely serious. A young, lovely society woman enters. She has been his love for the week, the understanding being that the affair is to terminate as it began, brusquely, without arriere-pensee. But she loves Gerardo. She clamours to be taken to Brussels. She will desert husband, children, social position, she will ruin her future to be with the man she adores. She is mad with the despair of parting. He is inexorable. He gently reminds her of their agreement. His contract does not permit him to travel in company with ladies, nor may he scandalise the community in which he resides. Tenors, too, must be circumspect.

She swears she will kill herself. He smiles and bids her remember her family. She does shoot herself, and he sends for a policeman, remembering that an arrest by superior force will but temporarily abrogate his contract. No policeman is found by the distracted hotel servants, and, exclaiming: "To-morrow evening I must sing Tristan in Brussels," the conscientious artist hurries away to his train, leaving the lifeless body of his admirer on the sofa. Played by a versatile actor, this piece ought to make a success in America, though the biting irony of the dialogue and the cold selfishness of the hero might not be "sympathetic" to our sentiment-loving audiences. The poet has protested in print against the alteration of the end of this little piece, _i. e._, one acting version made the impassioned lady only a pretended suicide, which quite spoils the motivation.

Ibsen must have felt sick when such an artist as Duse asked him to let her make Nora in Doll's House return to her family. But he is said to have consented. Wedekind consented, because he was ill, but he made his protest, and justly so.

The Marquis of Keith is a larger canvas. It is a modern rogues' comedy. Barry Lyndon is hardly more entertaining. The marquis is the son of an humble tutor in the house of a count whose son later figures as Ernest Scholtz. The marquis is a swindler in the grand manner. He is a Get-Rich-Quick Wallingford, for he has lived in the United States, but instead of a lively sketch is a full-length portrait painted by a master. You like him despite his scampishness. He is witty. He has a heart--for his own woes--and seems intensely interested in all the women he loves and swindles. He goes to Munich, where he invents a huge scheme for an exhibition palace and fools several worthy and wealthy brewers, but not the powerful Consul Casimir, the one man necessary to his comprehensive operation. When his unhappy wife tells him there is no bread in the house for the next day, he retorts: "Very well, then we shall dine at the Hotel Continental." Nothing depresses his mercurial spirits. He borrows from Peter to pay Paul, and an hour later borrows from Paul to pay himself. His boyhood friend he simply plunders. This Ernest, in reality the Graf von Trautenau, is an idealist of the type that Wedekind is fond of delineating. He would save the world from itself, rescue it from the morass of materialism, but he relapses into a pathological mysticism which ends in a sanitarium for nervous troubles. The marquis is a Mephisto; he is not without a trace of idealism; altogether a baffling nature, Faust-like, and as chock-full of humour as an egg is full of meat. He goes to smash. His plans are checkmated. His beloved deserts him for the enemy. His wife commits suicide. His life threatened, and his liberty precarious, he takes ten thousand marks from Consul Casimir, whose name he has forged in a telegram, and with a grin starts for pastures new. Will he shoot himself? No! After all, life is very much like shooting the chutes. The curtain falls. This stirring and technically excellent comedy has never been a favourite in Germany. Perhaps its cynicism is too crass. It achieved only a few performances in Berlin to the accompaniment of catcalls, hisses, and derisive laughter. I wonder why? It is entertaining, with all its revelation of a rascally mean soul and its shady episodes.

Space, I am sorry to say, forbids me from further exposition of such strong little pieces as Musik, a heart-breaking drama of a betrayed girl studying singing who goes to jail while the real offender, the man, remains at liberty (1907), or of Die Zensur, with its discussion of art and religion--the poet intrudes--and its terrible cry at the close: "Oh, God! why art thou so unfathomable?" Or of the so-called Lulu tragedy (Erdgeist and The Box of Pandora) of which I like the first act of the former and the second act of the latter--you are reminded at this point of the gambling scene in Sardou's Fernande--but as I do not care to sup on such unmitigated horrors, I prefer to let my readers judge for themselves from the printed plays.

Karl Hetman is an absorbing play in which a man loses the world but remains captain of his soul; actually he ends his life rather than exhibit himself as motley to the multitude. As a foil for the idealist Hetman--who is a sort of inverted Nietzsche; also a self-portrait in part of the dramatist--there is the self-seeking scamp Launhart who succeeds with the very ideas which Hetman couldn't make viable, ideas in fact which brought about his disaster. They are two finely contrasted portraits, and what a grimace of disgust is aroused when Launhart tells the woman who loves Hetman: "O Fanny, Fanny, a living rascal is better for your welfare than the greatest of dead prophets." What Dead-Sea-fruit wisdom! The pathos of distance doesn't appeal to the contemporary soul of Wedekind. He writes for the young, that is, for to-morrow.

The caprice, the bizarre, the morbid in Wedekind are more than redeemed by his rich humanity. He loves his fellow man even when he castigates him. He is very emotional, also pragmatic. The second act of his Franziska, a Karnevalgroteske, was given at the Dresden Pressfestival, February 7, 1913, with the title of Matrimony in the Year 2000, the author and his wife appearing in the leading roles with brilliant success. It contains in solution the leading motives from all his plays and his philosophy of life. It is fantastic, as fantastic as Strindberg's Dream Play, but amusing. In 1914 his biblical drama, Simson (Samson), was produced with mixed success.

Translated Wedekind would lose his native wood-note wild, and doubtless much of his dynamic force--for on the English stage he would be emasculated. And I wonder who would have the courage to produce his works.

Musik, for example, if played in its entirety might create a profound impression. It is pathetically moving and the part of the unhappy girl, who is half crazy because of her passion for her singing-master, is a role for an accomplished actress. If the public can endure Brieux's Damaged Goods, why not Musik? The latter is a typical case and is excellent drama; the French play is neither. For me all the man is summed up in the cry of one of his characters in Erdgeist: "Who gives me back my faith in mankind, will give me back my life." An idealist, surely.

The last time I saw him was at the Richard Strauss festival in Stuttgart, October, 1912. He had changed but little and still reminded me of both David Belasco and an Irish Catholic priest. In his eyes there lurked the "dancing-madness" of which Robert Louis Stevenson writes. A latter-day pagan, with touches of the perverse, the grotesque, and the poetic; thus seems to me Frank Wedekind.

VII

THE MAGIC VERMEER

I

Who owns the thirty-fifth canvas by Jan Vermeer of Delft? And are there more than thirty-five works by this master of cool, clear daylight? I have seen nearly all the pictures attributed to the too little known Dutchman, and as far as was in my power I have read all the critical writings by such experts as Havard, Obreen, Bredius, Hofstede de Groot (Jan Vermeer van Delft en Carel Fabritius, 1907), Doctor Bode, Wauters, Arsene Alexandre, G. Geoffroy, Buerger, Taine, John Smith, Gustave Vanzype, and several others.

Doctor A. Bredius has printed an article entitled: A Pseudo-Vermeer in the Berlin gallery, which I have not been able to procure, but then the same worthy authority has contested the authenticity of the portrait of a young man in the Brussels Museum. It is not signed, this beautiful head, and at one time it was in the English collections of Humphry Ward and Peter Norton, and later in the Collection Otlet at Brussels. Smith catalogued it as a Rembrandt; indeed, it had the false signature of the great master. Much later it was accredited to Jan Victoors, a Rembrandt pupil, and to Nicolas Maes, and under this name was sold in Paris in 1900. A. J. Wauters finally declared it a Vermeer, though neither Bredius nor Hofstede de Groot are of his opinion. And now we hear the question: Who owns the thirty-fifth Vermeer, Vermeer of the magical blue and yellow?

First let us ask: Who was Jan Vermeer, or Van der Meer? "What songs did the sirens sing?" puzzled good old Sir Thomas Browne, and we know far more about William Shakespeare or Sappho or Memling than we do of the enigmatic man from Delft who died a double death in 1675; not only the death of the body, but the death of the spirit, of his immortal art. For several centuries he was not accorded the paternity of his own pictures. To Terburg, Pieter de Hooch, Nicolas Maes, Metsu they were credited. Even the glorious Letter Reader of the Dresden gallery has been attributed to De Hooch, and by no less an authority than Charles Blanc. Fromentin, of all men, does not mention his name in his always admirable book on the art of the Low Countries; no doubt one cause for his neglect.

This is precisely what we know of Jan Vermeer of Delft, in which city--oddly enough--there is not a single canvas of his. In 1632 he was born there. In 1653 he married Catherine Bolnes; he was just twenty-one years old. His admission to the corporation of painters as a master occurred the same year, as the books attest. In 1662 he was elected dean of the corporation, and again in 1670. In 1675 he died, in his forty-third year, and at the apogee of his powers.

When he became a member of the corporation of painters at Delft he could not pay in full the initiation fee, six florins, and he gave on account one florin ten cents--the entry in the books attests this astounding fact. He was poor, but he had youth and genius, and he loved.

He had also eight or ten children and lived happily--as do most people without a history--on the Oude Langendyck, where he became at least a local celebrity, according to a mention of him in the Journal des Voyages, by Balthazar de Moncouys (published 1665). Moncouys also recorded another interesting fact. "At Delft I saw the painter Vermeer," he writes, "but none of his works were at his atelier; at a baker's I saw a figure--for which was paid six hundred livres." At a bakeshop! Vermeer, then, literally painted for his bread.

In 1696, twenty years after his death, certain of his works (forty in the catalogue) brought only 100 florins, pictures that to-day are worth hundreds of thousands of dollars. And in 1719 the superb Milk Girl, now in the Rijks Museum, formerly from the Six Collection, was sold for 126 florins (it brought $100,000 when Mr. Six sold it to the museum), while at the same sale the mediocre Gerard Dou fetched 6,000 florins for a canvas. Even nowadays the public has not been converted to the idea of the greatness of Vermeer. Go any time of the day into the Mauritshuis at The Hague and you will always discover a crowd before that clumsy, stupid bull with the wooden legs, by no means Paul Potter's masterpiece, while the gem of The Hague gallery, the View of Delft, with its rich pate, its flowing rhythms, its clear daylight, seldom draws a large audience. And I do not doubt that only the propinquity of Rembrandt's Young Saskia to Vermeer's Merry Company (otherwise known as The Courtesan) in the Dresden gallery attracts an otherwise indifferent public.

In 1696 there were 21 pictures of Vermeer sold at public auction in Amsterdam. Of these 21 the experts claim to have discovered 16. But the bother of the question is that 100 other pictures were also sold at the same time; furthermore, the sale is said to have taken place after the death of a venerable mediocrity, also named Vermeer, but hailing from Haarlem. (He died in 1691.) This confusion of names may have had something to do with the obscuring of the great Vermeer. But he had no vogue in 1696, as the prices at the sale prove only too well.

Vanzype gives the list, and its importance in any research of the Vermeer pictures is paramount. Here are the 21 canvases that are extant, and the prices paid: No. 1--A young woman weighing gold, 155 florins; 2--A milk girl, 175 florins; 3--The portrait of the painter in his studio, 45 florins; 4--A young woman playing the guitar, 70 florins; 5--A gentleman in his chamber, 95 florins; 6--A young lady playing the clavecin, with a gentleman who listens, 30 florins; 7--A young woman taking a letter from her servant, 70 florins; 8--A servant who has drunk too much asleep at a table, 62 florins; 9--A merry company, 73 florins; 10--A young lady and a gentleman making music, 81 florins; 11--A soldier with a laughing girl, 44 florins; 12--A young lacemaker, 28 florins; 13--View of Delft, 200 florins; 14--A house at Delft, 72 florins; 15--A view of some houses, 48 florins; 16--A young woman writing, 63 florins; 17--A young woman, 30 florins; 18--Young woman at a clavecin, 42 florins; 19--A portrait in antique costume, 36 florins; 20 and 21--Two pendants, 34 florins.

The subsequent history of these pictures, while too copious for transcription here, may be skeletonised. This may answer the question posed at the beginning of this little story. Gustave Vanzype asks: What has become of the young woman weighing gold, which reappeared at a sale in the year 1701, which Buerger thought he had found in the canvas, The Weigher of Gold. And the Intoxicated Servant? The latter is in the Altman collection; the former at Philadelphia, in Mr. Widener's gallery. But let us see how the wise doctors of paint dispute among themselves. How many Vermeers are there in existence, that is, known to the world, for there may be others, for all we know, hidden in the cabinets of collectors or sporting other names? Buerger, who called Vermeer the Sphinx among artists, has generously attributed to him 76 pictures. This was in 1866, and since then a more savant authority has reduced the number to 40. Havard admits 56. The Vermeer of Haarlem was to blame for this swollen catalogue. Bredius and De Groot have attenuated the list. The Morgan Vermeer in the Metropolitan Museum, a Vermeer of first-class quality, is not in some of the catalogues, nor is the Woman Weighing Pearls, now in the possession of P. A. B. Widener, of Philadelphia, to be found accredited to Vermeer in Smith's Catalogue Raisonne. But not much weight can be attached to the opinions of the earlier critics of Vermeer. For them he was either practically unknown or else an imitator of Terburg, De Hooch, or Mieris, he whose work is never tight, hard, or slippery.

The following list of thirty-four admittedly genuine Vermeers may clear up the mystery of the 1696 sale at Amsterdam. Remember that the authenticity of these works is no longer contested.

In Holland at The Hague there are four Vermeers: The Toilette of Diana, the Head of a Young Girl, An Allegory of the New Testament, and the View of Delft. At the Rijks Museum, Amsterdam, there are four: The Milk Girl, The Reader, The Letter, and A Street in Delft. (This latter is the House in Delft, which sold for seventy-two florins in 1696.) In Great Britain in the Coats collection at Castle Skalmorlie (Scotland) there is Christ at the House of Martha and Mary. In the National Gallery, a young woman standing in front of her clavecin. In the Beit collection, London, a young woman at her clavecin. Collection Salting, London, The Pianist. Windsor Castle, The Music Lesson. Beit collection, A Young Woman Writing. In the Joseph collection, A Soldier and a Laughing Girl. And the Sleeping Servant, formerly of the Kann collection, Paris, then in London, and later sold to Mr. Altman. In Germany we find the following: At the Berlin Museum, The Pearl Collar. The Drop of Wine, in the same museum, Berlin. The Coquette, Brunswick Museum. The Lady and Her Servant, in the private collection of James Simon, Berlin. The Merry Company and The Reader in the Dresden gallery. The Geographer at the Window, in the Staedel Institute, Frankfort. In France, The Astronomer of the A. de Rothschild collection at Paris, and the little Lacemaker, in the Louvre Gallery. In Belgium, there was at Brussels the portrait of a girl, which was formerly in the Arenberg gallery. When I tried to see it I was told that it had been sold to some one in Germany. Its type, judging from the head of a girl at The Hague, is not unlike The Geographer, in the collection of Viscount Du Bus de Gisegnies, Brussels. A Young Girl, collection of Jonkheer de Grez, Brussels. This last was discovered by Doctor Bredius in 1906, and is at the present writing in New York at the gallery of Mr. Knoedler.

In Austria-Hungary there are two noble Vermeers; one in the private gallery of Count Czernin, the portrait of the painter, the other in the Museum of Budapest, the portrait of a woman, the latter as solidly modelled as any Hals I ever viewed. The Czernin Vermeer is the only one in Vienna (the other Vermeer in this gallery is by Renesse). It is a masterpiece. In it he grazes perfection.

The United States is, considering the brevity of the list, well off in Vermeers. There is at Philadelphia the Mandoliniste of John G. Johnson (without doubt, as M. Vanzype points out, the Young Woman Playing the Guitar of the 1696 sale). At Boston Mrs. John Gardner owns The Concert. At the Metropolitan Museum there is the Woman with the Jug (Marquand); and the Morgan Letter Writer; H. C. Frick boasts The Singing Lesson (probably known at the 1696 sale as A Gentleman and Young Lady Making Music).

So the importance of the 1696 catalogue is indisputable. And now, after wading through this dry forest of figures and dates and haphazard or dogmatic attributions, we are at the fatal number, thirty-four--only thirty-four authentic Vermeers in existence. Some one must be mistaken. Who owns the thirty-fifth Vermeer? I again ask.

II

The works attributed only to our master in the list compiled by M. Vanzype are but six: Portrait of a Man, at the Brussels Museum; View of Delft, in the collection of Michel Van Gelder, at Uccle, Brussels; The Lesson, at the National Gallery, London; the Sleeping Servant, Widener collection, Philadelphia--another version, according to Buerger-Thore; Portrait of a Young Man, in the same collection; two interiors, collection Werner Dahl at Duesseldorf and collection Matavansky at Vienna, respectively. There is also to be accounted a small landscape in the Dresden gallery, a Distant View of Haarlem (probably by Vermeer of Haarlem), the Morgan and the Widener Vermeers. To deny the authenticity of either of these compositions would be to fly into the face of Vermeer himself. I have enjoyed the privilege and pleasure of viewing the Widener Vermeers, and I believe that the Sleeping Servant--she may not be intoxicated, a jug on the table being the only evidence; certainly her features are placid enough; besides, Vermeer did not indulge in paintings of low life as did Teniers, Ostrade, or Jan Steen--is about the same period as The Merry Company, in the Dresden gallery, that is, if paint, texture, and arrangement of still-life be any criterion. As for the Woman Weighing Gold, it is superb Vermeer.

There is little danger nowadays of any other painter being saddled with the name of Vermeer. It is usually the other way around, as we have seen. As was the case with Diaz and Monticelli, so has it been with Vermeer and De Hooch, Vermeer and Terburg (or Ter Borch). I have the highest admiration for the vivacious and veracious work of these two other men--possibly associates of Vermeer. Their surfaces are impeccably rendered. The woman playing a bass viol in the Berlin gallery and a certain interior in the National Gallery display the art of representation raised to the highest pitch; realism can go no further.

The psychology of a painter's household is revealed in the Count Czernin example (l'Atelier du Peintre). An artist sits with his back to us and on his canvas he broiders the image of his good wife. Again the miracle is repeated, "Let there be light!" Here is not only the subtle equilibrium between man and the things that surround him, but the things themselves--flesh-tints, drapery, garbs, polished floor, chairs, table, and wall tapestry--are saturated with light; absorbed by the inert matter which nevertheless vibrates and, like the flesh-tones, remains puissant and individual.

Humanity is the central and sounding note of his art. He is neither a pantheist in his worship of sunshine, nor is he a mystic in his pursuit of shadows. He is always virile, always tender, never trivial, nor coarse--an aristocrat of art.

In the Dresden Merry Company, and a large canvas it is--he comes to grips with Rembrandt in the matter of the distribution of lights and shades. The cavalier at the left of the picture--facing it--with the cynical smile, is marvellously depicted. There is a certain shadow on his wide-margined collar which also touches the lower part of his face--but now we are nearing the region of transcendental virtuosity. I always convince myself when in the presence of the other Dresden Vermeer, and the greater of the two, that this young Dutch lady reading a letter at an open window is my favourite.

And now it's high time to answer my question: Who owns the thirty-fifth Vermeer? We stopped, you may recall, at the thirty-fourth, The Singing Lesson, belonging to Mr. Frick. That would give the thirty-fifth to the Portrait of a Man in the Brussels Museum. But that is a contested canvas, while the Lesson in the National Gallery (not the young woman at her clavecin, a genuine Vermeer) is also doubtful, say the experts.

Setting aside the two interiors and the second View of Delft as not being in the field of the authentic, there remain the Morgan and the Widener Vermeers. Which of the pair is the thirty-fifth Vermeer? They are both masterpieces, though the Morgan is blacker and has been overcleaned.

Since writing the above I had on my return to America the pleasure of reading Philip L. Hale's wholly admirable study of Vermeer, and many dark places were made clear; especially concerning the place in the catalogue of 1696 of the Widener picture, Lady Weighing Gold, often called Lady Weighing Pearls, because there are pearls on the table about to be weighed. Mr. Hale, who, as a painter, knows whereof he speaks, styles Vermeer as "the greatest painter who ever lived," and meets all the very natural objections to such a bold statement. Certainly with Velasquez and Da Vinci, Vermeer (the three V's) is the one of the supreme magicians of paint in the history of art. Who doubts this should visit Berlin, Dresden, Vienna, and Amsterdam, and for ever after hold his peace.

VIII

RICHARD STRAUSS AT STUTTGART

I

After a week of Richard Strauss at Stuttgart one begins to entertain a profound respect for the originality of Richard Wagner. And Wagner during his embattled career was liberally accused of plagiarism, of drawing heavy drafts upon the musical banking houses of Beethoven, Weber, Marschner, Schubert, and how many others! Indeed, one of the prime requisites of success for a composer is to be called a borrower of other men's ideas. The truth is that there are only thirty-six dramatic situations and only seven notes in the scale, and all the possible permutations will not prevent certain figures, melodic groups, or musical moods from recurrence. Therefore, to say that Richard Strauss is a deliberate imitator of Wagner would be to restate a very common exaggeration. He is inconceivable without Wagner; nevertheless, he is individual. All his musical life he has been dodging Wagner and sometimes he succeeds in whipping his devil so far around the stump that he becomes himself, the glorious Richard Strauss of Don Quixote, of Till Eulenspiegel, of Hero's Life, and Elektra. But it may be confessed without much fear of contradiction that for him Wagner is his model--even in Salome, where the head of John the Baptist is chanted to the tune of Donner's motive from Rheingold.

At the Stuttgart festival, in 1912, which endured a week, I was struck by the Wagner obsession in the music of his only legitimate successor. To alter an old quotation, we may say: He who steals my ideas steals trash: ideas are as cheap and plentiful as potatoes in season; but he who steals my style takes from me the only true thing I possess. Now, Richard Strauss in addition to being a master of form, rather of all musical forms, is also the master-colourist of the orchestra. No one, not even Wagner, o'ertops him in this respect, though Wagner and Berlioz and Liszt showed him the way. Why, then, does he lean so heavily on Wagner, not alone on his themes--for Strauss is, above all, a melodist--but on his moods; in a word, the Wagnerian atmosphere? I noted that wherever a situation analogous to one in the Wagnerian music-drama presented itself the music of the protean younger Richard was coloured by memories of the elder composer. For example, in Ariadne at Naxos, the heroine is discovered outstretched on her island in the very abandonment of despair. We hear faint echoes of the last pages of Tristan and Isolde; no sooner do three women begin to sing than is conjured up a vision (aural, of course) of the Rhine maidens. In Feuersnot the legendary tone was unavoidable, yet there is too much of Die Meistersinger in this early work. Does a duenna appear with the heroine, at once you are reminded of Eva and Magdalena; and in the balcony scene, so different in situation from Lohengrin, Elsa nevertheless peers from behind the figure of Diemut. As for the lovers, Kunrad and Diemut, they, taking advantage of the darkness, as Mr. Henderson once remarked of another opera, Azrael, appropriated the musical colour--let me put the case mildly--of the duo of Walther and Eva. Wagner dead remains the imperious tyrant, a case of musical mortmain, the lawyers would put it; a hand reaching from his grave dictating the doings of the living. The great chorus in Feuersnot, after the fires are extinguished, because of the Alberich-like curse of Kunrad, is not without suggestions from the street fight in Die Meistersinger, and the wild wailings of the Walkyrie brood. Thus, if you are looking for reminiscences, I know of few composers whose work, vast and varied as it is, will afford such chances of spearing a Wagner motive as it appears for a moment on the swift and boiling stream of the Strauss orchestral narration. But if you have attained the age of discretion you will not ask too much, forget such childish and sinister play, and enjoy to the full the man's extraordinary gift of music-making.

For Richard Strauss is an extraordinary musician. To begin with, he doesn't look like a disorderly genius with rumpled hair, but is the mildest-mannered man who ever scuttled another's score and smoked Munich cigars or played "skat." And then he loves money! What other composer, besides Handel, Haydn, Mozart--yes, and also Beethoven--Gluck, Meyerbeer, Verdi, Puccini, so doted on the box-office? Why shouldn't he? Why should he enrich the haughty music publisher or the still haughtier intendant of the opera-house? As a matter of fact, if R. Strauss were in such a hurry to grow rich, he would write music of a more popular character. It would seem, then, that he is a millionaire malgre lui, and that, no matter what he writes, money flows into his coffers. Indeed, an extraordinary man. Despite his spiritual dependence upon Wagner, and in his Tone-Poems, upon Liszt and Berlioz, he has a very definite musical personality. He has amplified, intensified the Liszt-Wagner music, adding to its stature, also exaggerating it on the purely sensuous side. That he can do what no other composer has done is proved by the score of his latest opera Ariadne at Naxos, given for the first time in Stuttgart. Here, with only thirty-six in the orchestra, a grand pianoforte and a harmonium included, he produces the most ear-ravishing tones, thus giving a negative to those who assert that without a gigantic orchestral apparatus he is ineffectual. Strauss received a sound musical education; he could handle the old symphonic form, absolute music, before he began writing in the vein modern; his evolution has been orderly and consistent. He looked before he leaped. His songs prove him to be a melodist, the most original since Brahms in this form. Otherwise, originality is conditioned. He is, for instance, not as original as Claude Debussy, who has actually said something new. Strauss, a rhetorician with enormous temperamental power, modifies the symphonic form of Liszt, boils down the Wagnerian trilogy into an hour and thirty minutes of seething, white-hot passion, and paints all the moods, human and inhuman, with incomparable virtuosity. It is a question of manner rather than matter. He is even a greater virtuoso than Hector Berlioz, and infinitely more tender; he is Meyerbeer in his opportunism, but there the comparison may be dropped, for old Meyerbeer could shake tunes out of his sleeve with more facility than does Strauss--and that is saying a lot. No, the style of Strauss is his own, notwithstanding his borrowings from Liszt and Wagner. He is not as original as either one, for he employs them both as his point of departure; but when you begin to measure up the power, the scope, and the versatility of his productions you are filled with a wholesale admiration for the almost incredible activity of the man, for his ambitions, his marvellous command of every musical form, above all, for his skill as a colourist.

Sometimes he hits it and sometimes he doesn't. After two hearings of Ariadne at Naxos in the smaller of the two new royal opera-houses at Stuttgart, I came to the conclusion that both composer and librettist, while greatly daring, had attempted the impossible, and therefore their work, despite its many excellencies, missed fire. In the first place, Herr Hugo von Hofmannsthal, the poet of Elektra and Der Rosercavalier, conceived the unhappy idea that Moliere's Le Bourgeois Gentilhomme might be butchered to make a Straussian holiday and serve merely as a portico for the one-act opera that follows. But the portico turned out to be too large for the operatic structure. The dovetailing of play and music is at best a perilous proceeding. Every composer knows that. To give two acts of spoken Moliere (ye gods! and spoken in German) with occasional interludes of music, and then top it off with a mixture of opera seria and commedia del arte, is to invite a catastrophe. To be sure, the unfailing tact of Strauss in his setting of certain episodes of the Moliere play averted a smash-up, but not boredom. In the second place, the rather heavy fooling of the actors, excellent artists all, made Moliere as dull as a London fog. The piece is over two hundred and fifty years old; it must be played by French actors, therefore in the German version sadly suffers. I hear that it has been still further cut down, and at the present writing there is some gossip to the effect that Ariadne will be sung some day without the truncated version of Moliere by the ingenious Herr Hofmannsthal.

II

At the general rehearsal, the night before the opening, which was attended by the musical elite of Europe (whatever that may mean), poets, critics, managers, composers, princely folk, musical parasites, and other east winds, as Nietzsche has it, the performance went on leaden feet. The acting of Victor Arnold (Berlin) as prosy old Jourdain just bordered on the burlesque; Camilla Eibenschuetz, not unknown to New York, cleared the air with her unaffected merriment. Strauss, after a delightful overture in the rococo manner of Gretry, contributes some fascinating dance measures, a minuetto, a polonaise, a gavotte, and a march. The table-music is wholly delightful. A brilliant episode is that of the fencing-master, who is musically pictured by a trumpet and pianoforte (with Max von Pauer at the keyboard). Nothing could be more dazzling. You hear the snapping of the foil in the hand of the truculent bully. The music that accompanies the tailor is capital, as are also the two dances--parodies of the dances in Salome and Elektra--for the kitchen boy, who leaps out of a huge omelette (like the pie-girl years ago in naughty New York), and for a tailor's apprentice. These were both danced with seductive charm by the youthful Grete Wiessenthal (Vienna), and were the bright particular spot of the play.

After a transition, not particularly well done, the curtains part and disclose a stage upon a stage, a problematic question under the most favourable conditions. Herr Jourdain makes by-remarks and interrupts the mimic opera. It is all as antique as the clown at the circus. Finally the opera gets under way and Ariadne publishes her views. Von Hofmannsthal's figure of the deserted lady is not a particularly moving one. Naturally, much must be allowed for the obviously artificial character of the piece. Max Reinhardt, maker of stagecraft and contriver of "atmosphere," has caught the exact shades. In the dinner scene of the play his stage was chastely beautiful. In the gaudy foliage of the exotic island, with the three chandeliers of a bygone epoch, the sharp dissonance of styles is indicated. Aubrey Beardsley would have rejoiced at this mingling of genres; at the figures of Harlequin, Scaramuccio; at the quaint and gorgeous costuming; at the Dryad, Naiad, Echo, and all the rest of seventeenth-century burlesque appanage. And yet things didn't go as they should have gone. The music is sparkling for the minor characters, and for Zerbinetta Strauss has planned an aria, the coloratura of which was to have made Mozart's famous aria for the Queen of Night seem like thirty cents. (I quote the exact phrase of an over-seas admirer.) Well, if Mozart's music is worth thirty cents, then the Zerbinetta aria is worth five; that is the proportion. The fact is the composer burlesques the old-fashioned scene and air with trills and other vocal pyrotechnics, but overdoes the thing. Frieda Hempel was to have sung the part and did not. Margarethe Siems (Dresden) could not. She was as spiritless as corked champagne. To give you an idea of the clumsy humour of the aria it is only necessary to relate that in the middle of the music the singer comes down to the footlights, points to her throat, tells the conductor that she is out of breath, that she must have breathing time if she is to go on. At the general rehearsal this vaudeville act found no favour and the singer was without doubt vocally distressed. An ominous noise from the direction of the conductor's desk (Strauss himself) caused her some embarrassment. She eventually got under way, leaving the audience in doubt as to the success of the experiment--the score shows that it is all in deadly earnest. But the foot-stamping of Strauss and his remarks reminded me of Gumprecht's description of Liszt's B-minor Sonata as the Invitation to Hissing and Stamping. Zerbinetta's vocal flower-garden must be shorn of many roses and lilies before it will be shapely.

Mizzi Jeritza (what ingratiating names they have in Vienna!) was the first Ariadne. In addition to being heartbroken over the perfidy of Theseus she was scared to death. It took some time before her voice grew warm, her acting less stiff. Her new wooer, Hermann Jadlowker (Vienna), was the Bacchus. As you have seen and heard him in New York, I need hardly add that he didn't "look" the part, though he sang with warmth. The three Rhine maidens on dry land were shrill and out of tune. But for the life of me I couldn't become interested in the sorrow and ecstasy, chiefly metaphysical, of this pair. The scheme is too remote from our days and ways. These young persons were make-believe, after all, and while they sonorously declaimed their passion--hers for a speedy death, his for the new life--under a canopy with mother-of-pearl lining (Reinhardt, too, can be very Teutonic), I didn't believe in them, and, I fear, neither did Strauss. He has written sparkling music, Offenbachian music, rainbow music and music sheerly humouristic, yet the entire production reminded one of a machine that wouldn't work at every point.

There were three performances besides the general rehearsal given at the low price of fifty marks (twelve dollars and fifty cents) a performance. One of the jokes of Strauss is to make music-critics pay for their seats. Screams of agony were heard all over the Continent as far north as Berlin, as far south as Vienna. A music-critic dearly hates to pay for a ticket. Hence the Till Eulenspiegel humour of R. Strauss. Hence the numerous "roasts" all his new works receive. He is the most unpopular composer alive with the critical confraternity. No wonder. I simply glory in him. Talk about blood from a stone! Strauss always makes money, even when his operas do not. Stuttgart, most charming of residency cities (it holds over two hundred and fifty thousand souls), was so crowded when I arrived that I was glad I had taken the hint of a friend and engaged a room in advance. The place simply overflowed with strangers. Certainly, I thought, they order these things better in Germany, and was elated because of the enthusiasm openly displayed over Strauss and the two noble opera-houses. All for Strauss? Alas! no. The Gordon Bennet balloon contest had attracted the majority, and until it was fought and done for there was no comfort to be had in cafe, restaurant, or hotel.

III

The performances of earlier Strauss works were in the main well attended. Oddly enough the poorest house--and it was far from empty--was that of The Rosecavalier. Possibly because the composer had gone over to Tuebingen to conduct a concert there (he always makes hay while the Strauss shines), there was so little enthusiasm displayed; possibly also because Max Schillings conducted. He is an excellent composer, a practical conductor, but he couldn't extract the "ginger" in the score--and it's full of it, full of fire, of champagne, of dreamy sentiment and valses that would turn gray with envy the hair of Johann Strauss if he hadn't thought of them before his namesake Richard. I didn't grow enthusiastic over the Stuttgart production, mainly a local affair. The honours of the evening rightfully belonged to Alwin Swoboda, who looked like De Wolf Hopper, but sang a trifle better. A favourite there is Iracema-Bruegelmann; another, Erna Ellmenreich. One can sing, but acts amateurishly; the other screams, but is a clever actress. In Salome she was wonderful, singing out of tune as she often did. Her pose was hieratic as a sphinx when she watched the antics of the neurasthenic Herod. And her dance was one of the best I have yet seen, though Aino Acte's is said to rank them all. Wittich, Krull, Destinn, Rose, Walther, Acte, not one of them ever sang as sang Olive Fremstad at that memorable dress rehearsal of a certain Sunday morning in the Metropolitan Opera-House. Vocally she was the Salome of Richard Strauss, and she was lovely to behold. Salome herself should be a slight, cynical young person--half Flaubert, half Laforgue. Under Strauss the Salome is neither impossible nor vulgar. Very intense, an apparition rather than a human, she sounds the violet rays of eroticism (if I may be forgiven such a confusion of terms, of such a mixed metaphor). Another thing: the tempi were different from Campanini's--_i. e._, the plastic quality of the reading gave us new colours, new scents, new curves. Strauss is careless when he directs the works of others, but with his own he is all devotion. Take Elektra, for instance.

But I must finish my Salome budget. The Herod was not the actor that was Karl Burrian, but he sang better. His name is Josef Tyssen. The John was Herman Weil. Salome was preceded by Feuersnot, the folks-tone of which is an admirable foil to the overladen tints of Salome. (By the way, the sky in the latter opera showed the dipper constellation, Charles's Wain. Now, will some astronomer tell us if such a thing is possible in Syrian skies?) Herman Weil was the chief point of attraction. As for the so-called immoral ending of the composition, discovered by amateur critical prudes, to be forthright in my speech, it is all nonsense: it doesn't exist. But Wolzogen doesn't follow the lines of the Famine of Fire. His is a love scene with a joke for relief. The music is ultra-Wagnerian, the finale genuine Strauss, with its swelling melos, its almost superhuman forcing of the emotional line to the ecstatic point.

In Elektra, with the composer conducting, I again marvelled at the noisy, ineffective "reading" of a Hammerstein conductor, whose name I've forgotten. Yet New York has seen the best of Elektras, Mme. Mazarin--would that she had sung and danced here in Stuttgart! She might have surprised the composer--but New York is yet to hear Elektra as music-drama. Thus far I think (and it's only one man's opinion) that Strauss will endure because of his Till Eulenspiegel, Don

Quixote, and Elektra. The mists are gathering over the other works; Salome is too theatrical, Feuersnot a pasticcio of Wagner, Guntram is out of the question (for ten years I've used it to sit on when I played Bach's C-major invention), and even the mighty major-minor opening of Also Sprach Zarathustra begins to pall. But not Don Quixote, so full of irony, humour, and pathos; not Elektra, in the strictest sense of the word a melodrama, and certainly not the prankish and ever inimitable Till Eulenspiegel. These abide by one, whereas the head in Salome has become vieux chapeau. When Ellmenreich sang to it that night it might have been a succulent boar's head on a platter for all the audience cared. (I fancy they would have preferred the boar to the saint--deadliest of all operatic bores, for ever intoning a variant of the opening bars of the Fidelio overture.)

But the Stuttgart Elektra performance will live long in my memory, but not because of the lady who assumed the title role, Idenka Fassbender, of Munich. (She is not to be compared with the epileptic Mazarin for a moment. She is not Elektra vocally or histrionically.) The artiste of the evening was Anna von Mildenburg (Vienna), the wife of Herman Bahr, novelist and playwright, best known to America as the author of The Concert, one of David Belasco's productions. The Mildenburg is a giantess, with a voice like an organ. She is also an uneven singer, being hugely temperamental. The night in question she was keyed up to the occasion, and for the first time I realised the impressiveness of the part of Klytemnestra, its horrid tragic force, its abnormal intensity, its absolute revelation of the abomination of desolation. Mildenburg played it as a mixture of Lady Macbeth and Queen Gertrude, Hamlet's mother. And when she sang fortissimo all the Strauss horses and all the Strauss men were as supine, tonally speaking, as Humpty Dumpty. Her voice is of a sultry tonal splendour.

The two new opera-houses--also theatres--are set in a park, as should be art and opera houses. Facing the lake is the larger, a building of noble appearance, with a capacity for 1,400 persons seated. The smaller building only holds 800, but it looks as big as the old New York Sub-Treasury, and is twice as severe. Max Reinhardt calls the Hof-Oper the most beautiful in Europe. He is not exaggerating. A round 7,000,000 marks (about $1,750,000) was the cost of the buildings. His Majesty Wilhelm II, a liberal and enlightened monarch, dipped heavily into his private bank account. Stuttgart, according to the intendant, Graf zu Putlitz, must become the leading operatic and art city in Germany. The buildings are there, but not yet the singers. Dresden boasts its opera, and Berlin has better singers. Nevertheless, the pretty city, surrounded by villa-crowned hills, is to be congratulated on such classic temples of music and drama.

IV

Standing at the window of my hotel in Stuttgart, I watched a crowd before the Central railway station. Evidently something important was about to take place. What! Only the day previous all Stuttgart had strained its neck staring at a big Zeppelin air-ship. It was the week of the Gordon Bennett balloon race and every hotel, every lodging-house was full. It was also the Richard Strauss festival week, with the formal inauguration of the two magnificent opera-houses in the Schlossgarten. So it was not difficult to guess that an important visitor was due at the station. Hence the excitement, which increased when the King of Wuertemberg dashed up in an open carriage, the royal livery and all the rest making a brave picture for his loyal subjects.

I've seen several kings and kaisers, but I've never seen one that looked "every inch a king." The German Kaiser outwardly is a well-groomed Englishman; Franz Josef of Austria--I've not met him since 1903, when our carriage wheels locked and he, a lovable old man, gallantly saluted my companion--he is everything but kingly; the late King Edward when at Marienbad was very much the portly type of middle-aged man you meet in Wall Street at three o'clock in the afternoon; while William II of Wuertemberg is a pleasant gentleman, with "merchant" written over him. It is true he is an excellent man of affairs, harder working than any of his countrymen. He is also more democratic, and with his beloved Queen daily promenades the streets, lifting his hat half the time in response to the bowings and scrapings of patriotic Swabians.

The train arrived. The crowd grew denser. Zealous policemen intercepted passers-by from coming too close to the royal equipage; an old peasant woman carrying a market-basket was nearly guillotined by the harsh reproaches of the officers. She stumbled, but was shunted into the background just as the King reappeared in company with Prince August, greeted with wild cheering. The crowd, its appetite increasing by what it had fed on, remained. What next? Ah! The personal servants and valets of the youthful aristocrat from Berlin emerged from the station and entered a break. No baggage as yet. "Drat the folk!" I exclaimed, "why don't they clear out and leave the way for pedestrians." But it was not to be. A murmur arose when finally a baggage-wagon decked by the royal colours appeared. Trunks were piled on it, and only when it disappeared did the crowd melt. I thought of Gessler's cap on the pole and William Tell. Curiosity is perhaps the prime root of patriotism.

Finally, as too much Strauss palls, also too much Stuttgart. I first visited the pretty city in 1896 en route to Bayreuth, and on my return to New York I remember chiding Victor Herbert for leaving the place where he had completed his musical education. He merely smiled. He knew. So do I. A Residenzstadt finally ends in a half-mad desire to escape; anywhere, anywhere, only let it be a big town where the inhabitants don't stare at you as if you were a wild animal. Stuttgart is full of stare-cats (as is Berlin for that matter). And those hills that at first are so attractive--they hem in the entire city, which is bowl-shaped, in a valley--become monotonous. They stifle you. To live up there on the heights is another thing; then the sky is an accomplice in your optical pleasures, but below--especially when the days are rainy and the nights doleful, as they are in November--oh, then you cry: Let me see once more summer-sunlit Holland and its wide plains punctuated only by church spires and windmills!

Otherwise Stuttgart is an easy-going spot. It's cheaper than Dresden or Munich (though it was expensive during the Strauss week); the eating at the restaurants is about one-half the price of first-rate establishments in New York (and not as good by a long shot); lodgings are also cheap, and often nasty--Germany is not altogether hygienic, notwithstanding her superiority over America in matters musical; but the motor-cars are simply miraculous to the New Yorker accustomed to the bullies, bandits, and swindlers who pretend to be chauffeurs in our metropolis. For twenty-five cents you can ride nearly a half-hour in Stuttgart in cars faultlessly conducted. A two and a half hours' trip round the town--literally--in the hills, through the park cost seven marks (one dollar and seventy-five cents)--and even then the driver was distinctly apologetic when he showed his register.

Stuttgart, oddly enough, is a centre for all the engraving, etching, and mezzotint sales. I say, oddly, because the art museum contains the worst collection of alleged "old masters" I ever encountered off Fifth Avenue. Hardly an original in the whole lot, and then a third-rate specimen at that. But the engraving cabinets and the Rembrandt original drawings are justly celebrated. And now with the two new theatres, or opera-houses, Stuttgart ought soon to forge to the front as an art centre in Germany. Thanks to its energetic King and cultivated Queen.

The question with which I began this little talk--is Richard Strauss retrograding in his art?--may be answered by a curt negative. One broadside doesn't destroy such a record as Richard's. Like that sublime bourgeois Rubens, like that other sublime bourgeois Victor Hugo, like Bernini, to whose rococo marbles the music of Richard II is akin, he has essayed every department of his art. So expressive is he that he could set a mince-pie to music. (Why not, after that omelette in Ariadne?) So powerful is his imagination that he can paint the hatred of his epical Elektra or the half-mad dreams of Don Quixote. He is easily the foremost of living composers, and after he is dead the whirligig of fortune which has so favoured him may pronounce him dead for ever. But I doubt it.

IX

MAX LIEBERMANN AND SOME PHASES OF MODERN GERMAN ART

I

The importance of Max Liebermann in any critical consideration of modern German art is prime. Meister Max, no longer as active as he was, for he was born in 1847, is still a name to conjure with not only in Berlin, his birthplace and present home, but in all Germany, and, for that matter, the wide world. He is intensely national. He is a Hebrew, and proud of his origin. He is also cosmopolitan. In a word, he is versatile.

Some years ago, through the enthusiasm and enterprise of the late Hugo Reisinger and several other art lovers, New York had an opportunity of enjoying a peep at German paintings in the Metropolitan Museum. It was rather a disappointing exhibition, principally because the men shown were not represented at their best. Lenbach was not, nor Boecklin, nor a dozen others, though Menzel was. That is, we admired one of Menzel's least characteristic efforts but his most brilliant of canvases, the stage of the Theatre Gymnase, Paris. Never before nor since that pictorial performance did the wonderful Kobold of German art attain such mellowness. Just as he had been under the influence of Courbet when he painted his big iron forge picture--which, with the French theatre subject, hangs in the National Gallery, Berlin--so he felt in the latter the impact of the new Impressionistic school with its devotion to pure colour, air, and rhythm. Max Liebermann was best seen in his Flax Spinners of Laren, an early work, Dutch in spirit and execution, and not without traces of the influence of his friend Josef Israels. But of the real Liebermann, his scope, originality, versatility, America, I think, has not yet had an adequate idea.

Versatility is commonly regarded as an indication of superficiality. How, asks Mr. Worldly Wiseman, can that fellow Admirable Crichton do so many things so well when it takes all my time to do one thing badly? Therefore he must be regarded suspiciously. Now, there are no short cuts in the domain of the arts; Gradus ad Parnassum is always steep. But, given by nature a certain kind of temperament in which curiosity is doubled by mental energy, and you may achieve versatility. Versatility is often mainly an affair of energy, of prolonged industry. The majority of artists do one thing well, and for the remainder of their career repeat themselves. When Flaubert wrote Madame Bovary his admirers demanded a replica and were disappointed with Salammbo, with Sentimental Education, above all, with The Temptation of St. Anthony and Bouvard and Pecuchet. Being a creative genius, Flaubert taught himself to be versatile. Only through self-discipline, did he achieve his scheme, beside which the writing of the Human Comedy cannot be compared. There is more thought-stuff packed in his five masterpieces, apart from the supreme art, than in whole libraries: quality triumphing over quantity.

Greatly endowed by nature, by reason of his racial origin, and because of his liberal education, Liebermann was bound to become a versatile artist. That doesn't mean he is a perfectionist in many things, that he etches as well as he paints, that he composes as well as he draws.

As a matter of fact he is not as accomplished a master of the medium as is Anders Zorn; many a smaller man, artistically speaking, handles the needle with more deftness than Liebermann. But as a general impression counts as much as technique, your little etcher is soon forgotten when you are confronted with such plates as the self-portraits, the various beer-gardens, the houses on the dunes (with a hint of the Rembrandt magic), or the bathing boys. His skill in black and white is best seen when he holds a pencil, charcoal, or pen in his hand. The lightness, swiftness, elasticity of his line, the precise effect attained and the clarity of the design prove the master at his best and unhampered by the slower technical processes of etching or lithography.

I studied Liebermann's work from Amsterdam to Vienna, and out of the variety of styles set forth I endeavoured to disentangle several leading characteristics. The son of a well-known Berlin family, his father a comfortably situated manufacturer, the young Max was brought up in an atmosphere of culture and family affection. His love for art was so pronounced that his father, like the father of Mendelssohn, let him follow his bent, and at fourteen he was placed under the tutelage of Steffeck, an old-timer, whose pictures nowadays seem a relic from some nightmare of art. Steffeck had studied under Schadow, another of the prehistoric Dinosaurs of Germany, and boasted of it. He once told Liebermann that Adolf Menzel only made caricatures, not portraits. You rub your eyes and wonder. Liebermann has said that this rigid training did him good. But he soon forgot it in actual practice. Some good angel must have protected him, for he came under the influence of Munkaczy and, luckily for him, escaped the evil paint of that overrated mediocrity. But perhaps the Hungarian helped him to build a bridge between the antique formula of Steffeck and the modern French--that is, the Impressionists. Max had to burn many bridges behind him before he formed a style of his own. Individuality is not always born, it is sometimes made, despite what the copy-books assure us to the contrary. The wit and irony of the man and painter come both from Berlin and from his Jewish ancestry. He looks like a benevolent Mephistopheles, and is kindness personified to young artists.

Subjecting himself to the influence of Courbet, Millet, Rousseau, Corot, Troyon, he went to Holland, and there fell captive to the genius of Rembrandt. The mystic in Liebermann is less pronounced than one might expect. His clear picture of the visible world holds few secret, haunted spots. I do not altogether believe in his biblical subjects, in the Samson and Delilah, in the youthful Christ and the Doctors of the Law--the latter is of more interest than the former--they strike one as academic exercises. Nevertheless, the lion's paw of Rembrandt left its impress upon his art. The profounder note which the French painters sometimes miss is not missing in Liebermann. He has avoided both the pomp and rhetoric of the academic school and the sentimentality of the latter-day Germans. Liebermann is never sentimental, though pity for the suffering of life is easily detected in his canvases, particularly in his Old Men's Home, The Orphans, The Widower, and a dozen masterpieces of the sort.

In Frans Hals Liebermann found a congenial spirit and made many copies of his pictures to train his hand and eye. His portraits reveal the broad brush work of Hals. They are also psychological documents. Associated with Josef Israels, he was in sympathy with him, but never as sentimental as the Dutchman. Both reverenced Rembrandt and interpreted him, each after his own temperament. When Liebermann first knew Manet, Monet, Pissarro, Renoir, and Degas (particularly Degas) he had experimented in every key. Master of his materials, master of himself, a cultured man of the world and a sincere artist, the French group showed him the way to liberty, to a deliverance from the ruddy tones of Munich, from the dulness of Duesseldorf, from the bitter angularities of German draughtsmanship and its naivete which is supposed to stand for innocence of spirit--really the reverse, a complete poverty of spirit--and with it all the romantic mythology of German art, the bloated fighting fauns, leering satyrs, frogmen, fishwomen, monkeys, and fairies, imps, dryads, and nymphs. Liebermann discovered the glories of light, of spacing, of pure colour, and comprehended the various combinations by which tonalities could be dissociated and synthesised anew. He went back to Germany a painter of the first rank and an ardent colourist, and he must have felt lonely there--there were no others like him. Menzel was a master draughtsman, Leibl an admirable delineator of character, and to name these three is to name all. Henceforward, Liebermann's life task was to correlate his cosmopolitan art with German spirit, and he has nobly succeeded. To-day he is still the commanding figure in German art. No one can compete with him in maestria, in range, or as a colourist. And at last I have reached the goal of my discourse.

II

A visit to the National Gallery of Berlin makes me gnash my teeth. The sight of so much misspent labour, of the acres of canvases deluged with dirty, bad paint, raises my bile. We know that all things are relative, and because Germany has produced few painters worthy of the name that after all it doesn't much matter--there is Italy and Holland to fall back on; not to mention the Spain of El Greco, Velasquez, Goya, and the great Frenchmen. But there is something singularly exasperating in German painting, whether old or new, that sets us to wondering whether such museums as the National Gallery, Berlin; the new Pinakothek, Munich, and other repositories of ugly colour and absurd mythologies do not cause a deterioration in public taste. It is almost pathetic to see not only the general visitor but also students gazing admiringly at the monstrous art of Kaulbach, Schadow, Cornelius (the Nazarene school), or at the puerilities of the Swiss, Arnold Boecklin and his follower, Franz von Stuck, of Munich, who has simply brutalised the eternal Boecklin themes. It is all very well to say that these galleries, like the modern collection upstairs in the Dresden gallery (with its wonderful Rembrandts and Vermeers down-stairs) serve to preserve the historical art chain. But bad art should have no significance, history or no history--let such history appeal to the professors of aesthetics and other twaddlers. Furthermore, the evil example of Boecklin and the rest, shows in German contemporary painting. I don't mean the Cubists and other freaks, but in current art, the art that sells, that receives respectful critical treatment. We are continually forced to look at the menagerie, mermaids, and frogs, and fauns, painted in imitation of the hard, violent tones of Boecklin, himself a scene-painter, but not a great painter.

The critics in Germany don't bother themselves over paint quality, beautiful surfaces, or handling, but with books about the philosophy of the painter, his "weltanschauung," his ethics; you all the while wondering why he uses such muddy paints, why he is blind to the loveliness of atmosphere, pure colours, and sheer pictorial quality. Style and quality are, I believe, suspected in Germany as evidences of superficiality, of a desire to add ornament where plain speech should suffice. Like German prose and German singing--oh, how acrid is the Teutonic tone-production, a lemon in the larynx!--German painting limps heavily. Nietzsche is right; in certain matters the Germans are the Chinese of Europe; they refuse to see the light of modern discoveries in art.

Here is a violent instance: On the top floor of the National Gallery, Berlin, there is a room with fourteen masterpieces on its walls. Nothing in the galleries below--not even Zorn's Maja--nothing in all Berlin, excepting the old masters in the Kaiser Friedrich Museum, can be mentioned in the same breath with these beautiful compositions, condemned to perpetual twilight. They were secured by the late and lamented Von Tschudi, who left the National Gallery after their purchase and retired to Munich, where he bought a great example of El Greco for the old Pinakothek, the Laocoon, a service, I fancy, not quite appreciated by the burghers of Munich. The masters who have thus fallen under the ban of official displeasure are Manet, Monet, Pissarro, Renoir, Sisley, and Cezanne--the latter represented by two of the most veracious fruit-pieces I ever saw. The Manet is the famous Hothouse, and in the semi-darkness (not a ray of artificial light is permitted) I noted that the canvas had mellowed with the years. The Monets are of rare quality. Altogether a magnificent object-lesson for young Germany, in which tender colour, an exquisite vision (poetic without being sloppy-sentimental) of the animate and inanimate world. What a lesson for those rough daubers who growl at the dandyism of the Frenchmen, whose landscapes look like diagrams, surveyors' maps, or what-not; painters who, if they were told that they are not knee-high to a grasshopper when their pictures are set side by side with American landscapists, would roar as if at a good joke; and a lesson that will never be learned by the present generation, which believes that Max Klinger is a great etcher, a great sculptor (only think of that terrifying Beethoven statue in Leipsic), that Boecklin is a great poet as well as a marvellous painter, that--oh, what's the use! The nation that produced such world masters as Albrecht Duerer, Hans Holbein, Lucas Cranach, and the German Primitives has seemingly lost its lien in sound art.

Remember, I am not arguing with you, as Jemmy Whistler puts it, I'm just telling you; these things are not a matter of taste, but a matter of fact, of rotten bad paint. What Royal Cortissoz wrote of the German Exhibition and of the Scandinavians when in New York fits into this space with appositeness: "... an insensitiveness to the genius of their medium. They do not love paint and caress it with a sensuous instinct for its exquisite potentialities. They know nothing of the beauty of surface. Nor, by the same token, have they awakened to the lesson which Manet so admirably enforced of the magic that lies in pure colour for those who really know how to use it." I can hear our German friend discoursing on the subject of surface beauty! For him the underlying philosophic "idea," whatever that has to do with paint, is his shibboleth, and behold the result. Moreover, the German has not naturally a colour sense. It is only such a man as Reinhardt, with the Oriental feeling for sumptuous hues, that has succeeded in emancipating the German theatre from its garish taste. Some day the Richard Wagner music-drama will be renovated on the scenic side--Roller in Vienna has made a decided step in the right direction--and the old Munich travesties, which Wagner thought he wanted, will be relegated to the limbo of meretricious art.

III

Fancying, perhaps, that I had not been quite fair to modern German painters--later I may consider the ghastly sculpture which, like that cemetery of stone dolls and idols, the Siegesallee in the Berlin Tiergarten, has paralysed plastic art in that country--I determined early in the autumn of 1912 to visit again the principal cities, going as far down as Vienna and Budapest. I do not mind confessing that the thought of the glorious Jan Vermeer in the National Museum in the Magyar capital greatly tempted me. And to get an abiding pictorial flavour in my mind I began visiting The Hague, Haarlem, and Amsterdam. Any one who can admire modern German art after a course of Rembrandt, Hals, Vermeer, Josef Israels, and the brothers Maris (all three melting colourists), must have the powerful if somewhat uncritical stomach of an ostrich.

Leaving Holland, I found myself in London, and there, to add further to my distraction, I spent weeks at the National Gallery and the Wallace Collection. So I was ripe for revolt when I began at Stuttgart. While still in the rich tonal meshes of the Richard Strauss music, I wandered one grey afternoon into an exhibition of the Stuttgarter Kuenstlerbund. There were plenty of new names, but, alas! no new talent, only a sea of muddy paint, without nuance, clumsy drawing, harsh flesh-tints, and landscapes of chemical greens. Why mention names? Not even mediocrity was attained, though the next day I read in the papers that Professor This and Professor That were exhibiting masterpieces full of profound ideas. Ah! these paint professors, these philosophy-soaked critics, and that profound idea! Not, however, a word about the pictorial image.

In Munich, beside the standard galleries, I visited the Secession Gallery, and there I saw pictures by Becker-Gundhal, Louis Corinth, Paul Crodel, Josef Damberger, Julius Diez, Eichfeld, Von Habermann (a portraitist of distinction), Herterich (with much decorative ability), Von Heyden (deceased, and a capital delineator of chickens), Von Keller, Landenberger, Arthur Langhammer (deceased), Pietzsch, Bruno Piglhein (also deceased, I am sorry to say, for he had genuine ability), Leo Samberger (an interesting portraitist, monotonous in his colour-gamut), Schramm-Zitau, the inevitable Von Stuck (whose productions look like melodramatic posters), the late Fritz von Uhde, W. Volz, and others, mostly dead, and but recently. The portrait of Conrad Ansorge, a former Liszt pupil, by Louis Corinth, was not without character, the tempo slow, as is the tempo of Ansorge himself. Corinth, like Von Uhde, Leopold von Kalckreuth, O. H. Engel, Skarbina, Bantzer, Slevogt, Waldemar Roesler, is a follower of Max Liebermann, whose influence is easily discernible in the work of these younger men. To be sure, there are no landscapists in Germany, such as Davies, Ernest Lawson, Alden Weir, Childe Hassam, Metcalf--I mention a few at random--but the younger chaps are getting away from the sentimental panoramas of Hans Thoma and other "idealists" who ought to be writing verse or music, not painting, as too many ideas, like too many cooks, spoil the pictorial broth.

Grant the Germans fertility of fancy, invention, science in building up a figure, force, humour, sentiment, philosophy, and artistic ability generally, yet they have a deficiency in the colour sense and an absence of a marked personal style. An exhibition of new art on the Odeonplatz, Munich, did not give me much hope. There were some pictures so bad as to be humorous; a dancer by the Holland-Parisian, Kees van Dongen, had the merit at least of sincerity. Erbsloeh has joined the extremists, Kirchner, Guimi, Kanoldt, Kandinsky, Utrello--a good street effect; Werefkin and several Frenchmen were in evidence. The modelling was both grotesque and indecent. The human figure as an arabesque is well within the comprehension of the average observer, but obscenity is not art--great art is never obscene. The blacks and whites that I saw in Munich at this particular show were not clever, only bestial. I only wish that German art of the last decade had not gone over, bag and baggage, to the side of vulgar license. Certainly Matthew Arnold could say of it, as he once said of Paris, that the great goddess Lubricity reigned in state.

In the Moderne Galerie--I am still in Munich--I was reassured; I saw Israels, Gauguin, Van Gogh--what masters!--Truebner, Hodler, Zuegel, Von Uhde, Max Slevogt--a fine view of Frankfort--and some children at the seashore by my favourite, Max Liebermann. Then there were Langhammer and Reumaini, the clever Max Mayrshofer, Bechler of the snow scenes, Obwald, Tooby, Leibl, Marees, and a very strongly conceived and soundly modelled nude by the Munich artist, Ernest Liebermann, one of the most gifted of the younger men and no relation of Meister Max of the same name. Local art in Vienna did not give me a thrill. I attended a retrospective exhibition of two half-forgotten mediocrities, Carl Rahl and Josef Hasslwander, and also the autumn exhibition in the Kuenstlerhaus. There, amid miles of glittering, shiny, hot paint, I found the best manipulator of paint to be a man bearing the slightly American name of John Quincy Adams, whose residence is given in the catalogue as Vienna. He has studied John Sargent to advantage and knows how to handle his medium, knows values, an unknown art in Germany and Austria except to a few painters. The glory of Vienna art is in her museums and in the private collections of Prince Liechtenstein and Count Czernin.

Despite his patchwork of colour, Ignacio Zuloaga's exhibition at Dresden (on the Pragerstrasse) gave me the modern thrill I missed both at Vienna and Prague (though in the Bohemian city I saw some remarkable engravings by the native engraver Wenceslaus Hollar). Several of the Zuloagas have been seen in New York when Archer M. Huntington invited the Spanish artist to exhibit at the Hispanic Museum. Not, however, his Lassitude, two half-nudes, nor his powerful but unpleasant Bleeding Christ. What a giant Zuloaga seems when matched against the insipidity and coarseness of modern German art. The recent art of Arthur Kampf, who is a painter of more force than distinction, a one-man show in Unter den Linden, Berlin, did not impress me; nor did the third jury-free art show in Rudolph Lepkes's new galleries in the Potsdamerstrasse, except that it was much less objectionable than the one in 1911, then held across the street.

Therefore I don't think I exaggerate the claims of Max Liebermann, who is, for me, the most important of living German artists, and one of the few great painters of to-day in any land. His boys bathing, his peaceful Holland interiors, his sympathetic presentment of poor folk, superannuated survivals awaiting death, his spirited horses and horsemen, polo pony players, race-course, his vivid transcription of Berlin out-of-door life, the concert gardens, the Zoo, the crowded streets, his children, his portraits, his sonorous, sparkling colour, his etchings and drawings--the list is large; all these various aspects of the world he has recorded with a fresh, unfailing touch. His horses are not as rhythmic as those of Degas, his landscapes are not as sun-flooded as those of Monet, nor are his Holland bits so charged with homely sentiment as those of Josef Israels. But Liebermann is Liebermann, with a supple, flowing, pregnant line, his condensed style a versatile conception, a cynical, at times, outlook upon the life about him; enfin--a colourist.

My admiration for Liebermann's draughtsmanship shown in the Berlin Secession Gallery in the Kurfuerstdam was reproved by a German friend, who remarked that Anselm Feuerbach was a "sounder" draughtsman. No doubt, but I prefer Liebermann's more nervous graphic line, also more eloquent, for Feuerbach, who is still called a master in Munich--he made grey cartoons--is as frigid and academic as a painted nude in a blizzard.

X

A MUSICAL PRIMITIVE: MODESTE MOUSSORGSKY

One need not be a Slavophile to admire Russian patriotism. The love of the Russian for his country is a passion. And from lips parched by the desire of liberty--though persecuted, exiled, imprisoned--this passion is still voiced with unabated intensity. What eloquent apostrophes have been addressed Russia by her great writers! How Turgenieff praised her noble tongue! The youngest among the European nations, herself a nation with genius, must possess a mighty power thus to arouse the souls of her children. Russia right or wrong! seems to be the slogan, even of those whom injustice and cruelty have driven to desperation. It is the land of neuroses, and the form that patriotism assumes there may be one other specimen. Yet the Russian is a cosmopolitan man; he is more French than the Parisian, and a willing dweller in the depths of German thought. The most artistic of Russia's novelists, Turgenieff, was cosmopolitan; and it was a frequent reproach made during his lifetime that the music of Tschaikovsky was too European, not sufficiently national. Naturally, Anton Rubinstein suffered the same criticism; too German for the Russians, too Russian for the Germans. It was altogether different in the case of Modeste Moussorgsky.

To enter into sympathy with Russian music we must remember one thing: that the national spirit pervades its masterpieces. Even the so-called "cosmopolitanism" of Peter Ilitch Tschaikovsky is superficial. To be sure, he leaned on Liszt and the French, but booming melancholy and orgiastic frenzy may be found in some of his symphonies. According to the judgment of the Rubinsteins he was too much the Kalmuck; Nicolas Rubinstein severely criticised him for this trait. But of all the little group that gathered about Mila Balakirev fifty years ago there was no one so Russian as a certain young officer named Modeste Petrovitch Moussorgsky (born 1839, died 1881). Not Rimsky-Korsakof, Borodine, Cesar Cui were so deeply saturated with love of the Russian soil and folk-lore as this pleasant young man. He played the piano skilfully, but as amateur, not virtuoso. He came of good family, "little nobles," and received an excellent but conventional education. A bit of a dandy, he was the last person from whom to expect a revolution, but in Russia anything may happen. Moussorgsky was like other well-nurtured youths who went to Siberia for a mere gesture of dissent. With Emerson he might have agreed that "whoso would be a man must be a non-conformist." With him rebellion against law and order revealed itself in an abhorrence of text-books, harmony, and scholastic training. He wished to achieve originality without the monotonous climb to the peak of Parnassus, and this was his misfortune. Two anarchs of music, Richard Strauss and Arnold Schoenberg, reached their goals after marching successfully through the established forms: and the prose versicles of Walt Whitman were achieved only after he had practised the ordinary rules of prosody. Not so with Moussorgsky, and while few youthful composers have been so carefully counselled, he either could not, or would not, take the trouble of mastering the rudiments of his art.

The result almost outweighs the evil--his opera, Boris Godounow. The rest of his music, with a few notable exceptions, is not worth the trouble of resuscitating. I say this although I disagree with the enthusiastic Pierre d'Alheim--whose book first made me acquainted with the Russian's art--and disagree, too, with Colvocoressi, whose study is likely to remain the definitive one. I've played the piano music and found it banal in form and idea, far less individual than the piano pieces of Cui, Liadow, Stcherbatchef, Arensky, or Rachmaninof. The keyboard did not make special appeal to Moussorgsky. With his songs it is another matter. His lyrics are charming and characteristic. Liszt warmly praised La Chambre des Enfants, one of his most popular compositions. Moussorgsky would not study the elements of orchestration, and one of the penalties he paid was that his friend, Rimsky-Korsakof "edited" Boris Godounow (in 1896 a new edition appeared with changes, purely practical, as Colvocoressi notes, but the orchestration, clumsy as it is, largely remains the work of the composer) and La Khovanchtchina was scored by Rimsky-Korsakof, and no doubt "edited," that is, revised, what picture experts call "restored." So the musical baggage which is carried by Moussorgsky down the corridor of time is not large. But it is significant.

He was much influenced by Dargomyjski, particularly in the matter of realism. "I insist that the tone will directly translate the word," was an axiom of this musician. His friend and follower often carries this precept to the point of caricature. There are numerous songs which end in mere mimicry, parody, a pantomime of tone. The realism so much emphasised by the critic Stassow and others is really an enormous sincerity, and the reduction to an almost bare simplicity of the musical idea. His vigorous rhythmic sense enabled Moussorgsky to express bizarre motions and unusual situations that are at first blush extramusical. Many of his "reforms" are not reforms at all, rather the outcome of his passion for simplification. The framework of his opera--Boris Godounow--is rather commonplace, a plethora of choral numbers the most marked feature. In the original draught there was an absence of the feminine element, but after much pressure the composer was persuaded to weave several scenes into the general texture, and let it be said that these are the weakest in the work. The primal power of the composition carries us away, not its form, which, to tell the truth, is rather old-fashioned.

His stubbornness is both a failure and a virtue. His sincerity covers a multitude of ineptitudes, but it is a splendid sincerity. His preference for unrelated tones in his melodic scheme led to the dissociated harmonies of his operatic score, and this same Boris Godounow has much influenced French music,--as I have pointed out earlier in this volume--a source at which Claude Debussy drank--not to mention Dukas, Ravel, and others--whose more sophisticated scores prove this. Of Moussorgsky, Debussy has remarked that he reminded him of a curious savage who at every step traced by his emotions discovers music. And Boris Godounow is virgin soil. That is why I have called its creator a Primitive. He has achieved the naive attitude toward music which in the plastic arts is the very essence of the Flemish Primitives. Nature made him deaf to other men's music. In his savage craving for absolute originality--the most impossible of all "absolutes"--he sought to abstract from the art its chief components. He would have it in its naked innocence: rhythmic, undefiled by customary treatment, and never swerving from the "truth" of the poem. His devotion to the verbal text and dramatic action out-Wagners Wagner. Moussorgsky did not approve of Wagner's gigantic orchestral apparatus; he wished to avoid all that would distract the spectator from the stage--for him Wagner was too much "symphonist," not enough dramatist. Action, above all, no thematic development in the academic sense, were the Russian's watchwords. Paul Cezanne is a Primitive among modern painters, inasmuch as he discards the flamboyant rhetoric and familiar points d'appui of the schools and achieves a certain naivete. The efforts of Moussorgsky were analogous. He employed leading motives charily, and as he disliked intricate polyphony, his music moves in massive blocks, following the semi-detached tableaux of the opera.

But a man is never entirely the master of his genius, and while Moussorgsky fought the stars in their courses, he nevertheless poured out upon paper the richest colours and images, created human characters and glorified the "people." He "went to the people," to the folk-melody, and in Pushkin he found the historical story of Czar Boris, neuropathic, criminal, and half crazy, which he manipulated to serve his purpose. The chorus is the protagonist, despite the stirring dramatic scenes allotted to Boris. After all, the "people," that mystic quantity in Russian art, must have a spokesman. Notwithstanding this every tune to be found in Pratsch's Russian anthology, and utilised by the new men, was composed by an individual man. Art is never democratic, but it is all the stronger when it incarnates the woes and joys of the people--not quite the same thing as being composed by the "people." The tree is rooted in the soil, but the tree stands alone in the forest. The moujik dominates the stage, even after the generous lopping from the partition of some of the choruses.

The feeling for comedy which is to be found in many of the songs is not missing in the stage work. Moussorgsky loved Gogol, set his Le Mariage to music (only one act) and savoured the salty humour of the great writer. But the composer has his tragic side, and therein he reminds me of Dostoievsky--both men died during the same year--who but Dostoievsky, if he had been a composer, could have written the malediction scene in Boris? As a matter of fact he did write a play on the same historical subject, but it has disappeared. There are many other contacts with Dostoievsky--intense Slavophilism, adoration of Russia; its very soil is sacred; carelessness as to the externals of their art--a Chinese asymmetry is present in their architectonic; they both excel in portraying humour, broad, vulgar, uproarious, outrageous, reckless humour; and also in exposing the profundities of the Russian soul, especially the soul racked by evil and morbid thoughts. Dostoievsky said: "The soul of another is a dark place, and the Russian soul is a dark place...." The obsession of the abnormal is marked in novelist and composer. They are revolutionists, but in the heaven of the insurgent there are many mansions. (Beethoven--a letter to Zmeskell--wrote: "Might is the morality of men who distinguish themselves above others. It is my morality, anyhow.") Dostoievsky and Moussorgsky were not unlike temperamentally. Dostoievsky always repented in haste only to sin again at leisure; with Moussorgsky it was the same. Both men suffered from some sort of moral lesion. Dostoievsky was an epileptic, and the nature of Moussorgsky's "mysterious nervous ailment" is unknown to me; possibly it was a mild or masked epilepsy. Moussorgsky was said to have been a heavy drinker--his biographer speaks of him as being "ravaged by alcohol"--a failing not rare in Russia. The "inspissated gloom" of his work, its tenebrous gulfs and musical vertigoes are true indices of his morbid pathology. He was of a pious nature, as was Dostoievsky; but he might have subscribed to the truth of Remy de Gourmont's epigram: "Religion est l'hopital de l'amour." Love, however, does not play a major role in his life or art, yet it permeates both, in a sultry, sensual manner.

Boris Godounow was successfully produced January 24, 1874, at the St. Petersburg Opera with a satisfactory cast. At once its native power was felt and its appalling longueurs, technical crudities and minor shortcomings were recognised as the inevitable slag in the profusion of rich ore. A Russian opera, more Russian than Glinka! It was the "high noon," as Nietzsche would say, of the composer--the latter part of whose career was clouded by a morose pessimism and disease. There is much ugly music, but it is always characteristic. Despite the ecclesiastical modes and rare harmonic progressions the score is Muscovite, not Oriental--the latter element is a stumbling-block in the development of so many Russian composers. The melancholy is Russian, the tunes are Russian, and the inn-scene, apart from the difference of historical periods, is as Russian as Gogol. No opera ever penned is less "literary," less "operatic," or more national than this one.

Rimsky-Korsakof, who died only a few years ago, was the junior of Moussorgsky (born 1844), and proved during the latter's lifetime, and after his death, an unshaken friendship. The pair dwelt together for some time and criticised each other's work. If Balakirev laid the foundation of Moussorgsky's musical education (in composition, not piano-playing) Rimsky-Korsakof completed it; as far as he could. The musical gift of the latter was more lyrical than any of his fellow students' at Balakirev's. Without having a novel "message," he developed as a master-painter in orchestration. He belongs in the category of composers who are more prolific in the coining of images than the creation of ideas. He "played the sedulous ape" to Berlioz and it was natural, with his fanciful imagination and full-blooded temperament, that his themes are clothed in shining orchestration, that his formal sense would work to happier ends within the elastic form of the Liszt symphonic poem. He wrote symphonies and a "symphoniette" on Russian themes, but his genius is best displayed in freer forms. His third symphony, redolent of Haydn, with a delightful scherzo, his fugues, quartet, ballets, operas--he composed fifteen, some of which are still popular in Russia--prove him a past master in his technical medium; but the real engaging and fantastic personality of the man evaporates in his academic work. He is at his top notch in Sadko, with its depiction of both a calm and stormy sea; in Antar, with its evocation of vast, immemorial deserts; in Scheherazade, and its background of Bagdad and the fascinating atmosphere of the Arabian Nights.

The initial Sunday in December, 1878, at Paris, was a memorable afternoon for me. (I was then writing "special" stories to the Philadelphia _Evening Bulletin_, and the rereading of my article in print has refreshed my memory.) I heard for the first time the music of Rimsky-Korsakof, also the name of Modeste Moussorgsky. The symphonic poem, Sadko, was hissed and applauded at a Pasdeloup concert in the Cirque d'Hiver, for the new music created, on the whole, a disturbing impression. To quiet the rioting in the audience--it came to shouts and fisticuffs--the conductor, Jacques Pasdeloup (whose real name was Jacob Wolfgang) played Weber's Invitation to the Valse, arranged by Berlioz, which tribute to a national composer--neglected when alive, glorified after death--put the huge gathering of musical "chauvinistes" into better humour. Sitting next to me and rather amused, I fancy, because of my enthusiasm for Sadko, was a young Russian, a student at the Sorbonne. He liked Rimsky-Korsakof and understood the new music better than I, and explained to me that Sadko was too French, too much Berlioz, not enough Tartar. I didn't, at the time, take all this in, nor did I place much credence in his declaration that Russia had a young man living in St. Petersburg, its greatest composer, a truly national one, as national as Taras Boulba, or Dead Souls. Moussorgsky was his name, and despite his impoverished circumstances, or probably because of them, he was burning the candle at both ends and in the middle. He had finished his masterpieces before 1878. I was not particularly impressed and I never saw the Russian student again though I often went to the Sorbonne. I was therefore interested in 1896 when Pierre d'Alheim's monograph appeared and I recalled the name of Moussorgsky, but it was only several seasons ago and at Paris I heard for the first time both his operas.

In 1889 Rimsky-Korsakof directed two concerts of Russian music at the Trocadero and Paris fell in love with his compositions. He not only orchestrated the last opera of his friend Moussorgsky, but also Dargomyjski's The Stone Guest, and with the assistance of his pupil, Glazounow, completed the score of Prince Igor, by Borodine. He was an indefatigable workman, and his fame will endure because of "handling" of gorgeous orchestral tints. He is an impressionist, a stylist, the reverse of Moussorgsky, and he has the "conscience of the ear" which his friend lacked. Praised by Liszt, admired by Von Buelow, he revealed the influence of the Hungarian. Profound psychologist he was not; an innovator, like Moussorgsky he never would have been; the tragic eloquence vouchsafed Tschaikovsky was denied him. But he wielded a brush of incomparable richness, he spun the most evanescent and iridescent web, previous to the arrival of Debussy: he is the Berlioz of Russia, as Moussorgsky is its greatest nationalist in tone.

I make this discursion because, for a period, the paths of the two composers were parallel. Tschaikovsky did not admire Moussorgsky, spoke slightingly of his abilities, though he conceded that with all his roughness he had power of a repellent order. Turgenieff did not understand him. The opera La Khovanchtchina, notwithstanding the preponderance of the chorus--in Russia choral singing is the foundation of musical culture--I found more "operatic" than Boris Godounow. The Old Believers become as much of a bore as the Anabaptists in Meyerbeer; the intrigue of the second plan not very vital; but as a composition it is more finished than its predecessor. The women are more attractive, the lyric elements better developed, but the sense of barbaric grandeur of Boris is not evoked; nor is its dark stream of cruelty present. Doubtless the belief that Modeste Moussorgsky is a precursor of much modern music is founded on truth, and while his musical genius is not to be challenged, yet do I believe that he has been given too lofty a position in art. At the best his work is unachieved, truncated, a torso of what might have been a noble statue. But it will endure. It is difficult to conceive a time when, for Russia, Boris Godounow will cease to thrill.

XI

NEW PLAYS BY HAUPTMANN, SUDERMANN, AND SCHNITZLER

I

In the present volume I have examined, more out of curiosity than interest, the figures of Zola's book sales. To my astonishment, not to say chagrin, I noted that Nana and The Downfall had bigger sales than the other novels; Nana probably because of its unpleasant coarseness, and The Downfall because of its national character. Now, neither of these books gives Zola at his best. Huysmans had not only preceded Nana by two years, but beat his master, with Marthe--the Paris edition was quickly suppressed--as it is a better-written and truer book than the story of the big blonde girl, who was later so wonderfully painted by Edouard Manet as she stood in her dressing-room at the theatre.

How far we are away from the powerful but crass realism of 1880 I thought as I sat in the Lessing Theatre, Berlin, and waited for the curtain to rise on Gerhart Hauptmann's latest play, The Flight of Gabriel Schilling (Gabriel Schilling's Flucht). And yet how much this poet and mystic owes to the French naturalistic movement of thirty odd years ago. It was Arno Holz and the young Hauptmann who stood the brunt of the battle in Germany for the new realism. Sudermann, too, joined in the fight, though later. Arthur Schnitzler was then a medical student in Vienna, and it was not till 1888 that he modestly delivered himself in a volume of verse, while Frank Wedekind, was just beginning to stretch his poetical limbs and savour life in Paris and London. (Eleven years later (1891) he gave us his most pregnant drama, young as he was, Spring's Awakening.) It is only fair, then, to accord to the recent winner of the Nobel Prize, Gerhart Hauptmann, the credit due him as a path breaker in German literature, for if Arno Holz showed the way, Hauptmann filled the road with works of artistic value; even at his lowest ebb of inspiration he is significant and attractive.

But Hauptmann is something more than a realist; if he were only that I should not have begun my story with a reference to the Zola book sales. There were published a short time ago the complete works of Gerhart Hauptmann--poems, social plays, novels, and tales in six stately volumes. In glancing at the figures of his sales I could not help thinking of Zola. Whereas Nana stands high on the list, The Sunken Bell (Die Versunkene Glocke, translated by Charles Henry Meltzer, and played in English by Julia Marlowe and Edward Sothern), has reached its eightieth edition, and remember that the German editions are sometimes two thousand or three thousand an edition. What the translation figures are I have no idea. The next in number to The Sunken Bell is The Weavers, forty-three editions. Its strong note of pity, its picture of poignant misery, and its eloquent cry for social justice, had much to do with the large sales. Hannele is number three in the order of sales, twenty-three editions being assigned to it. The same number stands for Der Arme Heinrich, not the best Hauptmann, and for that most moving human play, Rose Bernd--so marvellously enacted by Else Lehmann at the Lessing Theatre--there are eighteen editions. (These are 1913 figures.)

You can't help contrasting Parisian and Berlin taste, though the German capital is in the grip of pornographic literature and art. But it does indicate that a nation has not lost its idealism when it reads such a beautiful work, a work of such imagination as The Sunken Bell, does it not? I wish I could admire other of Hauptmann's work, such as Michael Kramer, Der Biberpalz, or the depressing Fuhrmann Henschel. And I also wish that I could include among his big works his latest, The Flight of Gabriel Schilling (written in 1906).

It is a drama, the story of slender interest, because the characters do not particularly interest--the misunderstood humbug of a woman--but in an original setting, a little island on the east coast of Germany, called Fischmeisters Oye, the scenic side is very effective. The piece plays in five acts, one act too many, and is slow in action, and unusually wordy, even for the German stage, where the public likes dialogues a half-hour at a stretch. I shall not bore you with more than a glance at the chief situations. Gabriel Schilling is a young Berlin painter who is too fond of the Friedrichstrasse cafe life, which means wine, wenches, and an occasional song. His friend the sculptor, Professor Mauerer, has persuaded Gabriel to leave Berlin during the dog-days, leave what the text calls the "hot, stinking asphalt," and join him at the seaside. Gabriel has a wife, to whom he is not exactly nice, being fond of a Vienna lady, who bears the name of Hanna Elias. This Hanna Elias has played, still plays, the chief role in his miserable existence. He has promised to give her up, she has promised to go back to her husband and child (the latter supposed to be the offspring of Gabriel). So his flight to the east coast is a genuine attempt to gain his liberty; besides, his health is bad, he suffers from heart trouble. The play opens with the sculptor talking of Schilling in the ears of a young violinist, a dear friend, who is summering with him. Unconventional folk, all of them. Hauptmann gets his character relief by setting off the town visitors with a background of natives, fishermen, working people. I wish there had been more of them, for with their uncouth accent, salt speech, and unconscious humour they are more refreshing than the city folk. Gabriel arrives. He looks sadly in need of sea air. I suppose Theodore Loos, who played the part, was coached by the dramatist, so I dare not criticise the validity of his interpretation. I only know that he did not make the character sympathetic; perhaps that were an impossibility. In a word, with his mixture of vapid idealism and old-fashioned fatalism, he proved monotonous to me. The sculptor is a formidable bore, the antique raisonneur of French drama, preaching at every pore every chance he has. The actor who played him, Hans Marr, made up as a mixture of Lenbach the painter--when he was about forty-five--and the painter, etcher, and sculptor, Max Klinger. The violinist was Lina Lossen, and excellent in the part.

Act II is a capitally arranged interior of the inn, with the wooden shoes of the servant maid clopping around, where the inevitable happens. Hanna Elias, accompanied by a young Russian girl--whose German accent furnishes mild humour--promptly swoops down on the anaemic painter. There is brief resistance on his part. She tells him she can't, can't live without him--oh, thrice-familiar feminine music!--and with a double sob that shakes you in your seat the pair embrace. Curtain. The next act is frittered away in talk, the principal object seemingly to show how much the sculptor hates Hanna. In Act IV Gabriel is ill. He has had a fall, but it is really a heart attack. A doctor, an old friend, is summoned from a neighbouring island. Unfortunately Mrs. Schilling, the neglected wife is informed by the not very tactful doctor that her husband is ill. She rushes up from Berlin, and the best, indeed the only, dramatic scene then ensues. She is not permitted to see the sick man. She demands the reason. She is naturally not told, for Hanna is nursing him. She can't understand, and it is the difficult task of Lucie Heil, the violinist, to get her away before the fat is in the fire. Unfortunately, at that critical moment, Hanna Elias walks calmly from Gabriel's sleeping chamber. The row is soon on. Hanna was enacted by an emotional actress, Tilla Durieux, whose personality is forthright, whose methods are natural. (Her Hedda Gabler is strong.) She dressed the character after the approved Friedrichstrasse style. You must know that the artistic Bohemienne wears her hair plastered at the sides of her head a la Merode. The eyes are always "done up," the general expression suggested, if the lady is dark, being that of Franz von Stuck's picture, Sin. To look mysterious, sinister, exotic, ah! that appeals to the stout, sentimental German beer heroes of the opera, theatre, and studio. Fraeulein Durieux is entirely successful in her assumption of a woman who is "emancipated," who has thrown off the "shackles" of matrimony, who drinks beer in the morning, tea in the afternoon, coffee at night, and smokes cigarettes all the time. It is a pronounced type in Berlin. She talks art, philosophy, literature, and she daubs or plays or models. She is the best portrait in the play, though a thrice-familiar one. The poet showed this "misunderstood woman" in one of his early works, Before Sunrise.

Hanna Elias stands the reproaches and berating of Evelin Schilling until her patience fades. Then the two women, despite the warning of the doctor that his patient must not be disturbed, as it might prove fatal, go for each other like a pair of fishwives. It is exciting, though hardly edifying. If you have ever seen two chickens, two hens, fight over the possession of a shining slug in a barnyard, then you will know what kind of a quarrel this is between the outraged wife, a feeble creature, and the bold, strong-willed Hanna. And the disputed booty is about as worthless as the slug. Gabriel appears. He is half dead from the excitement. A plague on both the women, he cries, and the scene closes with his whispered request to the doctor for poison to end his life. You remember Oswald Alving and his cry: "The sun, mother, give me the sun!" Act last shows the first scene, the beach, and a figurehead from a brig which had stranded during a storm some years before. This carved head and bust of a woman with streaming hair serves as a symbol. Gabriel is attracted by the wooden image, as is Lucie. The painter is fascinated by the tale of the shipwreck. He has escaped the nurse and is out on the dunes watching the figure as it is intermittently illuminated by the gleam of a revolving lighthouse further up the coast. He is in an exalted mood. There is some comic relief in the grave-digger manner between him and a joiner, who is also the undertaker of the island, a well-conceived character. A storm is rising. Gabriel, after many wild and whirling words, leaves a message for his friends. He is bathing. And so he makes by suicide his last flight, his escape from the horns of the dilemma, too weak to decide one way or the other. The ending is ineffective, and the sudden repentance of the middle-aged sculptor (fat men with forty-five-inch waists never do seem wicked), who promises to marry his Lucie, the fiddle player, is very flat. Nor does the storm strike terror as it should. What the moral? I don't know, except that it is dangerous to keep late hours on the Friedrichstrasse. A clock can't always strike twelve, and The Flight of Gabriel Schilling, notwithstanding some striking episodes and at moments poetic atmosphere, is not a masterpiece of Hauptmann.

II

Ever since I heard and saw Agnes Sorma in Liebele, I have admired the dramatic writings of Arthur Schnitzler, and, remember, that charming, withal sad, little play was written in 1895. I haven't seen all his works, but I have read many. The latest adapted into English for the American stage is the Anatol one-act cyclus (1893), and his new play I witnessed at the Kleines Theatre, Berlin. It bears the singularly unpromising title Professor Bernhardi, and is a five-act comedy. Its performance was interdicted in Vienna. The reason given by the Austrian authorities seems a simple one, though it is specious: for fear of stirring up religious animosities Professor Bernhardi was placed on the black books of the censor. The Jewish question, it appears, is still a live one in Austria, and this new play of Schnitzler's, himself of Semitic descent, is the very frank discussion of a certain incident which occurred in Vienna in which a Roman Catholic clergyman and a Jewish doctor were embroiled. The dramatist is fair, he holds the scales evenly. At the end of the piece both priest and surgeon stand alike in your regard. That the incident hardly suggests dramatic treatment is beside the mark; Schnitzler, with his invariable deftness of touch, has painted a dozen vital portraits; the priest is superb, the character values of exquisite balance. The hero, if hero he be, Professor Bernhardi, is carved out of a single block and the minor personalities are each and every one salient. I can't altogether believe in the thesis. Any one who has lived in Vienna must know that, except in certain restricted circles, there is no Judenhetz, no social ostracism for Hebrews. At the eleven-o'clock high mass in St. Stefan's Cathedral, the numbers of Oriental faces that one sees would be surprising if we did not hear of so many conversions. It is considered rather fashionable in Vienna to join the Christian fold. And on the score of business certainly the Austrian Hebrews have little to complain of, as they are said to be the leading factors in commerce. However, Henry James has warned us not to question too closely the theme of an artist; that is his own affair; his treatment should concern us. Has Schnitzler succeeded in making a play of heterogeneous material? I don't think he has altogether, yet I enjoyed several acts and enjoyed still more the reading of it in book form.

Professor Bernhardi is the professor of a medical institute in Vienna known as the Elizabethinum. A patient, a young woman, is dying in one of the wards, the victim of malpractice. But her passing away will be painless. She is happy because she believes that she is on the road to recovery, that she will live to marry her beloved young man. Euphoria, the doctor calls her condition. To tell her the truth would be in his eyes criminal. She would die in anguish. Why not let her go out of the world in bliss? But a female nurse, a conscientious Roman Catholic, thinks differently. With the aid of a budding student she sends for Father Franz Reder in the near-by Church of the Holy Florian. The priest obeys the summons, anxious to shrive a sinning soul, and to send her out of the world if not to Paradise, at least to Purgatory. In the office he encounters Professor Bernhardi, who tells him politely but firmly that he won't allow his patient to be disturbed. The priest, without excitement but painfully impressed, argues that, even if there are a few moments of sorrow, the saving of the girl's immortal soul is of paramount importance. The physician shrugs his shoulders. His business is with the body, not the soul, and he continues to bar the way. The priest makes one last appeal, uselessly; but, unperceived, the nurse has slipped out, and going to the bedside of the dying woman announces the advent of the holy man. The patient screams in agony: "I am dying!" and she does die, from fright. Bernhardi is enraged, though he never loses his air of sardonic politeness. The act ends. The result of the incident, magnified by a partisan press, is serious. A great lady, an archduchess, refuses to head the list of the Elizabethinum annual charity ball. She also snubs the wife of an aristocratic doctor. The politicians make fuel for their furnace, and presently the institution finds itself facing a grave deficit, perhaps ruin, for the minister of instruction does not favour further subventions, though he is a school friend of Bernhardi; worse follows, the board of directors is split, some of its Jewish members going so far as to say that Bernhardi should not have refused the consolations of religion to the dying. Wasn't the Elizabethinum Roman Catholic, after all?

There can be no doubt that the reason Arthur Schnitzler enjoyed handling the difficulties of such a theme is because his father was a well-known laryngologist of the University of Vienna, and he himself studied medicine and was an assistant doctor from 1886 to 1888 in the principal hospital of Vienna. With his father he helped to write a book entitled: The Clinical Atlas of Laryngology (1895). Hence his opportunity of studying the various types of Viennese professors in a little world must have been excellent. The veracity of his characters seems unimpeachable. There are all kinds of Jews--in Europe there is no such false sensitiveness if a Jewish type is portrayed on the boards, so long as it is not offensive; for example, there is the Jew who believes himself the victim of anti-Semitism, and, while the dramatist makes him "sympathetic," nevertheless he is funny with his mania of persecution. Then there is Doctor Goldberg, the lawyer, the counsel for Professor Bernhardi, in the prosecution case for insulting religion. He sends his boy to a Catholic college, his wife has Christian friends, and in his zeal not to seem friendly to Bernhardi, he loses the case. There are several others, all carefully sketched and with a certain wit that proves Schnitzler is as fair to his coreligionists as to the Gentiles. Let me hasten to add that there is nothing that would cause offence to either race throughout the piece. Its banning in Austria is therefore a mystery to me, as it must have been to the author.

What is more serious is the absence of marked dramatic movement in the play. It reads much like a short story made long in its dramatic garb. Fancy a play all men, chiefly bewhiskered; one woman in Act I, and only for ten minutes; fairly long-winded arguments for and against the ethics of the case. Not for more than one act would this capitally written work be tolerated on the English or American stage. Until Act IV there is hardly one genuine dramatic episode, though Bernhardi at a

directors' meeting is forced to resign and is eventually sent to
prison for two months. But in the penultimate act the priest calls on
him, and for fifteen minutes the situation is strong and splendidly
conceived. The conscience of the ecclesiastic brings him to Bernhardi,
not to confess, but to explain.

At the trial he positively insisted that he did not believe Bernhardi
had wished to insult religion, but that he followed the dictates of
his conscience; he believed that he was doing his duty in sparing the
girl the pain of discovery. But this statement was of no avail, for
the nurse swore that the professor had employed physical violence to
prevent the priest from entering the hospital ward. Later she
confesses her perjury. Bernhardi is pardoned, is convoyed home in
triumph by enthusiastic medical students, but is so disgusted by the
perfidy of some of his friends and associates that he returns to his
private practice. His argument with the priest throws light on his
obstinate character; in reality neither man retreats a jot from his
original position. I must add that the priest, because of his honest
attitude, although pressure had been put upon him, was relieved of his
duties at St. Florian's and sent to a little village on the Polish
border. He had displeased the powers that be. Again I must admire this
portrait of a sincere man, obsessed by his sense of duty, a fanatic,
if you will, but upheld by his supreme faith.

The acting throughout was artistic, Professor Bernhardi impersonated
by Bruno Decarli, and Father Reder by Alfred Abel, the latter a subtle
characterisation. The "team play" of the Kleines Theatre company was
seen at its best in the third act, where the directors hold a stormy
meeting. It was the perfection of ensemble work. The creator of Das
Suesse Maedel type of Vienna has painted a large canvas and revealed a
grip on the essentials of characterisation. To Ibsen's An Enemy of the
People he is evidently under certain obligations; Professor Bernhardi
is a variation of Doctor Stockmann, plus not a little irony and
self-complacency. But the thesis of Ibsen is less academic, sounder,
of more universal interest than Schnitzler's. There is no metaphysical
hair-splitting in An Enemy of the People, nor sentimental talk about
euphoria and going happily to death. Grim old Daddy Ibsen told us
that people were being poisoned by impure spring water, and, as Alan
Dale said, was the first man to write a drama around a drain-pipe.
Arthur Schnitzler, shedding for the nonce his accustomed Viennese
charm and nonchalance, has written a comedy about a very grave
subject, and has not uttered a single word that can be construed as
disrespectful to either religion, Jewish or Roman Catholic. He is a
genre painter almost to the point of perfection.

III

Once upon a time I called Hermann Sudermann the Klingsor of the German
stage, meaning thereby that he was a master of black magic. Of course,
like most comparisons, this was a far-fetched one. Yet Sudermann is a
master of theatrical machinery. With a pressure of his little finger
he can set the wheels whirring and make their noise attractive if not
precisely significant. This is the case with his latest offering, Der
gute Ruf (Good Reputation), which captured Berlin at the Deutsches
Schauspielhaus on the Friedrichstrasse. The play, in four acts, is a
variation on its author's early theme, Honour. It is also a variant of
his Joy of Life (Es lebe das Leben), translated by Edith Wharton, but
with the difference that the motive of Honour was more malleable for
the purpose of dramatic treatment, and also truer to life, while in
Reputation (as I suppose it will be called when translated) the thesis
is too incredible for belief; hence the magician, wily as he is,
scrambles about aimlessly in the last two acts, sparring for wind, and
seemingly anxious to escape from a blind alley of situations. That he
does it so well is a tribute to his technical prowess.

He knows how to write a play. This play would succeed in foreign
countries where the Hauptmann and Schnitzler plays would fall down.

The reason is because of the strong theatrical quality of the piece, and the grateful role for the heroine, a role that might have been written in Paris; indeed, the entire work, despite its local flavour, recalls the modern Parisian theatre of Bernstein & Co., because of its cynical satire, its mysterious intrigue, its doors and bells, its numerous exits and entrances.

A woman, rather a superwoman, the Baroness von Tanna, sacrifices her name--not of the best because she flirts--to save the good, nay, spotless reputation of her dearest friend, a millionaire's wife--who, in a "mad moment" (Aha!) becomes the beloved of a certain fascinating Max, a young and handsome ne'er-do-well. To add to the piquancy of the situation, the baroness, a beautiful woman, and not, like her friend, the mother of children, is entangled in the same net; she, too, adores Max the heart crusher, though she will not cross the Rubicon for his silly sake. The usual "triangle" becomes star-shaped, for a new feminine presence appears, a girl who is matched to marry the fatal Max. That makes five live wires; two husbands, two wives, a naive virgin, with Max as inaccessible as a star. But after a capital exposition, Sudermann gets us in a terrible state of mind by making the lady with the good reputation go off in a hysterical crisis, and almost confess to her stiff, severe husband--who is a maniac on the subject of his house being above suspicion. The charming, reckless baroness intervenes at the crucial point, becomes a lightning-rod that draws the electric current, and pretends to be the real culprit. Her husband, a sinister baron and ex-lieutenant in the Hussars, is present. A duel with Max is the result. In the last act, after she has been subjected to all kinds of ignominy, Baroness Dorrit von Tanna, without confessing, is socially rehabilitated. Skim-milk in this instance has passed for cream, the prudish millionaire's wife, her honour saved for the world at large, is now revealed as a hypocrite to her astounded and snobbish husband. The curtain falls on a maze of improbabilities, with the baroness in the centre.

For people who don't take their theatre seriously, _i. e._, neither as a fencing ground for propagandists nor for puling poets, this new Sudermann piece will please. It has triumphed in Berlin and Munich. Its people are portraits taken from fashionable West End Berlin, while the dialogue, witty, incisive, and also characteristic, is one of the consolations of a play that does not for a moment produce any illusion. There are plenty of striking episodes, but logic is lacking, not only the logic of life, but the logic of the theatre. No living playwright knows better how to arouse suspense than Sudermann, and he can't make us believe in his false theme, consequently his motivation in the last two acts is false and disappointing. But there is the old Sudermann pyrotechnical virtuosity, the fireworks dazzle with their brilliancy, and you think of Paris, and also that some drama may be divorced from life and literature and yet be interesting. Insincere as is the denouement, the note of insincerity was absent in the acting of the cast. The honours were easily borne away by a pretty Viennese actress from the Volks Theatre there, Elsa Galafres by name, whose methods are Gallic, whose personality is charming. Critical Berlin has taken her to itself, and her theatrical fortune is made. It may be confessed that her part, despite its artificiality, is one that any actress in the world would jump at. Sudermann is a conjurer. His puppets are all agreeable, and, in one instance, vital: the father of the baroness, a financier, who could be easily turned into a "heavy" conventional father, but, as played by Hermann Nissen, is a positively original characterisation. Max the butterfly (Ernst Dumcke) was wholly admirable. I shall be very much surprised if Der gute Ruf does not soon appear on the stage of other lands. Its picture of manners, its mundane environment, its epigrams and dramatic bravoura will make it welcome everywhere. Sudermann is still Klingsor, the evoker of artificial figures, not the poet who creates living men and women.

KUBIN, MUNCH, AND GAUGUIN: MASTERS OF HALLUCINATION

I

Because it is a simpler matter to tell the truth than casuists admit I shall preface this little sermon on three hallucinated painters by a declaration of my artistic faith.

I believe in Velasquez, Vermeer, and Rembrandt; the greatest harmonist, the greatest painter of daylight, and the profoundest interpreter of the human soul--Rembrandt as pyschologist is as profound as Beethoven.

The selection of this triune group of genius, one Spaniard and two Dutchmen, doesn't mean that I'm insensible to the purity of Raphael, the rich colouring of Titian, or the giant power of Michael Angelo. Botticelli is probably, so Mr. Berenson thinks, the most marvellous draughtsman thus far produced by European art (we can still go to old China and Japan for his masters), and who shall say him nay? Ruskin, on the strength of one picture, averred that Tintoretto was the greatest of painters. For William Blake, England's visionary painter, Rubens was an emissary from Satan let loose on this sinful globe to destroy art. And Leonardo da Vinci--what of that incomparable genius?

After Haarlem and Frans Hals you may realise that Manet and Sargent had predecessors; after a visit to The Hague the View of Delft may teach you that Vermeer was an Impressionist long before the French Impressionists; also that he painted clear light as it never before was painted, nor since. As for Rembrandt, the last word will never be said. He is the eternal Sphinx of art, whether as portraitist, landscape painter, etcher, or revealer of the night side of life, of its bestiality, madness, cruelty, and terrific visions. But Velasquez and Vermeer are more sane.

Anything I may write of Kubin, Munch, and Gauguin should be read in the light of my artistic credo. These three names do not swim in main currents, rather are they to be found in some morbid morass at the equivocal twilight hour, not the hour exquisite, but that indeterminate moment when the imagination recoils upon itself and creates shadows that flit, or, more depressing, that sit; the mood of exasperated melancholy when all action seems futile, and life a via crucis. Nor is this mood the exclusive possession of perverse poets; it is an authentic one, and your greengrocer around the corner may suffer from its presence; but he calls it the blues and resorts to alcohol, while the artist, ever conscious of the "values" of such a psychic state of soul, resorts to ink or colour or tone (not always despising wine).

This Alfred Kubin has done; with his etching-needle he has aroused images from the plate that alternately shock and exalt; occasionally he opens the valves of laughter for he can be both witty and humorous. His Slavic blood keeps off the encroaching danger of himself taking his own work too seriously. I wish his German contemporaries boasted such gifts of irony. Kubin is a Bohemian, born in 1877, the son of an Austrian Army officer. His boyhood was given over to caprice, and he appears to have passed through the various stages familiar in the career of romantic pathological temperaments. Disillusionment succeeded disillusionment; he even contemplated Werther's end.

He found himself in Munich at the beginning of this century with a slender baggage of ideals, much scorn of life, and a determination to express his tortured and complicated personality in art. No matter what comical old women professors (in trousers) tell you of "objective art" and the superior advantage of drawing from plaster casts, that is the ultimate aim of an artist (naturally I don't refer to fashionable face painters, who make a lucrative trade of their slippery paint). Nevertheless, a more rigid discipline might have smoothed the way for Kubin, who has not yet mastered the tools of his art. He has always practised his scales in public.

A man's reading proclaims the man. Kubin's favourite authors for years were Schopenhauer and Mainlaender, the latter a disciple of the mighty Arthur and one who put into practice a tenet of his master, for he attained Nirvana by his own hand.

Now, a little Schopenhauer is an excellent thing to still restless, egotistic spirits, to convince them of the essential emptiness of life's coveted glories; but a surfeit of Schopenhauer is like a surfeit of lobster--mental indigestion follows and the victim blames the lobster (_i. e._, life) instead of his own inordinate appetite. Throughout Kubin's work I detect traces of spleen, hatred of life, delight in hideous cruelty, a predisposition to obscurity and a too-exclusive preoccupation with sex; indeed, sex looms largest in the consciousness of the new art.

To burlesque the human figure, to make of it a vile arabesque, a shameful sight, is the besetting temptation of the younger generation. Naturally, it is good to get away from the saccharine and the rococo, but vulgarity is always vulgarity and true art is never vulgar. However, Kubin has plenty of precedents. A ramble through any picture-gallery on the Continent will prove that human nature was the same five hundred years ago as it was in the Stone Age, as it is to-day, as it always will be. Some of Rembrandt's etched plates are unmentionable, and Goya even went to further lengths.

Now, Kubin is a lineal descendant of this Spaniard, minus his genius, for our young man is not a genius, despite his cleverness. He burlesques the themes of Goya at times, and in him there is more than a streak of the cruelty which causes such a painful impression when viewing the Proverbs or the Disasters of War.

Kubin has chosen to seek earlier than Goya for his artistic nourishment. He has studied the designs of the extraordinary Pieter Breughel, and so we get modern versions of the bizarre events in daily life so dear to old Pieter. On one plate Kubin depicts a hundred happenings. Cruelty and broad humour are present and not a little ingenuity in the weaving of the pattern. He, too, like Breughel, is fond of trussing up a human as if he were a pig and then sticking him with a big knife. Every form of torture from boiling oil to retelling a stale anecdote is shown. The elder Teniers, Hieronymus Bosch, Breughel, Goya, and among later artists, Rops, Toulouse-Lautrec, and Aubrey Beardsley, are apparent everywhere in Kubin's work. Neither is Rembrandt missing.

Beardsley is, perhaps, the most marked influence, and not for the best, though the Bohemian designer is a mere tyro when compared to the Englishman, the most extraordinary apparition in nineteenth-century art.

Kubin has illustrated Poe--notably Berenice; of course the morbid grimace of that tale would attract him--Gerard de Nerval's Aurelia, Maerchen by W. Hauff, and his own volume of short stories entitled, Die andere Seite, written in the fantastic Poe key and with literary skill. The young artist is happy in the use of aquatint, and to judge from his colour combinations one might call him a rich colourist. Singularly enough, in his woodcuts he strangely resembles Cruikshank, and I suppose he never saw Cruikshank in his life, though if he has read Dickens he may have. In his own short stories there are many illustrations that--with their crisp simplicity, their humour and force--undoubtedly recall Cruikshank, and a more curious combination than the English delineator of broad humour and high animal spirits and the Bohemian with his predilection for the interpretation in black and white of lust, murder, ghosts, and nightmares would be hard to find. Like Rops, Kubin is a devil-worshipper, and his devils are as pleasant appearing as some of the Belgian's female Satans.

I've studied the Sansara Blaetter, the Weber Mappe, and Hermann Esswein's critical edition of various plates, beginning with one executed when Alfred was only sixteen; but in it may be found his principal qualities. Even at that age he was influenced by Breughel. Quaint monsters that never peopled our prehistoric planet are being bound in captivity by dwarfs who fire cannon, stab with lances, and attack enemies from the back of impossible elephants. The portrait of what Kubin calls his muse looks like a flamingo in an ermine skirt posing previous to going to jail. Then we see the shadow, a monstrous being pursuing through a lonely street at night a little burgher in a hurry to reach his bed. The "shudder" is there. Kubin has read Baudelaire. His Adventure resembles a warrior in No Man's Land confronted by a huge white boa-constrictor with the head of a blind woman, and she has a head upon which is abundant white hair. Puerile, perhaps, yet impressive.

I shall skip the numerous devil's laboratories wherever people are being stewed or sawn asunder, also the scenes of men whipped with leather thongs or broken on the rack. One picture is called The Finger. An aged man in night-dress cowers against the wall of his bedroom and gazes with horror at an enormous index-finger which, with the hand to which it is attached, has crawled across the floor as would a devilfish, or some such sort of monster. The finger threateningly points to the unhappy person. Unquestionably it symbolises a guilty conscience. Franz von Stuck has left his impression on Kubin. He portrays mounds of corpses, the fruit of war, which revolt the spectator, both on account of the folly and crime suggested and the morbid taste of the artist.

Kubin's Salome is the last word in the interpretation of that mellifluous damsel. It is a frank caricature of Beardsley, partially nude, the peculiar quality of the plate being the bestial expression of the face. No viler ugliness is conceivable. And, according to Flaubert, who created the "modern" Salome, she was fascinating in her beauty. I fancy foul is fair nowadays in art. Never before in its history has there been paid such a tribute to sheer ugliness. Never before has its house been so peopled by the seven devils mentioned in the Good Book.

In the domain of fantasy Kubin is effective. A lonely habitation set in nocturnal gloom with a horde of rats deserting it, is atmospheric; two groups of men quarrelling in sinister alleys, monks of the Inquisition extinguishing torches in a moonlit corridor, or a white nightmare nag wildly galloping in a circular apartment; these betray fancy, excited perhaps by drugs. When in 1900 or thereabouts the "decadence" movement swept artistic Germany, the younger men imitated Poe and Baudelaire, and consumed opium with the hope that they might see and record visions. But a commonplace brain under the influence of opium or hasheesh has commonplace dreams. To few is accorded by nature (or by his satanic majesty) the dangerous privilege of discerning la-bas, those visions described by De Quincey, Poe, or De Nerval. Alfred Kubin has doubtless experienced the rapture of the initiate. There is a certain plate in which a figure rushes down the secret narrow pathway zigzagging from the still stars to the bottommost pit of hell, the head crowned as if by a flaming ecstasy, the arms extended in hysteria, the feet of abnormal size. A thrilling design with Blake-like hints--for Blake was master of the "flaming door" and the ecstasy that consumes.

A design that attracts is a flight of steps feebly lighted by a solitary light, hemmed in by ancient walls; on the last step lurks an anonymous person. A fine bit of old-fashioned romance is conjured up; also memories of Piranesi.

The drowning woman is indescribable, yet not without a note of pathos.

Buddha is one of the artist's highest flights. The Oriental mysticism, the Kef, as ecstasy is called in the East, are admirably expressed. His studies of deep-sea life border on the remarkable. I have seldom encountered such solicitude for exact drawing, such appreciation of the beauties of form and surface colouring, as these pictures of shells, sea flora, and exotic pearls. The Cardinal series must not be forgotten, those not easily forgotten portraits of a venerable ecclesiastic.

It is difficult to sum up in a brief article all the characteristics of this versatile Bohemian, as it is difficult to find a picture that will give a general idea of his talent. I select the Nero, not because it exhibits any technical prowess (on the contrary, the arms are of wood), but because it may reveal a tithe of the artist's fancy. Nero has reached the end of a world that he has depopulated; there remains the last ship-load of mankind which he is about to destroy at one swoop. The design is large in quality, the idea altogether in consonance with the early emotional attitude of Kubin toward life.

II

Edvard Munch, the Norwegian, is a much bigger man and artist. The feminine note, despite his sensibility, is missing. He has control of his technical forces and he never indulged in such nervous excesses as Kubin. Besides, he is sincere, while the other is usually cynical. He deals with the same old counters, love and death, debauchery and consequent corruption. He is an exponent of feverish visions, yet you never feel that he is borne down by his contact with dwellers on the threshold. A border-lander, as is Maurice Maeterlinck, Munch has a more precise vision; in a word he is a mystic, and a true mystic always sees dreams as sharp realities.

It was Mr. Saintsbury who first called attention to the clear flame of Flaubert's visions as exemplified by his Temptation of St. Anthony. So Munch, who pins to paper with almost geometrical accuracy his personal adventures in the misty mid-region of Weir. And a masculine soul is his. I can still recall my impressions on seeing one of his early lithographs entitled, Geschrei. As far as America is concerned, Edvard Munch was discovered by Vance Thompson, who wrote an appreciation of the Norwegian painter, then a resident of Berlin, in the pages of _M'lle New York_ (since gathered to her forefathers). The "Cry" of the picture is supposed to be the "infinite cry of nature" as felt by an odd-looking individual who stands on a long bridge traversing an estuary in some Norwegian harbour. The sky is barred by flaming clouds, two enigmatic men move in the middle distance. To-day the human with the distorted skull who holds hands to his ears and with staring eyes opens wide a foolish mouth looks more like a man overtaken by seasickness than a poet mastered by cosmic emotion.

In 1901 I visited Munich and at the Secession exhibition at the Glass Palace I saw a room full of Munches. It was nicknamed the Chamber of Horrors, and the laughter and exclamations of disgust indulged in by visitors recalled the history of Manet's Dejeuner sur l'herbe and the treatment accorded it by Parisians (an incident utilised by Zola in L'Oeuvre). But nowadays, in company with the Neo-Impressionists, the Lampost Impressionists, Cubists, and Futurists, Munch might seem tame, conventional; nevertheless he was years ahead of the new crowd in painting big blocks of colour, juxtaposed, not as the early Impressionists juxtaposed their strokes of complementary colour to gain synthesis by dissociation of tonalities, but by obvious discords thus achieve a brutal optical impression.

His landscapes were those of a visionary in an Arcadia where the ugly is elevated to the tragic. Tragic, too, were his representations of his fellow men. Such every-day incidents as a funeral became transfigured in the sardonic humour of this pessimist. No one had such a quick eye in detecting the mean souls of interested mourners at the interment of a relative. I possess an original signed lithograph called, The Curious Ones, which shows a procession returning afoot from a funeral. Daumier, himself, could not beat the variety of expressions shown in this print. The silk hat (and Goya was the first among modern artists to prove its value as a motive) plays a role in the Munch plates. His death-room scenes are unapproachable in seizing the fleeting atmosphere of the last hour. The fear of death, the very fear of fear, Maeterlinck has created by a species of creeping dialogue. (The Intruder is an example), but Edvard Munch working in an art of two dimensions where impressions must be simultaneous, is more dynamic. The shrill dissonance in his work is instantly reflected in the brain of the speaker. In his best work--not his skeletons dancing with plump girls, or the youthful macabre extravagances after the manner of Rops, Rethel, De Groux, or James Ensor--he does invoke a genuine thrill.

Psychologic, in the true sense of that much-abused word, are his portraits; indeed, I am not sure that his portraits will play second fiddle to his purely imaginative work in the future. There is the Strindberg, certainly the most authoritative presentment of that strange, unhappy soul. The portraits of Hans Jaeger, the poet (in oil), the etched head of Doctor A., the etched head of Sigbjorn Obstfelder, poet who died young, as well as the self-portraits and the splendidly constructed figure and eloquent expression in the portrait of a woman, an oil-painting now in the National Gallery, Christiania, these and many others serve as testimony to a sympathetic divination of character. His etched surfaces are never as silvery as those of Anders Zorn, who is a virtuoso in the management of the needle. Not that Munch disdains good craftsmanship, but he is obsessed by character; this is the key-note of his art. How finely he expresses envy, jealousy, hatred, covetousness, and the vampire that sometimes lurks in the soul of woman. An etching, Hypocrisy, with its faint leer on the lips of a woman, is a little masterpiece. His sick people are pitiful, that is, when they are not grotesque; the entire tragedy of blasted childhood is in his portrait of The Sick Child.

As a rule he seldom condescends to sound the note of sentimentality. He is an illustrator born, and as such does not take sides, letting his parable open to those who can read. And his parable is always legible. He distorts, deforms, and with his strong, fluid line modulates his material as he wills, but he never propounds puzzles in form, as do the rest of the experimentalists. The human shape does not become either a stovepipe or an orchid in his hands. His young mothers are sometimes dithyrambic (as in Madonna) or else despairing outcasts. One plate of his which always affects me is his Dead Mother, with the little daughter at the bedside, the cry of agony arrested on her lips, the death chamber exhaling poverty and sorrow. By preference Munch selects his themes among the poor and the middle class. He can paint an empty room traversed by a gleam of moonlight and set one to thinking a half day on such an apparently barren theme. He may suggest the erotic, but never the lascivious. A thinker doubled by an artist he is the one man north who recalls the harsh but pregnant truths of Henrik Ibsen.

III

Every decade, or thereabouts, a revolution occurs in the multicoloured world of the Seven Arts; in Paris, at least a half dozen times in the year, a new school is formed on the left bank of the Seine or under some tent in the provinces. Without variety--as well as vision--the people perish. Hence the invention known as a "new art," which always can be traced back to a half-forgotten one. After the hard-won victories of Impressionism there was bound to ensue a reaction. The symbolists crowded out the realists in literature and the Neo-Impressionists felt the call of Form as opposed to Colour. Well, we are getting form with a vengeance, and seldom has colour been so flouted in favour of cubes, cylinders, and wooden studio models and muddy paste.

Paul Gauguin, before he went to the equator, saw the impending change. He was weary of a Paris where everything had been painted, described, modelled, so he sailed for Tahiti, landing at Papeete. Even there he found the taint of European ideas, and after the funeral of King Pomare and an interlude of flirtation with an absinthe-drinking native princess, niece of the departed royalty (he made a masterly portrait of her), he fled to the interior and told his experiences in Noa Noa, The Land of Lovely Scents. This little book, illustrated with appropriate sketches by the author-painter, is a highly important contribution to the scanty literature dealing with Gauguin. I've read Charles Morice and Emil Bernard, but beyond telling us details about the Pont-Aven School and the art and madness of gifted Vincent Van Gogh, both are reticent about Gauguin's pilgrimage to the South Seas. We knew why he went there, now we know what he did while he was there. The conclusion of the book is illuminating. "I returned to Paris two years older than when I left, but feeling twenty years younger."

The cause of this rejuvenation was a complete change in his habits. With an extraordinary frankness, not at all in the perfumed manner of that eternal philanderer, Pierre Loti, this one-time sailor before the mast, this explosive, dissipated, hard-living Paul Gauguin became as a child, simulating as well as could an artificial civilised Parisian with sick nerves the childlike attitude toward nature that he observed in his companions, the gentle Tahitians. He married a Maori, a trial marriage, oblivious of the fact that he had left behind him in France a wife and children, and, clothed in the native girdle, he roamed the island naked, unashamed, free, happy. With the burden of European customs from his shoulders, his almost moribund interest in his art revived. Gauguin there experienced visions, was haunted by exotic spirits. One picture is the black goddess of evil, whom he has painted as she lies on a couch with a white background, a colour inversion of Manet's Olympe. With the cosmology of the islanders the Frenchman was familiar.

He has, in addition to portraying the natives, made an agreeable exposition of their ways and days, and their naive blending of Christian and Maori beliefs. His description of the festival called Areosis is startling. Magical practices, with their attendant cruelties and voluptuousness, still prevail in Tahiti, though only at certain intervals. Very superstitious, the natives see demons and fairies in every bush.

The flowerlike beauty of the brown women comes in for much praise, though to be truthful, the ladies on his canvases seem far from beautiful to prejudiced Occidental eyes. This Noa Noa is a refreshing contribution to the psychology of a painter who, in broad daylight dreamed fantastic visions, a painter to whom the world was but a painted vision, as the music of Richard Wagner is painted music overheard in another world.

"A painter is either a revolutionist or a plagiarist," said Paul Gauguin. But the tricksy god of irony has decreed that, if he lasts long enough, every anarch will end as a conservative, upon which consoling epigram let us pause.

If I were to write a coda to the foregoing, loosely heaped notes, I might add that beauty and ugliness, sickness and health, are only relative terms. The truth is the normal never happens in art or life, so whenever you hear a painter or professor of aesthetics preaching the "gospel of health in art" you will know that both are preaching pro domo. The kingdom of art contains many mansions, and in even the greatest art there may be found the morbid, the feverish, the sick, or the mad. Such a world-genius as Albrecht Duerer had his moment of "Melencolia," and what can't you detect in Da Vinci or Michael Angelo if you are overcurious?

"Beauty," like that other deadly phrase, "beautiful drawing," is ever the shibboleth of the mediocre, of imitators, in a word, of the academy. These men of narrow vision pin their faith to Ingres (which is laudable enough), but groan if the "mighty line" of Degas is mentioned; yet Degas, a pupil of Ingres, has continued his master's tradition in the only way tradition should be continued, _i. e._, by further development and by adding an individual note. Therefore, when I register my overwhelming admiration for Velasquez, Vermeer, and Rembrandt I do not bind myself to close my eyes to originality, personal charm, or character in the newer men. There is no such thing as schools of art; there are only artists.

XIII

THE CULT OF THE NUANCE LAFCADIO HEARN

Lafcadio Hearn, shy, complex, sensuous, has in Elizabeth Bisland a sympathetic biographer. In her two volumes, the major portion is devoted to the letters of this exotic and extraordinary writer; he was both, without being either a great man or a great artist. The dominant impression made by his personality, so much and often so unhappily discussed, is itself impressionistic. Curiously enough, as he viewed the world, so has he been judged by the world. His life, fragmentary, episodic, restless, doubtless the result of physical and psychical limitations, is admirably reflected in his writings with their staccato phrasing, overcoloured style, their flight from anything approaching reality, their uneasy apprehension of sex, and their flittings among the folk-lore of a half dozen extinct civilisations. His defective eyesight was largely the cause of his attitude toward life and art--for with our eyes we create our world--and his intense sufferings and consequent pessimism must be set down to the inevitable tragedy of a soul that greatly aspired, but a soul that had the interior vision though not the instrument with which to interpret it. Lafcadio Hearn was a poetic temperament, a stylist, but an incomplete artist.

His biographer, Miss Bisland, speaks of him as a "stylist." Unfortunately this is not far from the truth; he was a "stylist," though not always with an individual style. The real Hearn had superimposed upon him the debris of many writers, usually Frenchmen. He began his literary life as a worshipper and translator of Theophile Gautier and died in the faith that Pierre Loti had said the last word of modern prose. Gautier attracted him by his sumptuousness of epithet, the perfectly realised material splendours of gold, of marble, of colour. To the neurasthenic Hearn, his brain big with glorious dreams, the Parisian pagan must have seemed godlike in his half-smiling, half-contemptuous mastery of language, a mastery in its ease not outrivalled even by Flaubert. Gautier was a gigantic reflector of the visible world, but without genuine sympathy for humanity, and he boasted that his periods, like cats, always fell on their feet, no matter how high or carelessly he tossed them. And then he was Greek in his temperament, Greek grafted upon a Parisian who loved form and hue above all else, and this appealed to Hearn, whose mother was Greek, whose tastes were exotic. It was only after he had passed the half-century mark and when he was the father of three sons that some apprehension of the gravity of Occidental ethical teaching was realised by him.

When M. Loti-Viaud, that most exquisite of French prose artists and sentimental sensualists, made his appearance, Lafcadio was ravished into the seventh heaven. Here was what he had sought to do, what he never would do--the perfection of impressionism, created by an accumulation of delicate details, unerringly presented, with the intention of attacking the visual (literary) sense, not the ear. You can't read a page of Loti aloud; hearing is never the final court of appeal for him. Nor is the ear regarded in Hearn's prose. He is not "auditive"; like Loti and the Goncourts, he writes for the eye. Fr. Paulhan calls writers of this type rich in the predominance des sensations visuelles. Disconnected by his constant abuse of the dash--he must have studied Poe not too wisely--infinitesimal strokes of colour supplying the place of a large-moulded syntax, this prose has not unity, precision, speed, euphony. Its rhythms are choppy, the dabs of paint, the shadings within shadings, the return upon itself of the theme, the reticent, inverted sentences, the absence of architectonic and the fatal lack of variety, surprise, or grandeur in the harmonic sense, these disbar the prose of Lafcadio Hearn from the exalted position claimed for it by his admirers.

Yet it is a delicate prose; the haunted twilight of the soul has found its notations in his work. With Amiel he could say of a landscape that it was a state of soul. His very defects became his strength. With normal eyesight we should not have had the man of ghostly reveries, the patient, charming etcher on a miniature block of evanescent prose, the forger of tiny chords, modulating into Chopin-like mist. His mania for the word caused him to neglect the sentence; his devotion to the sentence closed for him any comprehensive handling of the paragraph; he seldom wrote a perfect page; never an entire chapter or book. At his best he equals Loti in his evocation of the mystery that encompasses us, a mystery that has been sounded in music, seldom in language. His cast of mind was essentially romantic. Hearn does not mention the name of Goncourt in his letters, and yet it is a certain side of the brothers, the impressionistic side, that his writings resemble. But he had not their artistry. Nor could he, like Maupassant, summon tangible spirits from the vasty deep, as did the Norman master in Le Horla. When Rodin was told by Arthur Symons that William Blake saw visions, the sculptor, after looking at the drawings, replied: "Yes, he saw them once; he should have seen them three or four times." Hearn seldom pinned down to the paper his dreams, though he had a gift of suggestion, of spiritual overtones, in a key of transcendentalism, that, in certain pages, far outshines Loti or Maupassant. Disciple of Herbert Spencer--he was forced because of his feminine fluidity to lean on a strong, positive brain--hater of social conventions, despiser of Christianity, a proselyte to a dozen creeds, from the black magic of Voodooism to Japanese Shintoism, he never quite rid himself of the spiritual deposits inherited from his Christian ancestry. This strain, this contradiction, to be found in his later letters, explains much of his psychology, all of his art. A man after nearly two thousand years of Christianity may say to himself: "Lo! I am a pagan." But all the horses from Dan to Beersheba cannot drag him back to paganism, cannot make him resist the "pull" of his hereditary faith. The very quality Hearn most deplored in himself gives his work an exotic savour; he is a Christian of Greek and Roman Catholic training, a half Greek, half Celt, whole gipsy, masquerading as an Oriental. The mask is an agreeable one, the voice of the speaker sweet, almost enticing, but one more mask it is, and therefore not the real Hearn. He was Goth, not Greek; he suffered from the mystic fear of the Goth, while he yearned for the great day flame of the classics. Even his Japonisme was skin-deep.

Miss Bisland relates the uneventful career of Hearn in an unaffected manner. He was loved by his friends, while he often ran away from them. Solitary, eccentric, Hearn was an unhappy man. He was born June 27, 1850, on one of the Ionian Isles, Santa Maura, called in modern Greek, Leokus, or Lafcada, the Sappho Leucadia, promontory and all. His father was Charles Bush Hearn, of an old Dorsetshire family--Hearn, however, is a Romany name--and an Irishman. His mother was Rosa Cerigote, a Greek, whose brothers, it is said, stabbed their sister's suitor, but she, Isolde-like, nursed him, and he married her. The marriage was not a happy one. Young Lafcadio drifted to Ireland, was adopted by a rich aunt of Doctor Hearn's, a Mrs. Brenane, and went with her to Wales. He is said to have been educated in the north of France at a Jesuit college. He learned the language there. Later he was at Ushan, the Roman Catholic college of Durham. His life long he hated this religion, hated it in a superstitious fashion, and seemed to have suffered from a sort of persecution mania--he fancied Jesuits were plotting against him. At school he lost the sight of one eye through an accident while at play. In 1869 Hearn was five feet three inches tall, weighed one hundred and thirty-seven pounds, and had a chest measurement of thirty-six and three-fourths inches. Disappointed of an expected inheritance--his grandaunt left him nothing--he went to London with his head full of dreams, but his pockets were empty. In 1869 he landed in New York, penniless, poor in health, half blind, friendless, and very ambitious.

In this biography you may follow him through the black and coiling poverty, a mean and bitter life compared with which the career of Robert Louis Stevenson was the triumphal procession of a Prince Charming of letters. He landed finally in Cincinnati, where he secured an unimportant position on _The Enquirer_. His friends at that time were H. E. Krehbiel, Joseph Tunison, and H. F. Farney, the artist. His letters, printed in this volume, and ranging from 1877 to 1889, addressed to Mr. Krehbiel, are the most interesting for the students of Hearn the literary aspirant. He envies the solid architecture of that music-critic's prose, but realises that it is not for him--lack of structure is his chief deficiency. But he passionately admired that quality in others wherein he felt himself wanting. He was generous to others, not to himself. It is unfortunate that he studied the prose of the seventeenth century. Mr. Krehbiel evidently knew of his tone-deafness. Hearn wrote him that he could listen to Patti after he had read Krehbiel. This proves him to be of the "literary" type of music lover; music must first be a picture before it makes a tonal image in the cortical cells. The most remarkable thing in the Hearn case is his intensity of vision without adequate optical organs. With infinite pains he pictured life microscopically. He was for ever excited, his brain clamouring for food, starving for the substance denied it by lack of normal eyesight. Hearn sickened of newspaper work, he loathed it, he often declared, and slipped away to New Orleans. There he found much material for his exotic cravings. He accumulated an expensive and curious library, for his was the type of talent that must derive from art, not life. At Martinique we find him hypnotised by the scenery, the climate, and the colourful life. He abhorred the cold, he always shivered in New York, and this tepid, romantic island, with its dreamy days and starry nights, filled him with languid joy. But he soon discovered that the making of literature was not possible in such a luxurious atmosphere, as he did later in Japan, and he returned to the United States. In 1890 he left for the East, never to return. He died at Tokio, September 26, 1904.

Hearn had an amazing acquaintance with the folk-lore of many nations. He was perpetually raving over the Finnish, the Voodoo, the Hindu. If he had gone to Paris instead of to Japan, we should have missed the impressionism of his Japanese tales, yet he might have found the artistic solace his aching heart desired. There his style would have been better grounded; there he would have found solid weapons fashioned for his ethnical, archaeological, and aesthetical excursions. Folk-lore is a treacherous byway of literature, and Hearn always worked in it with old-fashioned tools. As versatile in range as were his researches, the results are meagre, for he was not a trained observer nor thinker in any domain. So is it that in his later rovings among the metaphysics of Spencer and modern thought there is something feverishly shallow. His judgments of English writers were amateurish. He called Kipling a great poet, presumably on the strength of his exotic tang. Sir Edwin Arnold he rated above Matthew Arnold for the same reason.

In Japan, delicious, malodorous Japan, we leave him to the reader, who will find in these letters to Henry Edward Krehbiel, Ball, W. D. O'Connor, Gould, Elizabeth Bisland, Page M. Butler, Basil Hall Chamberlain, Ellwood Hendrick, and Mitchell McDonald the most entertaining, self-revealing literary correspondence published since the death of Robert Louis Stevenson. He interpreted the soul of old Japan at the critical moment when a new Western one was being assumed like a formidable carapace. He also warned us of Japan, the new Japan--though not in a friendly way; he would have been glad to see Western civilisation submerged by the yellow races.

Shy, complex, sensuous, Hearn is the real Lafcadio Hearn in these letters. Therein we discover the tenderness, the passion, the capacity for friendship, the genuine humanity absent in his books. His life, his art, were sadly misfitted with masks--though Nietzsche says: "All that is profound loves the mask"; and the symbolism of the Orient completed the disintegration of his baffling personality.

XIV

THE MELANCHOLY OF MASTERPIECES

I

Possibly it is a purely subjective impression, but I seldom face a masterpiece in art without suffering a slight melancholy, and this feeling is never influenced by the subject. The pastoral peace that hovers like a golden benison about Giorgione's Concert at the Louvre, the slow, widowed smile of the Mona Lisa, the cross-rhythms of Las Lanzas, most magnificent of battle-pieces, in the Velasquez Sala at the Prado, even the processional poplars of Hobbema at the National Gallery, or the clear cool daylight which filters through the window of the Dresden Vermeer--these and others do not always give me the buoyant sense of self-liberation which great art should. It is not because I have seen too often the bride Saskia and her young husband Rembrandt, in Dresden, that in their presence a tinge of sadness colours my thoughts. I have endeavoured to analyse this feeling. Why melancholy? Is great art always slightly morbid? Is it because of their isolation in the stone jails we call museums? Or that their immortality yields inch by inch to the treacherous and resistless pressure of the years? Or else because their hopeless perfection induces a species of exalted envy? And isn't it simply the incommensurable emotion evoked by the genius of the painter or sculptor? One need not be hyperaesthetic to experience something akin to muffled pain when listening to certain pages of Tristan and Isolde, or while submitting to the mystic ecstasy of Jan Van Eyck at Ghent. The exquisite grace of the Praxiteles Hermes or the sweetness of life we recognise in Donatello may invade the soul with messages of melancholy, and not come as ministers of joy.

One can't study the masters too much--I mean, from the amateur's view-point; in the case of an artist it depends on the receptivity of his temperament. Velasquez didn't like Raphael, and it was Boucher who warned Fragonard, when he went to Rome, not to take the Italian painters too seriously. Imitation may be the sincerest form of flattery, but it sometimes stifles individuality. I think it is probably the belief that never again will this planet have another golden age of painting and sculpture that arouses in me the melancholy I mention. Music has passed its prime and is now entering the twilight of perfections past for ever. So is it with the Seven Arts. Nevertheless, there is no need of pessimism. Even if we could, it would not be well to repeat the formulas of art accomplished, born as they were of certain conditions, social as well as technical. Other days, other plays. And that is the blight on all academic art. "Traditional art," says Frank Rutter, "is the art of respectable plagiarism," a slight variation on Paul Gauguin's more revolutionary axiom. No fear of any artist being too original. "There is no isolated truth," exclaimed Millet; but Constable wrote: "A good thing is never done twice." Best of all, it was R. A. M. Stevenson who said in effect that after studying Velasquez at the Prado he had modified his opinions as to the originality of modern art. Let us admit that there is no hope of ever rivalling the dead; yet a new beauty may be born, a new vision, and with it necessarily new technical procedures. When I say "new," I mean a new variation on the past. To-day the Chinese and Assyrian are revived. It is the denial of these very obvious truths that makes academic critics slightly ridiculous. They obstinately refuse to see the sunlight on the canvases of the Impressionists just as they deny the sincerity and power of the so-called post-Impressionists. The transvaluation of critical values must follow in the trail of revolutions.

It is a pity that New York as yet has not had an opportunity of viewing the best Cezannes, Gauguins, and Van Goghs. I did not see the exhibition several years ago at the Armory, which was none the less an eye-opener. But I have been told by those whose opinion and knowledge are incontrovertible that this trinity of the modern movement was inadequately represented; furthermore, Henri Matisse, a painter of indubitable skill and originality, did not get a fair showing. It would be a superfluous and thankless task to argue with critics or artists who refuse to acknowledge Manet, Monet, Degas. These men are already classics. Go to the Louvre and judge for yourself. Impressionism has served its purpose; it was too personal in the case of Claude Monet to be successfully practised by every one. Since him many have hopelessly attempted the bending of his bow. Manet is an incomplete Velasquez; but he is a great colourist, and interpreted in his fluid, nervous manner the "modern" spirit. Degas, master designer, whose line is as mighty as Ingres his master, is by courtesy associated with the Impressionistic group, though his methods and theirs are poles asunder. It seems that because he didn't imitate Ingres in his choice of subject-matter he is carped at. To-day the newest "vision" has reverted to the sharpest possible silhouettes and, to add confusion, includes rhythms that a decade ago would not have been thought possible.

II

I can't agree with those who call Paul Cezanne the "Nietzsche of painting," because Nietzsche is brilliant and original while the fundamental qualities of Cezanne are sincerity, a dogged sincerity, and also splendid colouring--the value of the pigment in and for itself, the strength and harmony of colour. His training was in the classics. He knew Manet and Monet, but his personal temperament did not incline him to their forms of Impressionism. A sober, calculating workman, not a heaven-storming genius, yet a painter whose procedure has served as a point of departure for the younger tribe. Like Liszt, Cezanne is the progenitor of a school, for Wagner founded no great school as much as he influenced his contemporaries; he was too complete in himself to leave artistic descendants, and Liszt, an intermediate type, influenced not only Wagner but the Russians and the Neo-Frenchman. The greatest disciples of Cezanne are Gauguin and Van Gogh. Mr. Brownell once wrote: "We only care for facts when they explain truths," and the facts of Cezanne have that merit. He is truthful to the degree of eliminating many important artistic factors from his canvases. But he realises the bulk and weight of objects; he delineates their density and profile. His landscapes and his humans are as real as Manet's; he seeks to paint the actual, not the relative. There is strength if not beauty--the old canonic beauty--and in the place of the latter may be found rich colour. A master of values, Cezanne. After all, paint is thicker than academic culture.

I saw the first Paul Gauguin exhibition at Durand-Ruel's in Paris years ago. I recall contemporary criticism. "The figures are outlined in firm strokes and painted in broad, flat tints on canvas that has the texture of tapestry. Many of these works are made repulsive by their aspect of multicoloured crude and barbarous imagery. Yet one cannot but acknowledge the fundamental qualities, the lovely values, the ornamental taste, and the impression of primitive animalism." Since that rather faint praise Gauguin is aloft with the Olympians. His art is essentially classic. Again his new themes puzzled critics. A decorative painter born, he is fit for the company of Baudry the eclectic, Moreau the symbolist, Puvis de Chavannes, greatest of modern mural painters, and the starlit Besnard. A rolling stone was Gauguin, one that gathered no stale moss. He saw with eyes that at Tahiti became "innocent." The novelty of the flora and fauna there should not be overlooked in this artistic recrudescence. His natural inclination toward decorative subjects rekindled in the presence of the tropical wilderness; at every step he discovered new motives. The very largeness of the forms about him, whether human, vegetable, or floral, appealed to his bold brush, and I think that critics should take this into consideration before declaring his southern pictures garish. They often seem so, but then the sunset there is glaring, the shadows ponderous and full of harsh complementary reflects, while humanity wears another aspect in this southern island where distance is annihilated by the clarity of the atmosphere. No, Paul Gauguin is certainly not a plagiarist. Clive Bell has written: "Great artists never look back." I believe the opposite; all great artists look back and from the past create a new synthesis.

Wells has said: "Better plunder than paralysis," the obverse of Gauguin's teaching, and if Vincent Van Gogh "plundered" in his youth it was not because he feared "paralysis." He merely practised his scales in private before attempting public performance. Remember that none of these revolutionary artists jumped overboard in the beginning without swimming-bladders. They were all, and are all, men who have served their technical apprenticeship before rebellion and complete self-expression.

The gods of Van Gogh were Rembrandt, Delacroix, Daumier, Monticelli, and Millet. The latter was a veritable passion with him. He said of him, and the remark was a sign-post for his own future: "Rembrandt and Delacroix painted the person of Jesus, Millet his teaching." This preoccupation with moral ideas lent a marked intensity to his narrow temperament. Ill-balanced he was; there was madness in the family; both his brother and himself committed suicide. His adoration of Monticelli and his jewelled style led him to Impressionism. But colour for colour's sake or optical illusion did not long hold him. The overloaded paint in his earlier works soon gave way to flat modelling. His effects are achieved by sweeping contours instead of a series of planes. There are weight, sharp silhouettes, and cruel analysis. His colour harmonies are brilliant, dissociated from our notions of the normal. He is a genuine realist as opposed to the decorative classicism of Gauguin. His work was not much affected by Gauguin, though he has been classed in the same school. Cezanne openly repudiated both men. "A sun in his head and a hurricane in his heart," was said of him, as it was first said of Delacroix by a critical contemporary. Vincent Van Gogh is, to my way of thinking, the greatest genius of the trio under discussion. After them followed the Uglicists and the passionate patterns and emotional curves of the Cubists.

Henri Matisse has science, he is responsive to all the inflections of the human form, and has at his finger-tips all the nuances of colour. He is one of those lucky men for whom the simplest elements suffice to create a living art. With a few touches a flower, a woman, grow before your eyes. He is a magician, and when his taste for experimenting with deformations changes we may expect a gallery of masterpieces. At present, pushed by friends and foes, he can't resist the temptation to explode fire-crackers on the front stoop of the Institute. But a master of line, of decoration, of alluring rhythms. Whistler went to Japan on an artistic adventure. Matisse has gone to China, where rhythm, not imitation, is the chiefest quality in art.

Such men as Matisse, Augustus John, and Arthur B. Davies excel as draughtsmen. The sketches of the first-named are those of a sculptor, almost instantaneous notations of attitudes and gestures. The movement, not the mass, is the goal sought for by all of them. The usual crowd of charlatans, camp-followers, hangers-on may be found loudly praising their own wares in this Neo-Impressionist school--if school it be--but it is only fair to judge the most serious and gifted painters and sculptors of the day. Already there are signs that the extremists, contortionists, hysterical humbugs, Zonists, Futurists, and fakers generally are disappearing. What is good will abide, as is the case with Impressionism; light and atmosphere are its lessons; the later men have other ideals: form and rhythm, and a more spiritual interpretation of "facts."

III

The Comparative Exhibition in New York over ten years ago proved that it is dangerous to mix disparate schools and aims and personalities. And while the undertaking was laudable, seeking as it did to dissipate our artistic provinciality, it but emphasised it--proved beyond the peradventure of a doubt American dependence on foreign art. Technically, to-day, the majority of our best painters stem from France, as formerly they imitated English models or studied at Duesseldorf and Munich. When the Barbizon group made their influence felt our landscapists immediately betrayed the impact of the new vision, the new technique. Our younger men are just as progressive as were their fathers and grandfathers. Every fresh generation uses as a spring-board for its achievements the previous generation. They have a lot to put on canvas, new sights that only America can show. What matter the tools if they have, these young chaps, individuality? Must they continue to peer through the studio spectacles of their grandfathers? They make mistakes, as did their predecessors. They experiment; art is not a fixed quantity, but a ceaseless experimenting. They are often raw, crude, harsh; but they deal in character and actuality. They paint their environment--the only true historic method--and they do this with a modern technique. Manet, Goya, Renoir, Monet, Pissarro, Toulouse-Lautrec, Degas, Whistler, and others may be noted in the technical schemes of nine out of ten native-born American artists. The question at issue is whether our new men have anything to say, and do they say it in a personal manner. I think the answer is a decided affirmative. We can't compete with the great names in art, but in the contemporary swim we fairly hold our own.

Consider our recent Academy exhibitions--and I prefer to take this stronghold of antiquated art and prejudices as a starting-point rather than the work of the out-and-out insurgents--consider, I repeat, the Academy, and then try to recall, say, ten years ago and the pictures that then hung on the line. Decidedly, as Zola would say, there has been a cleaning up of dirty old palettes, an inrush of fresh air and sunshine. In landscape we excel, easily leading the English painters. Of Germany I do not care to speak here: the sea of mud that passes for colour, the clumsiness of handling, and the general heavy self-satisfaction discourage the most ardent champion of the Teutonic art. In England, Burlington House still sets the fashion. At one Royal Academy I attended I found throngs before a melodramatic anecdote by John Collier, entitled The Fallen Ideal. It had the rigidity of a tinted photograph. But it hit the "gallery," which dearly loves a story in paint. The two Sargent landscapes did not attract, yet they killed every picture within optical range. Nor was Collier's the worst offence in an enormous gathering of mediocre canvases. One must go, nowadays, to the New English Art Club to see the fine flower of new English art. There Augustus John reigns, but he is not to be confined in parochial limits; he is a "European event," not merely Welsh. He dominates the club as he dominates English art. What's one man's paint may be another's poison. I never saw so many examples of his except in Mr. John Quinn's collection--who has the largest gathering in America of the work of this virile painter and draughtsman. His cartoon--The Flute of Pan (the property of Mr. Quinn)--hanging in the winter show of the English Art Club, reveals the artist's impulse toward large decorative schemes. At first the composition seems huddled, but the cross-rhythms and avoidance of facile pose are the reason for this impression. The work is magisterial. It grows upon one, though it is doubtful whether it will ever make the appeal popular. John's colour spots are seductive. He usually takes a single model and plays with the motive as varyingly as did Brahms in his variations on a theme by Paganini. But with all his transcendental virtuosity the Welsh painter is never academic; he is often rank in his expression of humanity, human, all-too-human, as Nietzsche would have said. A great personality (with greater potentialities) is that of Augustus John. But aside from his powerful personality and remarkable craftsmanship, who is there that can't be matched by our own men? There are no landscapists like ours--is it necessary to count them off name by name? Neither are our figure-painters excelled. I know comparisons are not courteous, and I forbear particularising. John S. Sargent, our greatest painter of surfaces, of the mundane scene, was not even born here, though he is of American parentage. Nevertheless, we claim him. Then there is Whistler, most elusive of our artists. Is he American? That question has been answered. He is, even if he deals with foreign subject-matter. Wonderfully wrought, magically coloured, rich and dim, are his pictures, and one, to employ the phrase of an English critic, is fain to believe that his brush was dipped in mist, not pigment.

Let us be catholic. Let us try to shift anew the focus of criticism when a fresh personality swims into our ken. Let us study each man according to his temperament and not insist that he should chime with other men's music. The Beckmesser style of awarding good and bad marks is obsolete. To miss modern art is to miss one of the few thrills that life holds. Your true decadent copies the past and closes his eyes to the insistent vibrations of his day. I know that it is not every one who can enjoy Botticelli and Monet, Duerer and Manet, Rembrandt and Matisse. Ready-made admiration is fatal to youthful minds; nevertheless, we should, all of us, as well as young--particularly the academic elderly--cultivate a broader comprehension of the later schools and personalities. Art is protean. But will, I ask myself, posterity sit before the masterpieces of Matisse, Picasso, and Van Dongen, and experience that nostalgia of the ideal of which I wrote at the beginning of these desultory notes? Why not? There may be other ideals in those remote times, ideals that may be found incarnate in some new-fangled tremendous Gehenna. But nature will always remain modern.

II

THE ITALIAN FUTURIST PAINTERS

Because I had strolled over to buy a newspaper at a kiosk hard by the Rijks Museum in Amsterdam, I discovered an announcement that the Italian Futurists were holding an exhibition in De Roos Gallery on the Rokindam. This was early in September, 1912. What a chance, I thought, to compare the new with the old. After that glorious trinity, Rembrandt, Frans Hals, and Vermeer, hanging in the Rijks, what a piquant contrast to study the new-fangled heresies and fantastic high-kicking of the Futurists! This group, consisting of five Italian painters in company with the poet Marinetti as a self-constituted chef d'ecole, is perfectly agreed that all the old conventions of pictorial art have outlived their usefulness; that drawing, colour, perspective, harmonious composition must walk the plank as far as they are concerned; in a word, classic, romantic, impressionistic art is doomed; only symbolism will endure; for symbolism only is there a future. Signor Marinetti, who coined the hideous word, "Futurism," goes still further. Literature, too, must throw off the yoke of syntax. The adjective must be abolished, the verb of the infinite should be always employed; the adverb must follow the adjective; every substantive should have its double; away with punctuation; you must "orchestrate" your language (this outrivals Rene Ghil); the personal pronoun is also to disappear with the rest of the outmoded literary baggage, which was once so useful to such moribund mediocrities (the phrase is of Marinetti's making) as Dante, Petrarch, Tasso, Alfieri; even D'Annunzio is become a moss-covered reactionary.

I purposely mention Marinetti and his manifesto for the reason that this movement in painting and sculpture is decidedly "literary," the very accusation of which makes the insurgents mightily rage. For example, I came across in _De Kunst_, a Dutch art publication in Amsterdam, a specimen of Marinetti's sublimated prose, the one page of which is supposed to contain more suggestive images and ideas than a library written in the old-fashioned manner. Here are a few lines (Battle is the title and the prose is in French):

"Bataille. Poids-odeur. Midi 3/4 flutes glapissement embrasement toumb toumb alarme gargaresch eraquement erepitation marche," etc.

This parrot lingo, a mere stringing together of verbs and nouns, reminds one of the way the little African child was taught to say, dog, man, horse, cow, pump. When at Turin in March, 1910, they threw rotten eggs at Marinetti, in the Chiarella Theatre, the audience was but venting its feelings of indignation because of such silly utterances. Baudelaire, patterning after Poe and Bertrand, fashioned poems in prose and created images of beauty; following him Huysmans added a novel nuance and made the form still more concentrated. But Signor Marinetti--there are no ideas in his prose and his images are nil--writes as if he were using a cable code, a crazy one at that. How far he is responsible for the "aesthetic" of the Futurist art I don't know. If he is responsible at all then he has worked much mischief, for several of the five painters are men of unquestionable ability, skilled brush workers and of an artistic sincerity that is without suspicion. Mind you, I don't say all of the groups; there are charlatans who hang on to the coat-tails of every talented man or are camp-followers in every movement. These five painters: Umberto Boccioni (Milan); Carlo D. Carra (Milan); Luigi Russolo (Milan); Giacomo Balla (Rome), and Gino Severini (Paris) do not paint for money. The pictures in this exhibition are not for sale; indeed, I doubt if the affair pays expenses, for it has travelled far; from Turin and Milan and Rome, to Paris, London, Berlin, Amsterdam. It will be in New York soon, and then look out for a repetition of the Playboy of the Western World scandal. Some of the pictures are very provocative.

Naturally the antithesis of old and new was unescapable the chilly September afternoon that I entered the "Roos" gallery. Fresh from The Milk Jug, that miracle in paint by Vermeer (formerly of the Jan Six Collection); from the Rembrandt Night watch (which was not much damaged by the maniac who slashed the right knee of the principal figure); from the two or three splendid portraits by Frans Hals; from the Elizabeth Bas and the Stallmeesters by Rembrandt--from all these masterpieces of great paint, poetry, humour, humanity, I confess the transition to the wild and whirling kaleidoscopes called pictures by these ferocious Futurists was too sudden for my eyes and understanding. It was some time before I could orient myself optically. If you have ever peered through one of those pasteboard cylinders dear to childhood, you will catch a tithe of my early sensations. All that I had read of the canvases was mere colourless phrase-making. After the first shudder had passed, the magnetism, a hideous magnetism, drew you to the walls, the lunatic patterns began to yield up vague meanings; arabesques that threatened one's sanity became almost intelligible. The yelling walls seemed to sing more in tune, the flaring tones softened a trifle, there was method in all this madness and presently you discovered that there was more method than madness, and that way critical madness lay. You are not in the least converted to this arbitrary and ignominious splashing of raw tints, but you are interested--you linger, you study and then you fall to reading the philosophy of the movement. It is the hour of your aperitive, l'heure exquise, when you take your departure, and out on

the noisy Rokindam, not far from the Central railway station, you rub
your eyes and then note that the very chaos you resented in the
canvases of the Futurists is in the streets--which are being repaved.
Snorting motor-cars and rumbling busses go by, people seem to be
walking up inclined planes, the houses lean over and their windows
leer and beckon to you; the sky is like a stage cloth and sweeps the
roofs; you hurry to your hotel and in strong tea you drown your
memories of the Italian Futurists.

It is only fair to give their side of the case. This I shall condense,
as the exuberant lyricism and defiant dithyramb soon became
monotonous. They write like very young and enthusiastic chaps, and
they are for the most part mature men and experienced painters.
Luckily for their public, Signor Marinetti and his friends did not
adopt his Siamese telegraphic style in their printed programme. They
begin by stating that they will sing the love of danger, the habit of
energy and boldness. The essential elements of their poetry will be
courage, daring, and rebellion. Literature has hitherto glorified
serene immobility, ecstasy, and sleep; they will extol aggressive
movement, feverish insomnia, the double-quick step, the somersault,
the box on the ear, the fisticuff. They declare that the world's
splendour has been enriched by a new beauty: the beauty of speed. A
racing car, its frame adorned by great pipes, like snakes with
explosive breath, a roaring motor-car, which looks as though running
on shrapnel, is more beautiful than the Winged Victory of Samothrace
in the Louvre. Note just here the speed-mania motive. There is no more
beauty except in strife. No masterpiece without aggressiveness. Poetry
must be a violent onslaught upon the unknown forces, commanding them
to bow before man. Now there is nothing particularly new in this.
Great poetry is dynamic as it is also reflective (the Futurists call
the latter "static"). They say they stand on the extreme promontory of
the centuries. Why, they ask, should we look behind us, when we have
to break into the mysterious portals of the impossible? Time and space
died yesterday. Already we live in the absolute, since we have already
created speed, eternal and ever present. This rigmarole of metaphysics
betrays the influence of the Henri Bergson philosophy, the philosophy
of rhythm and rhythmic motion. It is just as original; _i. e._, not
original at all. Mother Earth is still spinning through space at the
gait originally imparted to her by the sun's superior force. Mankind
on her outer rind spins with her. Because we have invented steam and
electric cars, we must not arrogate to ourselves the discovery of
speed. What has speed to do with painting on a flat surface, painting
in two dimensions of space? Wait a bit! We are coming to the
application of rhythm to paint.

The Futurists wish to glorify war--the only health-giver of the
world--militarism, patriotism, the destructive arm of the anarchist,
the beautiful ideas that kill, the contempt for woman. They wish to
destroy the museums, the libraries (unlucky Mr. Carnegie!), to fight
moralism, feminism, and all opportunistic and utilitarian measures.
Museums are for them cemeteries of art; to admire an old picture is to
pour our sensitiveness into a funeral urn, instead of casting it
forward in violent gushes of creation and action. So set fire to the
shelves of libraries! Deviate the course of canals to flood the
cellars of museums! Seize pickaxes and hammers! Sap the foundations of
the antique cities! "We stand upon the summit of the world and once
more we cast our challenge to the stars." Thus F. T. Marinetti, editor
of _Poesia_.

The manifesto of the new crowd is too lengthy to reproduce; but here
are a few of its tenets:

1st: That imitation must be despised, and all originality glorified.
(How novel!)

2d: That it is essential to rebel against the tyranny of the terms
"harmony" and "good taste" as being too elastic expressions, by the
help of which it is easy to demolish the works of Rembrandt, of Goya,

and of Rodin.

3d: That the art-critics are useless or harmful.

4th: That all subjects previously used must be swept aside in order to express our whirling life of steel, of pride, of fever, and of speed.

5th: That the name of "madman" with which it is attempted to gag all innovators, should be looked upon as a title of honour.

6th: That innate complementariness is an absolute necessity in painting, just as free metre in poetry or polyphony in music. Oh, ass who wrote this! Polyphony is not a modern invention. A man named Bach, Johann Sebastian Bach, wrote fugues of an extraordinary beauty and clearness in their most complicated polyphony. But polyphony (or many voices) is new in painting, and to the Futurists must be conceded the originality of attempting to represent a half dozen different things at the same time on canvas--a dog's tail, a woman's laughter, the thoughts of a man who has had a "hard night," the inside of a motor-bus, and the ideas of its passengers concerning its bumping wheels, and what-not!

7th: That universal dynamism must be rendered in painting as a dynamic sensation.

8th: That in the manner of rendering nature, the essential is sincerity and purity (more copy-book maxims for us!).

9th: That movement and light destroy the materiality of bodies (a truism in art well known to Watteau, Rembrandt, Turner, and latterly, to Claude Monet and the earlier group of Impressionists). And now for the milk in the cocoanut.

We fight, concludes the manifesto: 1st: Against the bituminous tints by which it is attempted to obtain the patina of tone upon modern pictures. (The chief objection against this statement is its absolute superfluousness. The Impressionists forty years ago attacked bituminous painting and finally drove it out; now it is coming back as a novelty. The Futurists are gazing backward.) 2d: Against the superficial and elementary archaism founded upon flat tints, which, by imitating the linear technique of the Egyptians, reduces painting to a powerless synthesis both childish and grotesque. 3d: Against the false claims of belonging to the future put forward by the Secessionists and the Independents, who have installed new academies no less trite and attached to routine than the preceding ones. 4th: We demand for ten years the total suppression of the nude in painting.

There are thirty-four pictures in the show, the catalogue of which is a curiosity. Boccioni's The Street Enters the Home has a note in the catalogue which points out that the painter does not limit himself to what he sees in the square frame of the window as would a simple photographer, but he also reproduces what he would see by looking out on every side from the balcony. Isn't this lucid? But you ought to see the jumble in the canvas caused by the painter casting aside the chief prerogative of an artist, the faculty of selection, or, rather, as Walter Pater puts it, the "tact of omission."

There is the motion of moonlight in one canvas and in No. 24, by Russolo, entitled Rebellion, there is an effort to delineate--better say express, as the art of delineation is here in abeyance--the collision of two forces, that of the revolutionary element made up of enthusiasm and red lyricism against the force of inertia and reactionary resistance of tradition. The angles are the vibratory waves of the former force in motion. The perspective of the houses is destroyed just as a boxer is bent double by receiving a blow in the wind (refined image!). As this picture is purely symbolical, it is not open to objections; but isn't it rather amusing?

Memory of a Night, by Russolo (No. 23), is "a fantastic impression produced not by line but by colour." An elongated insect or snail--is it a man or a grasshopper?--is in the first plane; back of him is a girl's face with pleading eyes; an explosion of light in the background is evidently intended for an electric lamp; the rest is chaos.

The Milliner (No. 32) by Severini, the painter calls: "An arabesque of the movement produced by the twinkling colours and iridescence of the frills and furbelows on show; the electric light divides the scene into defined zones. A study of simultaneous penetration." The deathly grin of the modiste is about the only "simultaneous penetration" that I could see in the canvas.

As confused as is No. 27, The Pan-Pan Dance at the Monico, by Severini, there are some vital bits, excellent modelling, striking detail, though as a whole, it is hard to unravel; the point d'appui is missing; the interest is nowhere focussed, though the dancer woman soon catches the eye. No doubt a crowded supper room in a Continental cafe, the white napery, variegated colours of the women's attire, the movement and blinding glare of the lights are a chaotic blur when you first open your eyes upon them; but the human eye with its almost infinite capacity for adaptation soon resolves disorder into order, formlessness into form. The trouble with the Futurist is that he catches the full force of the primal impression, then later loads it with his own subjective fancies. The outcome is bound to be a riddle.

I confess without hesitation there are several pictures in the exhibition which impressed me. Power is power, no matter the strange airs it may at times assume. Browning's Sordello, despite its numerous obscure passages, is withal a work of high purpose, it always stirs the imagination. I found myself staring at Carra's Funeral of the Anarchist Galli and wondering after all whether a conflict shouldn't be represented in a conflicting manner. Zola reproached both De Goncourt and Flaubert for their verbal artistry. "Vulgar happenings," he said, "should be presented in the bluntest fashion." And then he contradicted himself in practice by attempting to write like Hugo and Flaubert. Signor Carra, who probably witnessed the street row at the funeral of Galli between the students and the police, sets before us in all its vivacity or rhythm--or rhythms--the fight. It is a real fight. And while I quite agree with Edgar Degas, who said he could make a crowd out of four or five figures in a picture, it is no reflection on Carra's power to do the same with a dozen or more. A picture as full of movement and the clash of combatants as is the battle section of the Richard Strauss Symphony, A Hero's Life. Realism is the dominating factor in both works. The cane and club swinging sympathisers of the anarchist are certainly vital.

In what then consists the originality of the Futurists? Possibly their blatant claim to originality. The Primitives, Italian and Flemish, saw the universe with amazing clearness; their pictorial metaphysics was clarity itself; their mysticism was never muddy; all nature was settled, serene, and brilliantly silhouetted. But mark you! they, too, enjoyed depicting a half-dozen happenings on the same canvas. Fresh from a tour through the galleries of Holland, Belgium, and France, after a special study of the Primitives, I quite understand what the Futurists are after. They emulate the innocence of the eye characteristic of the early painters, but despite their strong will they cannot recover the blitheness and sweetness, the native wood-note wild, nor recapture their many careless moods. They weave the pattern closer, seeking to express in paint a psychology that is only possible in literature. And they endeavour to imitate music with its haunting suggestiveness, its thematic vagueness, its rhythmic swiftness and splendour of tonalities. In vain. No picture can spell many moods simultaneously, nor paint soul-states successively within one frame. These painters have mistaken their vocation. They should have been musicians or writers, or handle the more satisfactory, if less subtle, cinematograph.

Will there ever be a new way of seeing as well as representing life, animate and inanimate? Who shall say? The Impressionists, working on hints from Watteau, Rembrandt, Turner, gave us a fresh view of the universe. Rhythm in art is no new thing. In the figures of El Greco as in the prancing horses of Gericault, rhythm informs every inch of the canvas. The Futurists are seeking a new synthesis, and their work is far from synthetic; it is decomposition--in the painter's sense of the word--carried to the point of distraction. Doubtless each man has a definite idea when he takes up his brush, but all the king's horses and all the king's men can't make out that idea when blazoned on the canvas. The Futurists may be for the future, but not for to-day's limited range of vision.

XV

IN THE WORKSHOP OF ZOLA

Taine once wrote: "When we know how an artist invents we can foresee his inventions." As to Zola, there is little need now for critical judgments on his work. He is definitely "placed"; we know him for what he is--a romancer of a violent idealistic type masquerading as an implacable realist; a lyric pessimist at the beginning of his literary career, a sonorous optimist at the close, with vague socialistic views as to the perfectibility of the human race. But he traversed distances before he finally found himself a field in which stirred and struggled all human animality. And he was more Zola when he wrote Therese Raquin than in his later trilogies and evangels. As an artist it is doubtful if he grew after 1880; repetition was his method of methods, or, as he once remarked to Edmond de Goncourt: "Firstly, I fix my nail, and then with a blow of the hammer I send it a centimetre deep into the brain of the public; then I knock it in as far again--and the hammer of which I make use is journalism." And a tremendous journalist to the end was Zola, despite his books and naturalistic theories.

Again, and from the diary of the same sublimated old gossip, Goncourt, Zola speaks: "After the rarefied analysis of a certain kind of sentiment, such as the work done by Flaubert in Madame Bovary; after the analysis of things, plastic and artistic, such as you have given us in your dainty, gemlike writing, there is no longer any room for the younger generation of writers; there is nothing left for them to do, ... there no longer remains a single type to portray. The only way of appealing to the public is by strong writing, powerful creations, and by the number of volumes given to the world." Theory-ridden Zola's polemical writings, like those of Richard Wagner's, must be set down to special pleading.

Certainly Zola gave the world a number of volumes, and, if the writing was not always "strong"--his style is usually mediocre--the subjects were often too strong for polite nostrils. As Henri Massis, the author of an interesting book, How Zola Composed His Novels, says, "he founded his work on a theory which is the most singular of mistakes." The "experimental" novel is now a thing as extinct as the dodo, yet what doughty battles were fought for its shapeless thesis. The truth is that Zola invented more than he observed. He was myopic, not a trained scrutiniser, and Huysmans, once a disciple, later an opponent of the "naturalistic" documents, maliciously remarked that Zola went out carriage riding in the country, and then wrote La Terre. Turgenieff declared that Zola could describe sweat on a human back, but never told us what the human thought. And in a memorable passage, Huysmans couches his lance against the kind of realism Zola represented, admitting the service performed by that romancer: "We must, in short, follow the great highway so deeply dug out by Zola, but it is also necessary to trace a parallel path in the air, another road by which we may reach the Beyond and the Afterward, to achieve thus a spiritualistic naturalism."

Mr. Massis has had access to the manuscripts of Zola deposited by his widow in the National Library, Paris. They number ninety volumes; the dossier alone of Germinal forms four volumes of five hundred pages. Such industry seems fabulous. But, if it did not pass Zola through the long-envied portals of the Academy, it has won for his ashes such an honourable resting-place as the Pantheon. There is irony in the pranks of the Zeitgeist. Zola, snubbed at every attempt he made to become an Immortal (unlike his friend Daudet, he openly admitted his candidature, not sharing with the author of Sapho his sovereign contempt for the fauteuils of the Forty); Zola, in an hour becoming the most unpopular writer in France after his memorable J'accuse, a fugitive from his home, the defender of a seemingly hopeless cause; Zola dead, Dreyfus exonerated, and the powdered bones of Zola in the Pantheon, with the great men of his land. Few of his contemporaries who voted against his admission to the Academy will be his neighbours in the eternal sleep. His admission to the dead Immortals must be surely the occasion for much wagging of heads, for reams of platitudinous writing on the subject of fate and its whirligig caprice.

This stubborn, silent man of violent imagination, copious vocabulary, and a tenacity unparalleled in literature, knew that a page a day--a thousand words daily put on paper every day of the year--and for twenty years, would rear a huge edifice. He stuck to his desk each morning of his life from the time he sketched the Plan general; he made such terms with his publishers that he was enabled to live humbly, yet comfortably, in the beginning with his "dear ones," his wife and his mother. In return he wrote two volumes a year, and, with the exception of a few years, his production was as steady as water flowing from a hydrant. This comparison was once applied to herself by George Sand, Zola's only rival in the matter of quantity. But Madame Sand was an improviser; with notes she never bothered herself; in her letters to Flaubert she laughed over the human documents of Zola, the elaborate note taking of Daudet, for she was blessed with an excellent memory and a huge capacity for scribbling. Not so Zola. Each book was a painful parturition, not the pain of a stylist like Flaubert, but the Sisyphus-like labor of getting his notes, his facts, his characters marshalled and moving to a conclusion. Like Anthony Trollope, when the last page of a book was finished he began another. He was a workman, not a dilettante of letters.

In 1868 he had blocked out his formidable campaign. Differing with Balzac in not taking French society as a whole for a subject, he nevertheless owes, as do all French fiction writers since 1830--Stendhal alone excepted--his literary existence to Balzac; Balzac, from whom all blessings, all evils, flow in the domain of the novel; Balzac, realist, idealist, symbolist, naturalist, humourist, tragedian, comedian, aristocrat, bourgeois, poet, and cleric; Balzac, truly the Shakespeare of France. The Human Comedy attracted the synthetic brain of Zola as he often tells us (see L'Oeuvre, where Sandoz, the novelist, Zola himself, explains to Claude his scheme of a prose epic). But he was satisfied to take one family under the Second Empire, the Rougon-Macquarts--these names were not at first in the form we now know them. A friend and admirer of Flaubert, he followed, broadly speaking, his method of proceeding and work; though an admirer of the Goncourts, he did not favour their preference for the rare case or the chiselled epithet.

Every-day humanity described in every-day speech was Zola's ideal. That he more than once achieved this ideal is not to be denied. L'Assommoir remains his masterpiece, while Germinal and L'Oeuvre will not be soon forgotten. L'Oeuvre is mentioned because its finished style is rather a novelty in Zola's vast vat of writing wherein scraps and fragments of Victor Hugo, of Chateaubriand, of the Goncourts, and of Flaubert boil in terrific confusion. Zola never had the patience, nor the time, nor perhaps the desire to develop an individual style. He built long rows of ugly houses, all looking the same, composed of mud, of stone, brick, sand, straw, and shining pebbles. Like a bird, he picked up his material for his nest where he could find it. His faculty of selection was ill-developed. Everything was tossed pell-mell into his cellar; nothing came amiss and order seldom reigns. His sentences, unlike Tolstoy's, for example, are not closely linked; to read Zola aloud is disconcerting. There is no music in his periods, his rhythms are sluggish, and he entirely fails in evoking with a few poignant phrases, as did the Goncourts, a scene, an incident. Never the illuminating word, never the phrase that spells the transfiguration of the spirit.

Among his contemporaries Tolstoy was the only one who matches him in the accumulation of details, but for the Russian every detail modulates into another, notwithstanding their enormous number. The story marches, the little facts, insignificant at first, range themselves into definite illuminations of the theme, just as a traveller afoot on a hot, dusty road misses the saliency of the landscape, but realises its perspective when he ascends a hill. There is always perspective in Tolstoy; in Zola it is rare. Yet he masses his forces as would some sullen giant, confident in the end of victory through sheer bulk and weight. His power is gloomy, cruel, pitiless; but indubitable power he has.

After the rather dainty writing of his Contes a Ninon, Zola never reached such compression and clarity again until he wrote L'Attaque au Moulin, in Les Soirees de Medan. To be quite frank, he rewrote Flaubert and the Goncourts in many of his books. He was, using the phrase in its real sense, the "grand vulgariser" of those finished, though somewhat remote artists. To the Goncourts fame came slowly; it was by a process of elimination rather than through the voluntary offering of popular esteem. And it is not to be denied that Madame Bovary owed much of its early success to the fact that its author was prosecuted for an outrage against public morals--poor Emma Bovary whose life, as Henry James once confessed, might furnish a moral for a Sunday-school class. Thus fashions in books wax and wane. Zola copied and "vulgarised" Charles de Mailly, Manette Salomon, Germinie Lacerteux (Charles Monselet saluted the book with the amiable title "sculptured slime"), Madame Gervasais--for his Roman story---Soeur Philomene, all by Goncourt, and he literally founded his method on Madame Bovary and L'Education Sentimentale, particularly upon the latter, the greatest, and one is tempted to say the most genuine realistic novel ever written. Its grey colouring, its daylight atmosphere, its marvellous description of Fontainebleau, of masquerades, of dinners and duels in high and low life, its lifelike characters, were for Zola a treasure-trove. He took Rosanette, the most lifelike cocotte in fiction, and transformed her into Nana, into a symbol of destruction. Zola saw the world through melodramatic eyes.

Mr. Massis has noted Zola's method of literary travail, the formation of his style, the labour of style, the art of writing, the pain of writing, and his infinitely painstaking manner of accumulating heaps of notes, and building his book from them. The Massis study, the most complete of its kind, may interest the student, not alone of Zola, but of literature in general. Not, however, as a model, for Zola, with all his tiresome preparations, never constructed an ideal book--rather, to put it the other way, no one of his books reveals ideal construction. The multiplicity of details, of descriptions weary the reader. A coarse spirit his, he revelled in scenes of lust, bloodshed, vileness, and cruelty.

His people, with a few exceptions, are but agitated silhouettes. You close your eyes after reading La Bete Humaine and think of Eugene Sue, a Sue of 1880. Yet a master of broad, symphonic descriptions. There is a certain resemblance to Richard Wagner; indeed, he patterned after Wagner in his use of the musical symbol: there is a leading motive in each of Zola's novels. And like Wagner he was a sentimental lover of mankind and a hater of all forms of injustice.

From the conception of the work, with its general notes on its nature, its movement, its physiology, its determination, its first sketches of the personages, the milieu--he was an ardent adherent of Taine in this particular--the occupations of the characters, the summary plan with the accumulated details, thence to the writing, the entire method is exposed in this ingenious and entertaining book of Massis. He has no illusions about Zola's originality or the destiny of his works. Zola has long ceased to count in literary evolution.

But Emile Zola is in the Pantheon.

ZOLA AS BEST SELLER

The publication of the number of books sold by a young American novelist previous to his untimely taking off does not prove that a writer has to be alive to be a best seller. If that were the case, what about Dickens and Thackeray as exceptions? The publishers of Dickens say that their sales of his novels in 1910 were 25 per cent more than in 1909, and 750,000 copies were sold in 1911. In many instances a dead author is worth more than a live one. With Zola this is not precisely so, though his books still sell; the only interregnum being the time when the Dreyfus affair was agitating France. Then the source of Zola's income dried up like a rain pond in a desert. Later on he had his revenge.

The figures for the sale of Zola up to the end of 1911 are very instructive. His collected works number forty-eight volumes. Of the Rougon-Macquart series 1,964,000 have been sold; other novels, 764,000; essays and various works bring the total to 2,750,000, approximately. In a word, a few years hence Zola will easily pass 3,000,000. Nana still holds its own as the leader of the list, 215,000; La Terre, 162,000; L'Assommoir, 162,000. This would seem to prove what the critics of the French novelist have asserted: that books in which coarse themes are treated with indescribable coarseness have sold and continue to sell better than his finer work, L'Oeuvre, for example, which has only achieved 71,000. But L'Assommoir is Zola at his best; besides, it is not such a vile book as La Terre. And then how about La Debacle, which has 229,000 copies to its credit? The answer is that patriotism played a greater role in the fortune of this work than did vulgar curiosity in the case of the others. Another popular book, Germinal, shows 132,000.

On the appearance of La Terre in 1887 (it was first published as a feuilleton in _Gil Blas_, from May 28 to September 15), five of Zola's disciples, Paul Bonnetain, J. H. Rosny, Lucien Descaves, Paul Margueritte, and Gustave Guiches, made a public protest which is rather comical if you remember that several of these writers have not turned out Sunday-school literature; Paul Margueritte in particular has in L'Or and an earlier work beaten his master at the game. But a reaction from Zola's naturalism was bound to come. As Remy de Gourmont wrote: "There has been no question of forming a party or issuing orders; no crusade was organised; it is individually that we have separated ourselves, horror stricken, from a literature the baseness of which made us sick." Havelock Ellis, otherwise an admirer of the genius of Emile Zola, has said that his soul "seems to have been starved at the centre and to have encamped at the sensory periphery." Blunt George Saintsbury calls Zola the "naturalist Zeus, Jove the Dirt-Compeller," and adds that as Zola misses the two lasting qualities of literature, style, and artistic presentation of matter, he is doomed; for "the first he probably could not have attained, except in a few passages, if he would; the second he has deliberately rejected, and so the mother of dead dogs awaits him sooner or later." Yet Zola lives despite these predictions, as the above figures show, notwithstanding his loquacity in regard to themes that should be tacenda to every writer.

But in this matter of forbidden subjects Zola is regarded by the present generation as a trifle old-fashioned. When alive he was grouped with Aretino and the Marquis de Sade, or with Restif de la Bretonne. To-day Paris has not only Paul Margueritte, who when writing in conjunction with his brother Victor gave much promise, but also Octave Mirbeau. With Zola, the newer men assert that their work makes for morality, exposing as it does public and private abuses, an excuse as classic as Aristophanes.

In 1893 the figures for the principal novels of Zola stood thus: Nana, 160,000; L'Assommoir, 127,000; La Debacle, 143,000; Germinal, 88,000; La Terre, 100,000; La Bete Humaine, 83,000; the same number for Le Reve; Pot-Bouille, 82,000; whereas L'Oeuvre only counted 55,000; La Conquete de Plassans, 25,000; La Curee, 36,000, and La Joie de Vivre, 44,000. La Terre, then, the most unmentionable story of them all, has jumped since 1893 to the end of 1911 from 100,000 to 215,000, whereas L'Oeuvre moved only from 55,000 to 71,000 in fourteen years. But a Vulgarian can understand La Terre while L'Oeuvre would be absolutely undecipherable to him.

Zola always knew his market; even knew it after Dreyfus had intervened. Of the series called Les Trois Villes, Rome is the best seller, 121,000; and it is as profound a vilification of the Eternal City as was La Terre of the French peasants, as Pot-Bouille of the French bourgeois. Indeed, all Zola reads like the frenzied attack of a pessimist to whom his native land is a hideous nightmare and its inhabitants criminals or mad folk. His influence on a younger generation of writers, especially in America, has been baneful, and he has done much with his exuberant, rhapsodical style to further the moon-madness of socialism; of a belief in a coming earthly paradise, where no one will labour (except the captive millionaires) and from whose skies roasted pigeons will fall straightway into the mouths of its foolish inhabitants.

Zola as a money-maker need not be considered now; his gains were enormous; suffice to say that he was paid large sums for the serial rights. Nana, in _Voltaire_, brought 20,000 francs; Pot-Bouille, in _Gaulois_, 30,000 francs; Bonheur des Dames, La Joie de Vivre, Germinal, L'Oeuvre, La Terre, in _Gil Blas_, each 20,000 francs; L'Argent, in the same journal, 30,000 francs; Le Reve, in the _Revue Illustree_, 25,000 francs; La Bete Humaine, in _Vie Populaire_, 25,000 francs; La Debacle, in the same, 30,000 francs, and Docteur Pascal in _Revue Hebdomadaire_, 35,000 francs. That amounts to about 300,000 francs. Each novel cost from 20,000 to 25,000 francs for rights of reproduction, and to all this must be added about 500,000 francs for the theatrical works, making a total of 1,600,000 francs. And it was in 1894 that these figures were compiled by Antoine Laporte in his book on Naturalism, which contains a savage attack on Zolaism. Truly, then, Zola may be fairly called one of the best sellers among all authors, dead or living.

XVI

A STUDY OF DE MAUPASSANT

In 1881 Turgenieff gave Tolstoy a book by a young Frenchman, telling him that he would find it amusing. This book was La Maison Tellier. Tolstoy revolted at the theme, but could not deny the freshness and power of the author. He found Maupassant "deficient in the moral sense"; yet he was interested and followed the progress of Flaubert's pupil. When Une Vie appeared, the Russian novelist pronounced it incomparably the best work of its author--perhaps the best French novel since Hugo's Les Miserables. He wrote this in an article entitled Guy de Maupassant and the Art of Fiction. It was doubtless the Norman's clear, robust vision that appealed to Tolstoy, who, at that period was undergoing a change of heart; else how could he call Les Miserables the greatest novel of France, he the writer of Anna Karenina--the antipodes of that windy apotheosis of vapid humanitarianism, the characteristic trait of Hugo's epic of pity and unreality.

But Maupassant affected Tolstoy as he had affected Turgenieff. Guy has told us of his first meeting with the latter, an artist superior to Tolstoy. "The first time I saw Turgenieff was at Gustave Flaubert's--a door opened; a giant came in, a giant with a silver head, as they would say in a fairy tale." This must have been in 1876, for in a letter dated January 24, 1877, Turgenieff writes: "Poor Maupassant is losing all his hair. He came to see me. He is as nice as ever, but very ugly just at present." In 1880 the young man published a volume of poetry, Des Vers. He was thirty years old (born August 5, 1850).

The literary apprenticeship of Guy to Gustave Flaubert is a thrice-told tale, and signifies only this: If the pupil had not been richly endowed all the lessons of Flaubert would have availed him little. Perhaps the anecdote has been overdone; Maupassant has related it in the preface to Pierre et Jean, and in the introduction to the George Sand-Flaubert correspondence--now at the head of the edition of Bouvard et Pecuchet. There are letters of Flaubert to his disciple full of his explosive good nature, big heart, irascibility and generous outpouring on the subject of his art. The thing that surprises a close student of this episode and its outcome is that Maupassant was in reality so unlike his master. And when I further insist that the younger man appropriated whole scenes from Flaubert for his longer stories, especially from L'Education Sentimentale, I feel that I am uttering a paradox.

What I mean is this: Maupassant's temperament was utterly different from Flaubert's. They were both prosecuted for certain things they wrote, Guy for a poem in 1880, at Estampes; there had been a detraque nervous system in both cases. Yet, similar in ideals and physical peculiarities as were these two men, there was a profound psychical gulf between their temperaments. Flaubert was a great genius, a path breaker, a philosophic poet, and the author of La Tentation de St. Antoine, the nearest approach that France can show to a prose epic, and a book of beauty and originality. Maupassant was a great talent, and a growing one when disease cut him down. He imitated the externals of Flaubert, his irony, his vivid power of picture-making; even his pessimism he developed--though that was personal, as we shall soon see. And yet his work is utterly unlike Flaubert, probably unlike what Flaubert had hoped for--the old man died in 1881 and therefore did not live to enjoy Maupassant in full bloom. If it did not sound quite heretical I should be tempted to assert that the writer Maupassant most patterned after, was Prosper Merimee, an artist detested by Flaubert because of his hard style. It is this precise style that Maupassant exhibits but coupled with a clarity, an ease, and a grace that Merimee could not boast. Of Flaubert's harmonious and imaginatively coloured manner, Maupassant shows no trace in his six novels and his two hundred and odd tales.

Maupassant was not altogether faithful to Flaubert's injunctions regarding the publication of his early attempts. He made many secret flights under different pen-names, though Boule de Suif was the first prose signed by him. It appeared in Les Soirees de Medan, and its originality quite outshone the more solid qualities of Zola's L'Attaque au Moulin, and a realistic tale of Huysmans's, Sac au dos. It was this knapsack of story, nevertheless, that opened the eyes of both Zola and Goncourt to the genuine realism of Huysmans as opposed to the more human but also more sentimental surface realism of Maupassant. Huysmans proved himself devoid of the story-telling gift, of dramatic power; yet he has, if compared to Maupassant, without an iota of doubt, the more vivid vision of the two; "the intensest vision of the modern world," says Havelock Ellis. Pictorial, not imaginative vision, be it understood. In his mystic latter-day rhapsodies it is the realist who sees, the realist who makes those poignant, image-breeding phrases. Take up Maupassant and in his best tales and novels, such as La Maison Tellier, Boule de Suif, Une Vie, Fort Comme la Mort, to mention a few, you will be surprised at the fluidity, the artful devices to elude the harshness of reality, the pessimistic poetry that suffuses his pages after reading Huysmans's immitigable exposition of the ugly and his unflinching attitude before the unpleasant. And Huysmans's point of departure is seldom from an idea; facts furnish him with an adequate spring-board. Maupassant is more lyric in tone and texture. Edmond de Goncourt, jealous of the success of the newcomer, wrote in his diary that Maupassant was an admirable conteur, but a great writer, never. Zola admitted to a few intimates that Guy was not the realist that Huysmans was. All of which is interesting, but proves nothing except that Maupassant wrote a marvellous collection of short stories, real, hyphenated short-stories, as Mr. Brander Matthews makes the delicate distinction, while Huysmans did not.

Edouard Maynial's La Vie et l'Oeuvre de Guy de Maupassant is the most recent of the biographical studies devoted to our subject, though Baron Albert Lumbroso, who escapes by a single letter from being confounded with the theory-ridden Turin psychiatrist, has given us, with the approval of Guy's mother, the definitive study of Maupassant's malady and death. It is frequently quoted by Maynial; there is a careful study of it which appeared in _Mercure de France_, June, 1905, by Louis Thomas. And there is that charming volume, Amitie amoureuse, in which Guy is said to figure as the Philippe, by Henri Amic and Madame Lecomte du Nouy. Here we get another Maupassant, not the taureau triste of Taine, but a delightful, sweet-tempered, unselfish, and altogether lovable fellow. What was the cause of his downfall? Dissipation? Mental overwork--which is the same thing? Disease? Maynial, Lumbroso, and Thomas offer us such a variety of documents that there can be no doubt as to the determining element. From 1880 to his death in 1893 Guy de Maupassant was "a candidate for general paralysis." These are the words of his doctor, later approved by Doctor Blanche, to whose sanitarium in Paris he was taken, January 7, 1893.

The father of Guy was Gustave de Maupassant, of an ancient Lorraine family. This family was noble. His mother was of Norman extraction, Laure de Poittevin, the sister of Alfred de Poittevin, Flaubert's dearest friend, a poet who died young. There is no truth in the gossip that Guy was the son of Flaubert. Flaubert loved both the Poittevins; hence his lively interest in Guy. There was a younger brother, Herve de Maupassant, who died of a mental disorder. His daughter, Simone, is the legatee of her uncle. The marriage of the elder Maupassants proved a failure. They are both dead now, and the subject may be discussed to the point of admitting that the father was not a domestic man; Guy inherited his taste for Bohemian life, and Madame Laure de Maupassant, after separating from her husband, was subject to nervous crises in which she attempted her life by swallowing laudanum and by strangling herself with her own hair. She was rescued both times, but she was an invalid to the last. A loving mother, she overlooked the education of Guy, and let it be said that no happier child ever lived. His early days were passed at Etretat, at the Villa Verguies, and generally in the open air.

The future writer adored the sea; he has written many tales of the water, of yachts and river sports. He went to the seminary at Yvetot and the lyceum of Rouen, but his education was desultory, his reading principally of his own selection--like most men of individual character. He was a farceur, fond of mystifications, of rough practical jokes, of horseplay. His physique was more Flemish than French--a deep chest, broad shoulders, heavy muscular arms and legs, a small head, a bull-neck. He looked like the mate of a deep-sea ship rather than a literary man. Add to this a craze for rowing, canoeing, swimming, boxing, fencing, and running. An all-round athlete, as the phrase goes, Guy, it is related, once paid a hulking chap to let himself be kicked. So hard was Guy's kick, done in an experimental humour, that the victim became enraged and knocked the kicker off his pins. Flaubert, the apostle of the immobile, objected. Too many flirtations, too much exercise! he admonishingly cried. A writer must cultivate repose.

In sooth Maupassant went a terrific pace. He abused his constitution from the beginning, seemingly tormented by seven restless devils. He spent five hours a day at his office in the Ministry, in the afternoon he rowed on the Seine, in the evening he wrote. After he had resigned as a bureaucrat he worked from seven until twelve every morning, no matter the excesses of the previous night; the afternoon he spent on the river, retiring very late. "Toujours les femmes, petit cochon," wrote Flaubert in 1876, "il faut travailler." But it was precisely work that helped to kill the man. Those six pages a day, while they seldom showed erasures, were carefully written, and not until after much thought. Guy was the type of the apparently spontaneous writers. His manuscripts are free from the interlineations of Flaubert. He wrote at one jet; but there was elaborate mental preparation. Toward the last began the ether inhalations, the chloroform, hasheesh, the absinthe, cocaine, and the "odour symphonies"--Huysmans's des Esseintes, and his symphonic perfume sprays were not altogether the result of invention. On his yacht _Bel Ami_ Guy never ceased his daily travail. It was Taine who called him un taureau triste. Paul Bourget relates that when he told Maupassant of this epigram, he calmly replied: "Better a bull than an ox."

His output--as they say in publishing circles--was breath-catching. It is whispered that he worked all the better after a "hard night." Now there can be but one end to such an expenditure of nervous energy, and that end came, not suddenly, but with the treacherous, creeping approach of paralysis. "Literary" criticism of the Nordau type is usually a foolish thing; yet in Maupassant's case one does not need to be a skilled psychiatrist to follow and note the gradual palsy of the writer's higher centres. Such stories as Qui Sait? Lui, Le Horla--a terrifying conception that beats Poe on his own chosen field--Fou, Un Fou, and several others show the nature of his malady. Guy de Maupassant came fairly by his cracked nervous constitution, and instead of dissipation, mental and physical, being the determining causes of his shattered health, they were really the outcome of an inherited predisposition to all that is self-destructive. The French alienists called it une heredite chargee. (No doubt the dread Spirochaeta pallida.)

He never relaxed his diligence, even writing criticism. He saluted the literary debuts of Paul Hervieu and Edouard Rod in an article which appeared in _Gil Blas_. At the time of his death he was contemplating an extensive study of Turgenieff. Edmond de Goncourt did not like him, suspecting him of irreverence because of some words Guy had written in the preface to Pierre et Jean about complicated exotic vocabularies; meaning the Goncourts, of course. It is to be believed that Flaubert also had some quiet fun with the brothers and with Zola regarding their mania for note taking; read Bouvard et Pecuchet for confirmation of this idea of mine.

Maupassant was paid one franc a line for his novels in the periodicals, and 500 francs for the newspaper rights of publication only; good prices twenty-five years ago in Paris.

His annual income was about 28,000 to 35,000 francs, and it kept up for at least ten years. A table shows us that to December, 1891, the sale of his books was as follows: short stories, 169,000; novels, 180,000; travel, 24,000; in all 373,000 volumes. Maupassant was even for these days of swollen figures a big "seller." His mother had an income of 5,000 francs, but she far excelled the amount in her living expenses. Guy was an admirable son--tender, thoughtful, and generous.

He made her an allowance, and at his death left her in comfort, if not actually wealthy. She died at Nice, December 8, 1904, his father surviving him until 1899.

And that death was achieved by the most hideous route--insanity. Restless, travelling incessantly, fearful of darkness, of his own shadow, he was like an Oriental magician who had summoned malignant spirits from outer space only to be destroyed by them. Not in Corsica or Sicily, in Africa nor the south of France, did Guy fight off his rapidly growing disease. He worked hard, he drank hard, but to no avail; the blackness of his brain increased. Melancholia and irritability supervened; he spelled words wrong, he quarrelled with his friends, he instituted a lawsuit against a New York newspaper, _The Star_; then the persecution craze, folie des grandeurs, frenzy. The case was "classic" from the beginning, even to the dilated pupils of his eyes, as far back as 1880. The 1st of January, 1892, he had promised to spend with his mother at Villa de Ravenelles, at Nice. But he went, instead, against his mother's wishes, to Ste.-Marguerite in company with two sisters, society women, one of them said to have been the heroine of Notre Coeur.

The next day he arrived, his features discomposed, and in a state of great mental excitement. He was tearful and soon left for Cannes with his valet, Francois. What passed during the night was never exactly known, except that Guy attempted suicide by shooting, and with a paper-knife. The knife inflicted a slight wound; the pistol contained blank cartridges--Francois had suspected his master's mood, and told the world later of it in his simple loving memoirs--and his forehead was slightly burned. Some months previous he had told Doctor Fremy that between madness and death he would not hesitate; a lucid moment had shown him his fate, and he sought death. After a week, during which two stout sailors of his yacht, _Bel Ami_, guarded him, as he sadly walked on the beach regarding with tear-stained cheeks his favourite boat, he was taken to Passy, to Doctor Blanche's institution. One of his examining physicians there was Doctor Franklin Grout, who later married Flaubert's niece, Caroline Commanville.

July 6, 1893, Maupassant died, as a lamp is extinguished for lack of oil. But the year he spent at the asylum was wretched; he became a mere machine, and perhaps the only pleasure he experienced was the hallucination of bands of black butterflies that seemed to sweep across his room. Monsieur Maynial does not tell of the black butterflies, the truth of which I can vouch for, as I heard the story from Lassalle, the French barytone, a friend of Maupassant's.

It may be interesting to the curious to learn that the good-hearted, brave heroine of Boule de Suif was a certain Adrienne Legay of Rouen, and that she heartily reprobated the writer for giving her story to the world. She even went so far as to say that Guy did it in a spirit of revenge. Madame Laure de Maupassant made inquiries about the patriotic little sinner so as to help her. It was too late. She had died in extreme poverty. The heroine of Mademoiselle Fifi was a brunette, Rachel by name; the hero was a young German officer, Baron William d'Eyrick.

Would Maupassant have reached the sunlit heights, as Tolstoy believed? Who may say? Truth lies not at the bottom of a well, but in suffering; suffering alone reveals the truth of himself, of his soul to man, and Guy had suffered as few; he had passed into the Inferno that later Nietzsche entered, passed into though not through it. Turgenieff, for whom Guy entertained a profound regard, had influenced him more than he, with his doglike fidelity for Flaubert, would have cared to acknowledge. Paul Bourget gives us chapter and verse for this statement; furthermore, the same authority, has described--in his Etudes et Portraits--the enormous travail of Maupassant in pursuit of style--he, seemingly, the most spontaneous writer of his generation. His books offend, delight, startle, and edify thousands of readers. That they have done absolute harm we are not prepared to say; book wickedness is, after all, an academic, not a vital question. If all the wicked books that have seen the light of publication had wrought the evil predicted of them the earth would be an abomination. In reality, we discuss with varying shades of enthusiasm or detestation such frank literature--naturally when it is literature--and after the hullabaloo of the moral bell-boys has ceased, the book is quietly forgotten on its shelf. Flaubert once wrote of the vast fund of indifference possessed by society. Dramas, books, pictures, statues have never ruined our overmoral world. The day for such things--if there ever was such a day--has passed. Besides, among the people of most nations, the hatred of art and literature is pushed to the point of lecturing boastfully about that same hatred.

XVII

PUVIS DE CHAVANNES

Although he has been dead since October 24, 1898, critical battles are still fought over the artistic merits of Puvis de Chavannes. Whether you agree with Huysmans and call this mural painter a pasticheur of the Italian Primitives, or else the greatest artist in decoration since Paolo Veronese, depends much on your critical temperament. There are many to whom Henri Martin's gorgeous colour--really the methods of Monet applied to vast spaces--or the blazing originality of Albert Besnard make more intimate appeal than the pallid poetry, solemn rhythms, and faded moonlit tonal gamut of Puvis. Because the names of Gustave Moreau and Puvis were often associated, Huysmans, ab irato, cries against the "obsequious heresy" of the conjunction, forgetting that the two men were friends. Marius Vauchon, despite his excessive admiration for Puvis has rendered a service to his memory in his study, because he has shown us the real, not the legendary man. With Vauchon, we are far from Huysmans, and his succinct, but disagreeable, epigram: C'est un vieux rigaudon qui s'essaie dans le requiem. The truth is, that some idealists were disappointed to find Puvis to be a sane, healthy, solidly built man, a bon vivant in the best sense of the phrase, without a suggestion of the morbid, vapouring pontiff or haughty Olympian. Personally he was not in the least like his art, a crime that sentimental persons seldom forgive. A Burgundian--born at Lyons, December 14, 1824--he possessed all the characteristics of his race. Asceticism was the last quality to seek in him. A good dinner with old vintage, plenty of comrades, above all the society of his beloved Princess Cantacuzene, whose love of her husband was the one romance in his career; these, and twelve hours' toil a day in his atelier made up the long life of this distinguished painter. He lived for a half-century between his two ateliers, on the Place Pigalle, and at Neuilly. Notwithstanding his arduous combat with the Institute and public indifference, his cannot be called an unhappy existence. He had his art, in the practice of which he was a veritable fanatic; he was rich through inheritance, and he was happy in his love; affluence, art, love, a triad to attain, for which most men yearn, came to Puvis. Yet the gadfly of ambition was in his flesh. He was a visionary, even a recluse, like his friend Moreau, but a fighter for his ideas; and those ideas have shown not only French artists, but the entire world, the path back to true mural tradition. It is not an exaggeration to say that Puvis created modern decorative art.

His father was chief engineer of mines, a strong-willed, successful man. Like father, like son, was true in this case, though the young De Chavannes, after some opposition, elected painting as his profession. He had fallen ill, and a trip to Italy was ordained. There he did not, as has been asserted, linger over Pompeii, or in the Roman Catacombs, but saved his time and enthusiasm for the Quattrocentisti. He admired the old Umbrian and Tuscan masters, he was ravished by the basilica of St. Francis at Assisi, and by Santa Maria Novella, Florence. Titian,

Tintoretto, finally Veronese, riveted his passion for what has been falsely styled the "archaic." Returning to Paris he was conducted by his friend Beauderon to the studio of Delacroix, whom he adored. He remained just fifteen days, when the shop was closed. Delacroix, in a rage because of the lack of talent and funds among his pupils, sent them away. Puvis had been under the tuition of Henri, the brother of Ary Scheffer, and for years spoke with reverence of that serious but mediocre painter. He next sought the advice of Couture, and remained with him three months, not, however, quarrelling with the master, as did later another pupil, Edouard Manet. Puvis was tractable enough; he had one failing--not always a sign of either talent or the reverse--he refused to see or paint as he was told by his teachers, or, indeed, like other pupils. Because of this stubbornness, his enemies, among whom ranked the most powerful critics of Paris, declared that he had never been grounded in the elements of his art, that he could not draw or design, that his colour-sense only proved colour-blindness. To be sure, he does not boast a fulgurant brush, and his line is often stiff and awkward; but he had the fundamentals of decorative art well in hand.

After his death thousands of sketches, designs, pencilled memoranda, and cartoons were found, and then there was whistled another tune. His draughtsmanship is that of a decorative artist, as the Rodin drawings are those of a sculptor, not of a painter. Considering the rigid standard by which the work of Puvis was judged, criticism was not altogether wrong, as was claimed when the wave of reaction set in. His easel pictures are not ingratiating. He does not show well in a gallery. He needs huge spaces in which to swim about; there he makes the compositions of other men seem pigmy. [It is the case of Wagner repeated, though there is little likeness between the ideas of the Frenchman and the German, except an epical bigness. Judged by the classical concert-room formulas, Wagner must not be compared with the miniaturist Mendelssohn. His form is the form of the music-drama, not the symphonic form.] Puvis adhered to one principle: A wall is a wall, and not an easel picture; it is flat, and that flatness must be emphasised, not disguised; decoration is the desideratum. He contrived a schematic painting that would harmonise with the flatness, with the texture and the architectural surroundings, and, as George Moore has happily said: "No other painter ever kept this end so strictly before his eyes. For this end Chavannes reduced his palette almost to a monochrome, for this end he models in two flat tints, for this end he draws in huge undisciplined masses.... Mural decoration, if it form part of the wall, should be a variant of the stonework." One might take exception to the word "undisciplined"--Puvis was one of the most calculating painters that ever used a brush, and one of the most cerebral. His favourite aphorism was: "Beauty is character." His figures have been called immobile, his palette impoverished; the unfair sex abused his lean, lanky female creatures, and finally he was named a painter for Lent--for fast-days. Even the hieratic figures of Moreau were pronounced opulent in comparison with the pale moonlighted spectres of the Puvis landscapes. Courbet, in Paris, was known as the "furious madman"; Puvis, as the "tranquil lunatic." Nine of his pictures were refused at the Salon, though in 1859 he exhibited there his Return from Hunting, and, in 1861, even received a second-class medal. His fecundity was enormous. His principal work comprises the Life of Ste. Genevieve (the saint is a portrait of his princess), at the Pantheon; Summer and Winter at the Hotel de Ville, the decorations for the amphitheatre of the Sorbonne, the decorations at Rouen, Inter Artes et Naturam; at Rouen, The Sacred Wood, Vision Antique, The Rhone, The Saone; the decorations at Amiens, War, Peace, Rest, Labour, Ave Picardia Nutrix, and two smaller grisailles, Vigilance and Fancy; at Marseilles, the Marseilles, Porte d' Orient, and Marseilles, the Greek Colony; the decorations for the Boston Public Library, and his easel picture, The Poor Fisherman, now in the Luxembourg. As to this latter, the painter explained that he had found the model in the person of a wretchedly poor fisherman at the estuary of the Seine; the young girl is a sister, and the landscape is that of the surroundings, though, as is the case with Puvis, greatly generalised. The above is but a slender list. New York has at the Metropolitan Museum at least one of his works, and in the collection here of John Quinn, Esq., there is the brilliant masterpiece, The Beheading of John the Baptist, and two large mural decorations, The River and The Vintage. They were painted in 1866. They are magnificent museum pictures.

All his frescoes are applied canvases. He didn't worry much over antique methods, nor can it be said that his work is an attempt to rehabilitate the Italian Primitives. On the contrary, Puvis is distinctly modern, and that is his chief offence in the eyes of official French art; while the fact that his "modernity" was transposed to decorative purposes, and appeared in so strange a guise, caused the younger men to eye him suspiciously. (Just as some recalcitrant music-critics refuse to recognise in certain compositions of Johannes Brahms the temperamental romantic.) Thus in the estimation of rival camps Puvis fell between two stools. He has been styled a latter-day Domenico Ghirlandajo, but this attribution rings more literary than literal.

Mr. Brownell with his accustomed sense of critical values has to our notion definitely summed up the question: "His classicism is absolutely unacademic, his romanticism unreal beyond the verge of mysticism and so preoccupied with visions that he may almost be called a man for whom the actual world does not exist--in the converse of Gautier's phrase. His distinction is wholly personal. He lives evidently on a high plane, dwells habitually in the delectable highlands of the intellect. The fact that his work is almost wholly decorative is not at all accidental. His talent, his genius, if one chooses, requires large spaces, vast dimensions. There has been a good deal of profitless discussion as to whether he expressly imitates the Primitives or reproduces them sympathetically; but really he does neither, he deals with their subjects occasionally, but always in a completely modern as well as a thoroughly personal way. His colour is as original as his general treatment and composition."

His men and women are not precisely pagan, nor are they biblical. But they reveal traits of both strained through a drastic "modern" intellect. They are not abstractions; the men are virile, the women maternal. There is the spirit of humanity, not of decadence. Puvis, like Moreau, did not turn his back to the rising sun. He admired Degas, Manet, Monet. At first he patterned after his friend Chasseriau, a fine and too-little-known painter, and at one time a mural decorator before he became immersed in Oriental themes. The lenten landscapes of Puvis are not merely scenic backgrounds, but integral parts of the general decorative web, and they are not conceived in No Man's Land, but selected from the vicinity of Paris. Puvis is by no means a virtuoso. His pace is usually andante; but he knows how to evoke a mood, summon the solemn music of mural spaces. His is a theme with variations. The wall or ceiling is ever the theme. His crabbed fugues soon melt into the larger austere music of the wall. His choral walls are true epopees. He is a master harmonist. He sounds oftener the symphonic than the lyric note. He gains his most moving effects without setting in motion the creaking allegorical machinery of the academy. He shows the simple attitudes of life transfigured without rhetoric. He avoids frigid allegory, yet employs symbols. His tonal attenuations, elliptical and syncopated rhythms, his atmosphere of the remote, the mysterious--all these give the spectator the sense of serenity, momentary freedom from the feverishness of every-day life, and suggest the lofty wisdom of the classic poets. But the serpent of futile melancholy, of the brief cadence of mortal dreams, and of the vanishing seconds that defile down the corridor of time, has stolen into this Garden of the Hesperides. Puvis de Chavannes, no more than Gustave Moreau, could escape the inquietude of his times. He is occasionally Parisian and often pessimist.

The inability of his contemporaries to understand his profound decorative genius, his tact in the handling of the great problem of lighting--the key is always higher because of the different or softer light of public buildings and the gloom of churches--and his feeling for the wall, purely as wall, a flat space, not to be confounded with the pseudo art that would make the picture like an open window in the wall, but based on the flatness of the material and the aerial magic of his spacing, sorely troubled him for half a century. Doubtless it was his refusal to visit Boston and study there the architectural conditions of the Public Library that resulted in the hang-fire of his decorations, though they are of an exalted order. One at least served as a spring-board for the decorative impulse of Besnard, as may be noted in his frescoes on the ceiling at the Hotel de Ville, Paris.

That Puvis de Chavannes was not an unfeeling Bonze of art, but a man of tender heart and warm affections was proved after the death of his much-loved Princess Marie Cantacuzene. Two months later sorrow over her loss killed him. He had painted the thousand and one expressive moments in the life of our species as a hymn to humanity, and their contours are eternal. Eternal? A vain phrase; but eternal till the canvas fades and the walls decay, that is nearer the truth. Art is long and appreciation sometimes a chilly consolation. Let us stick to the eternal verities. As D'Annunzio has it: Quella musica silenziosa delle linee immobili era cosi possente che creava il fantasma quasi visibile di una vita piu ricca e piu bella.

XVIII

THREE DISAGREEABLE GIRLS

I

HEDDA

Hazlitt tells us in a delightful essay about the whimsical notion of Charles Lamb that he would rather see Sir Thomas Browne than Shakespeare. A pleasant recreation is this same picking out "of persons one would wish to have seen." Causing great annoyance to Ayrton at an evening party, Lamb rejected the names of Milton and Shakespeare, selecting those of Browne and Fulke Greville--the friend of Sir Philip Sidney. For the prince of essayists there was mystery hovering about the personalities of this pair. I have often wondered if the most resounding names in history are the best beloved. Or in fiction. What is the name of your favourite heroine? Whom should you like to meet in that long corridor of time leading to eternity, the walls lined with the world's masterpieces of portraiture? I can answer for myself that no Shakespearian lovely dame or Balzacian demon in petticoats would ever be taken off the wall by me. They are either too remote or too unreal, though a word might be said for Valerie Marneffe. In the vasty nebula of the Henry James novel there are alluringly strange women, but if you summon them they fade and resolve themselves into everlasting phrases. In a word, they are not tangible enough to endure the change of moral climate involved in such a game as that played by Charles Lamb and his friends.

But Emma Bovary might come if you but ardently desired. And the fascinating Anna Karenina. Or Becky Sharp with her sly graces. Perhaps some of Dostoievsky's enigmatic, bewildering girls should be included in the list, for they brim over with magnetism, very often a malicious magnetism, and their glances are eloquent with suffering, haunt like the eyes one sees in a gallery of old masters. I do not speak of Sonia, but of the passionate Natasia Philipovna in The Idiot, or Aglaya Epanchin, in the same powerful novel, or Paulina in The Gambler. However, we cannot allow ourselves the luxury of so many favourites, even if they are only made of paper and ink. I confess I am an admirer of Emma Bovary. To the gifted young critics of to-day the work, and its sharply etched characters, has become a mere stalking horse for a new-fangled philosophy of Jules Gaultier, called Bovarysme, but for me it will always be the portrait of that unhappy girl with the pallid complexion, velvety dark eyes, luxuriant hair, and languid charm. Anna Karenina is more aristocratic; above all, she knew what happiness meant; its wing only brushed the cheek of Emma. Her death is more lamentable than Anna's--one can well sympathise with Flaubert's mental and physical condition after he had written that appalling chapter describing the poisoning of Emma. No wonder he thought he tasted arsenic, and couldn't sleep. Balzac, Dickens, and Thackeray were thus affected by their own creations, yet Flaubert is to this day called "impersonal," "cold," because he never made concessions to sentimentalism, never told tales out of his workshop for gaping indifferents.

As for Becky Sharp, that kittenish person seldom arouses in me much curiosity. I agree with George Moore that Thackeray, in the interests of mid-Victorian morality, suppressed many of her characteristics, telling us too little of her amatory temperament. Possibly, Mr. Moore may err, Becky may have had no "temperament," notwithstanding her ability to twist men around her expressive digits. That she was disagreeable when she set herself out to be I do not doubt; in fact, she is the protagonist of a whole generation of disagreeable heroines in English fiction. Bernard Shaw did not overlook her pertness and malevolence, though all his girls are disagreeable, even--pardon the paradox--his agreeable ones. But they are as portraiture far too "papery," to borrow a word from painters' jargon, for my purpose. They are not alive, they only are mouthpieces for the author's rather old-time ideas.

I mention the four heroines of a former period, Valerie, Becky, Emma, Anna, not because they are all disagreeable, but because they are my pets in fiction. Thoroughly disagreeable girls are Hedda Gabler, Mildred Lawson, and Undine Spragg. Of course, in a certain sense old Wotan Ibsen is the father of the latter-day Valkyrie brood. The "feminist" movement is not responsible for them; there were disagreeable females before the flood, yet somehow the latter part of the last and the beginning of the present century have produced a big flock in painting, music (Richard Strauss's operas), drama, and literature. Hedda boldly carved out of a single block stands out as the very Winged Victory of her species. In her there is a hint of Emma Bovary; both are incorrigible romanticists, snobs, girls for whom the present alone exists. She is decadent inasmuch as her nerves rule her actions, and at the rising of the curtain her nerves are in rags. Henry James finds in Ibsen a "charmless fascination," but by no means insists on the point that Hedda is disagreeable. Nor is he so sure that she is wicked, though he admits her perversity. The late Grant Allen once said to William Archer that Hedda was "nothing more nor less than the girl we take down to dinner in London, nineteen times out of twenty," which, to put it mildly, is an exaggeration. The truth is, Hedda is less a type than a "rare case," but to diagnose her as merely neurasthenic is also to go wide of the mark. Doubtless her condition may have added bitterness to her already overflowing cup; nevertheless Hedda is not altogether a pathological study. Approaching motherhood is not a veil for her multitude of sins. How soon are we shown her cruel nature in the dialogue with devoted Thea Rysing, whose hair at school had aroused envy in Hedda! She pulled it whenever she got a chance, just as she pulled from its hiding-place the secret of the timid Thea. Simply to say that Hedda is the incarnation of selfishness is but a half-truth. She is that and much more.

Charmless never, disagreeable always, she had the serpent's charm, the charm that slowly slays its victim. Her father succumbed to it, else would he have permitted her to sit in corners with poet Eiljert Loevborg and not only hold hands but listen to far from edifying discourses? Not a nice trait in Hedda--though a human, therefore not a rare one--is her curiosity concerning forbidden themes. She was sly.

She was morbid. Last of all she was cowardly. Yes, largely cerebral was her interest in nasty things, for when Eiljert attempted to translate his related adventures into action she promptly threatened him with a pistol. A demi-vierge before Marcel Prevost. Not as admirable as either Emma Bovary or Anna Karenina, Hedda Gabler married George Tesman for speculation. He had promised her the Falk villa--the scene plays up in Christiania--and he expected a professorship; these, with a little ready money and the selflessness of Aunt Julia, were so many bribes for the anxious Hedda, whose first youth had been heedlessly danced away without matrimonial success.

Mark what follows: Ibsen, the sternest moralist since old John Knox, doesn't spare his heroine. He places her between the devil of Justice Brack, libertine and house friend, and the deep sea of the debauched genius, Loevborg. To make a four-square of ineluctable fate she is flanked on either side by her mediocre husband and the devoted bore, Thea Rysing--Elvsted. Like a high-strung Barbary mare--she was of good birth and breeding--her nerves tugging in their sheaths, her heart a burnt-out cinder, Hedda saw but one way to escape--suicide. She took that route and really it was the most profound and significant act of her life, cowardly as was the motive. She was discontented, shallow, the victim of her false upbringing. In a more intellectual degree Eiljert, her first admirer, is her counterpart. Both could have consorted with Emma Bovary and found her "ideals" sympathetic. Emil Reich has called Hedda Gabler the tragedy of mesalliance. It is a memorial phrase. George Tesman and Charles Bovary are brothers in misfortune. They belong to those husbands "predestined" to betrayal, as Balzac puts it. Councillor Karenin completes the trio and Anna hated his large ears; but before Karenin, Charles Bovary was despised by Emma because of his clumsy feet and inexpressive bearing, and his habit of breathing heavily during dinner. George Tesman with his purblind faculties, amiable ways, and semi-idiotic exclamations will go down in the history of fiction with Georges Dandin, Bovary, and Karenin. As for Hedda, her psychological index is clear reading. In Peer Gynt one of the characters is described thus: "He is hermetically sealed with the bung of self, and he tightens the staves in the wells of self. Each one shuts himself in the cask of self, plunges deep down in the ferment of self." Imperfect sympathies, misplaced egoism--for there is a true as well as a false egoism--a craze for silly pleasures, no matter the cost, and a mean little vanity that sacrificed lives when not appeased. She is the most disagreeable figure in modern drama. Were it not for her good looks and pity for her misspent life and death she would be absolutely unendurable. The dramatic genius of Ibsen makes her credible. But what was the matter with George Tesman?

We cannot help noting that wherever the feminine preponderates, whether in art, politics, religion, society, there is a corresponding diminution of force in the moral and physical character of the Eternal Masculine. In the Ibsen dramas this is a recognised fact. Therefore, Strindberg called Ibsen an old corrupter. What is the matter with the men nowadays? Hadn't they better awaken to the truth that they are no longer attractive, or indispensable? Isn't it time for the ruder sex to organise as a step toward preserving their fancied inalienable sovereignty of the globe? In Thus Spake Zarathustra, Nietzsche wrote: "Thou goest to women. Remember thy whip." But Nietzsche, was he not an old bachelor, almost as censorious as his master, that squire of dames, Arthur Schopenhauer?

II

MILDRED

While Hedda Gabler is "cerebral" without being intellectual, you feel that she is more a creature of impulse than Mildred Lawson, who for me is George Moore's masterpiece in portraiture. Hedda is chilly enough, Mildred is distinctly frigid, yet such is the art of her creator that she comes to us invested with warmer colours; withal, about as disagreeable a girl as you may encounter in the literature of to-day. Now Mr. Moore is an outspoken defender of the few crumbling privileges of man at a time when the "ladies" are claiming the earth and adjacent planets. Yet I don't believe he wrote Mildred Lawson (in the volume entitled Celibates) with malice prepense. Too great an artist to use as a dialectic battering-ram one of his characters, for all that he makes Mildred very "modern." She doesn't despise men, nor does she care much for the ideas of her dowdy friend the "advanced" Mrs. Fargus; on the contrary, she makes fun of her clothes and ideas, though secretly regretting that she hadn't been sent by her parents to Girton College. Like Hedda she is ambitious to outshine any circle in which she finds herself. Modern she is, not because of her petty traits, but simply because Mr. Moore has painted a young woman of the day, rich, and so selfish that at the end her selfishness strangles the little soul she possesses. Her brother Harold, a sedate business man, is also a celibate whose ambition in life seems to be the catching of the 9:10 A.M. train to Victoria Station and the return to his suburban home on the 6 P.M. (He is not unlike a fussy little man, Willy Brooks, in the same Irish writer's early novel, Spring Days.) A rejected but ever hopeful suitor of Mildred's about comprises her domestic entourage.

She is ambitious. She hates the "stuffy" life of a hausfrau, but marriage makes no appeal, since the breaking of her engagement with Alfred--who is also a man with punctual business habits. She despises conventional men, and is herself compact of conventionality. In her most rebellious moods the leaven of Philistia (or the British equivalent, Suburbia) comes to the surface. She dares, but doesn't dare enough. "It needs both force and earnestness to sin." As in the case of Hedda Gabler, it is her social conscience that keeps her from throwing her bonnet over the moon, not her sense of moral values; in a word, virtue by snobbish compulsion. One thinks of Dante Gabriel Rossetti and the searing irony of his sonnet, Vain Virtues. The virtue of Mildred Lawson is vanity of vanities and the abomination of desolation.

She often argued that "it was not for selfish motives that she desired freedom." Her capacity for self-illuding is enormous. She didn't love her drawing-master, the unfortunate Mr. Hoskin, who had a talent for landscape, but no money, yet she allowed the man to think she did care a little and it sent him into bad health when he found she had fooled him. The scene in the studio, where the dead painter lies in his coffin, between Mildred and his mistress--a model from the "lower" ranks of life--is one of the most stirring in modern fiction. The "lady" comes off second-best; when she begins to stammer that she hoped the dead man hadn't suggested improper relations, the unhappy girl turns on her: "I dare say you were virtuous more or less, as far as your own body is concerned. Faugh! women like you make virtue seem odious." Mildred, indignant at such "low conversation," makes her escape, slightly elated at the romantic crisis. A real man has died for her sake. After all, life is not so barren of interest.

She goes to Paris. Studies art. Returns to London. Again to Paris and the forest of Fontainebleau, where she joins a student colony and flirts with a young painter; but it all comes to nothing, just as her work in the Julian Studio has no artistic result. Mr. Moore, who is a landscape-painter, has drawn a capital picture of the forest, though not with the fulness of charm to be found in Flaubert's treatment of the same theme in Sentimental Education. The little tale is a genuine contribution to fiction in which art is adequately dealt with. When Celibates appeared, Henry Harland said that Mildred Lawson was worthy of Flaubert if it had been written in good English, which is a manifest epigram. The volume is a perfect breviary of selfishness.

Tiring of art, Mildred takes up society, though she gets into a rather dubious Paris set. A socialist deputy and his wife protect her and she becomes a brilliant contributor--at least so she is made to believe--to a publication in which is eventually sunk a lot of her money. Her brother has warned her, but to no avail. At this juncture the tale becomes slightly mysterious. Mildred flirts with the deputy, his wife is apparently willing--having an interest elsewhere--and suddenly the bottom drops out of the affair, and Mildred poorer, also wiser, returns to her home in England. She has embraced the Roman Catholic religion, but you do not feel she is sincerely pious. It is one more gesture in her sterile career. At the end we find her trying to evade the inevitable matrimony, for she is alone, her brother dead, and she an heiress. Suspicious of her suitor's motives--it is the same faithful Alfred--she wearily debates the situation: "Her nerves were shattered, and life grows terribly distinct in the insomnia of the hot summer night.... She threw herself over and over in her burning bed, until at last her soul cried out in lucid misery: 'Give me a passion for god or man, but give me a passion. I cannot live without one.'" For her "mad and sane are the same misprint." And on this lyric note the book closes.

I believe if Hedda Gabler had hesitated and her father's pistol hadn't been hard by, she would have recovered her poise and deceived her husband. I believe that if Emma Bovary had escaped that snag of debt she would have continued to fool Charles. And I believe Mildred Lawson married at last and fooled herself into the belief that she had a superior soul, misunderstood by the world and her husband. There is no telling how vermicular are the wrigglings of mean souls. Mildred was a snob, therefore mean of soul; and she was a cold snob, hence her cruelty. That she was an eminently disagreeable girl I need hardly emphasise. Nevertheless the young chaps found her dainty and her poor girl friends, the artists, envied her pretty frocks. She had small shell-like ears, ears that are danger-signals to experienced men.

When I reread her history I was reminded of the princess in the allegory of Ephraim Mikhael, called The Captive. She was the cold princess held captive in the hall with the wall of brass. Wherever she turns or walks she sees a welcome visitor: it is always her own insolent image in the mirrors on the walls. These mirrors make of herself her own eternal jailer. When she gazes from the window of her prison tower she sees no one. No conquering lover comes to deliver her from the bondage of self. In the slave who offers rare fruits and precious wines in cups of emerald she sees only a mockery of herself, the words of consolation remind her of her own voice. "And that is why the sorrowful Princess drives away the beautiful loving slave, more cruel even than the mirrors." Egotist to the end, both Mildred and the Princess see naught in the universe save the magnified image of themselves.

III

UNDINE

Perhaps there is more than a nuance of caricature in the choice of such a name as "Undine Spragg" for the heroine of Edith Wharton's The Custom of the Country. Throughout that book, with its brilliant enamel-like surfaces, there is a tendency to make sport of our national weakness for resounding names. Undine Spragg--hideous collocation--is not the only offence. There is Indiana Frusk of Apex City, and Millard Binch, a combination in which the Dickens of American Notes would have found amusement. Hotels with titles like The Stentorian are not exaggerated. Miss Spragg's ancestor had invented "a hair waver"; hence the name Undine: "from undoolay, you know, the French for crimping," as the simple-hearted mother of the girl explained to a suitor. Mrs. Wharton has been cruel, with a glacial cruelty, to her countrywomen of the Spragg type. But they abound. They come from the North, East, South, West to conquer New York, and thanks to untiring energy, a handsome exterior, and much money, they "arrive" sooner or later. With all her overaccentuated traits and the metallic quality of technique in the handling of her portrait, Undine Spragg is both a type and an individual--she is the newest variation of Daisy Miller--and compared with her brazen charmlessness the figures of Hedda Gabler and Mildred Lawson seem melting with tenderness, aglow with subtle charm and muffled exaltation. Undine--shades of La Motte Fouque--is quite the most disagreeable girl in our fiction. She has been put under a glass and subjected to the air-pump pressure of Mrs. Wharton's art. She is a much more viable creature than the author's earlier Lily Bart, the heroine of The House of Mirth. At least Undine is not sloppy or sentimental, and that is a distinct claim on the suffrages of the intelligent reader. Furthermore, the clear hard atmosphere of the book is tempered by a tragic and humorous irony, a welcome astringent for the mental palate.

In Apex City Undine made up her mind to have her own way. She elopes and marries a vulgar "hustler," but is speedily divorced. She is very beautiful when she reaches New York. No emotional experience would leave a blur on her radiant youth, because love for her is a sensation, not a sentiment. By indirect and cumulative touches the novelist evokes for us her image. Truly a lovely apparition, almost mindless, with great sympathetic eyes and a sweet mouth. She exists, does Undine. She is not the barren fruit of a satirical pen. Foreigners, both men and women, puzzle over her freedom, chilliness, and commercial horse-sense. She doesn't long intrigue their curiosity, her brain is poorly furnished and conversation with her is not a fine art. She is temperamental in the sense that she lives on her nerves; without the hum and glitter of the opera, fashionable restaurants, or dances she relapses into a sullen stupor, or rages wildly at the fate that made her poor. She, too, like Hedda and Emma, lives in the moment, a silly moth enamoured of a millionaire. Mildred Lawson is positively intellectual in comparison, for she has a "go" at picture-making, while the only pictures Undine cares for are those produced by her own exquisitely plastic figure. No wonder Ralph Marvell fell in love with her, or, rather, in love with his poetic vision of her. He was, poor man, an idealist, and his fine porcelain was soon cracked in contact with her brassy egotism.

He is of the old Washington Square stock, as antique--and as honourable--as Methuselah. Undine soon tires of him; above all, tires of his family and their old-fashioned social code. For her the rowdy joys of Peter Van Degen and his set. The Odyssey of Undine is set forth for us by an accomplished artist in prose. We see her in Italy, blind to its natural beauties, blind to its art, unhappy till she gets into the "hurrah" of St. Moritz. We follow her hence, note her trailing her petty misery--boredom because she can't spend extravagantly--through modish drawing-rooms; then a fresh hegira, Europe, a divorce, the episode with Peter Van Degen and its profound disillusionment (she has the courage to jump the main-travelled road of convention for a brief term) and her remarriage. That, too, is a failure, only because Undine so wills it. She has literally killed her second husband because she wins from him by "legal" means their child, and in the end she again marries her divorced husband, Elmer Moffatt, now a magnate, a multimillionaire. She has at last followed the advice of Mrs. Heeny, her adviser and masseuse. "Go steady, Undine, and you'll get anywheres." We leave her in a blaze of rubies and glory at her French chateau, and she isn't happy, for she has just learned that, being divorced, she can never be an ambassadress, and that her major detestation, the "Jim Driscolls," had been appointed to the English court as ambassador from America. The novel ends with this coda: "She could never be an ambassador's wife; and as she advanced to welcome her first guests, she said to herself, that it was the one part she was really made for." The truth is she was bored as a wife, and like Emma Bovary, found in adultery all the platitudes of marriage.

You ask yourself, after studying the play, and the two novels, if the new woman is necessarily disagreeable. To my way of thinking, it is principally the craving for novelty in characterisation that has wrought the change in our heroines of fiction, although new freedom and responsibilities have evolved new types. Naturally the pulchritudinous weakling we shall always have with us, ugly girls with brains are a welcome relief from the eternal purring of the popular girl with the baby smile. But it would be a mistake to call Hedda, or Mildred, or Undine, new women. Mildred is the most "advanced," Hedda the most dangerous--she pulled the trigger far too early--and Undine the most selfish of the three. The three are disagreeable, but the trio is transitional in type. Each girl is a compromiser, Undine being the boldest; she did a lot of shifting and indulged in much cowardly evasion. Vulgarians all, they are yet too complex to be pinned down by a formula. Old wine in these three new bottles makes for disaster. Undine Spragg is the worst failure of the three. She got what she wanted for she wanted only dross. Ibsen's Button-Moulder will meet her at the Cross-Roads when her time comes. Hedda, like Strindberg's Julia, may escape him because, coward as she was when facing harsh reality, she had the courage to rid her family of a worthless encumbrance. If she had been a robust egoist, and realised her nature to the full, she would have been a Hedda Gabler "reversed," in a word, the Hilda Wangel of The Master Builder. But with Mildred she lacked the strength either to renounce or to sin. And Undine Spragg hadn't the courage to become downright wicked; the game she played was so pitiful that it wasn't worth the poor little tallow-dip. What is her own is the will-to-silliness. As Princess Estradina exclaimed in her brutally frank fashion: "My dear, it's what I always say when people talk to me about fast Americans: you're the only innocent women left in the world...." This is far from being a compliment. No, Undine is voluble, vulgar, and "catty," but she isn't wicked. It takes brains to be wicked in the grand manner. She is only disagreeable and fashionable; and she is as impersonal and monotonous as a self-playing pianoforte.

BOOKS BY JAMES HUNEKER

PUBLISHED BY CHARLES SCRIBNER'S SONS

```
=Ivory Apes and Peacocks.= 12mo.                        _net_, $1.50
=New Cosmopolis.= 12mo.                                 _net_, $1.50
=The Pathos of Distance.= 12mo.                         _net_, $2.00
=Franz Liszt.= Illustrated. 12mo.                       _net_, $2.00
=Promenades of an Impressionist.= 12mo.                 _net_, $1.50
=Egoists: A Book of Supermen.= 12mo.                    _net_, $1.50
=Iconoclasts: A Book of Dramatists.= 12mo.              _net_, $1.50
=Overtones: A Book of Temperaments.= 12mo.              _net_, $1.50
=Mezzotints in Modern Music.= 12mo.                     _net_, $1.50
=Chopin: The Man and His Music.= With Portrait. 12mo.   _net_, $2.00
=Visionaries.= 12mo.                                    _net_, $1.50
=Melomaniacs.= 12mo.                                    _net_, $1.50
```

TRANSCRIBER'S NOTES

1. Passages in italics are surrounded by _underscores_.

2. Passages in bold are surrounded by =bold=.

3. Certain words (L'Oeuvre, Soeur, Coeur) use oe ligature in the original.

4. The following misprints have been corrected:
    Missing period added at sentence end "a cosmopolitan." (page 29)

"Turgeneiff" corrected to "Turgenieff" (page 69)
Missing period added at sentence end "his admirers." (page 242)

5. Other than the corrections listed above, printer's inconsistencies in spelling, punctuation, hyphenation and ligature usage have been retained.